CHRISTIANITY'S MISSING PIECE

CHRISTIANITY'S MISSING PIECE

Thomas K. Siemer

urlink
PRINT & MEDIA

Christianity's Missing Piece

1603 Capitol Ave., Suite 310 Cheyenne, Wyoming USA 82001
1-888-980-6523 | admin@urlinkpublishing.com

URLink Print and Media is committed to excellence in the publishing industry.

Published in the United States of America

ISBN 978-1-64367-340-0 (Paperback)
ISBN 978-1-64367-339-4 (Digital)

Non-Fiction
03.04.19

THIS BOOK IS DEDICATED TO:

PHIL BERRIGAN AND DAN BERRIGAN, SJ, WHO FIRST CAUSED ME TO CHANGE FROM WAR TO PEACE WORK. AND TO MONICA AND JIM SIEMER, WHO FIRST HELPED ME. AND TO THOSE WHO KEEP ME WORKING FOR PEACE: BISHOP TOM GUMBLETON, RITA CLARK, ROY BOURGEOIS, MM, CHARLES LITEKY, LIZ MCALLISTER, MIGUEL D'ESCOTO, MM, RICHARD MCSORLEY,SJ, JOHN DEAR, SJ, ART LAFFIN, KATHY BOYLAN, MARIE DENNIS, BRIAN WILLSON, COLMAN MCCARTHY, MARY TROTOCHAUD, RICK MCDOWELL, DANIEL ELLSBERG, TOM AND FRANK CORDERO, DAVE ROBINSON, JACK RYAN, JIM WILLIS, ARDETH PLATTE, AND CAROL GILBERT.

Contact: Thomas Siemer, P.O.15633, Washington,
D.C. 20003, Tel. No. (703) 354-3098

Contents

INTRODUCTION 11
CHAPTER 1: THE POPE'S "STAR WARS REPORT" 17
CHAPTER 2: CHRISTIANS KILLING CHRISTIANS 34
CHAPTER 3: FLIGHT SCHOOL AND LOST LOVE 46
CHAPTER 4: FIRST INDIFFERENCE AND NEAR DEATH 60
CHAPTER 5: CHRISTIAN SOCIALISM 69
CHAPTER 6: PRIESTHOOD, OR A WOMAN? 80
CHAPTER 7: DECISION FOR SEMINARY 93
CHAPTER 8: FIRST HOMOSEXUAL DILEMMA 100
CHAPTER 9: SEMINARY LIFE 107
CHAPTER 10: FIRST JUSTIFICATION FOR WARS 120
CHAPTER 11: THE LONELINESS OF A CELIBATE 130
CHAPTER 12: MY DEAR WIFE AND WORK 146
CHAPTER 13: FIRST CAPITALIST EXPERIENCE 164
CHAPTER 14: MY CALLING AND VIETNAM 178
CHAPTER 15: MY CAPITALIST VENTURE 193
CHAPTER 16: SECOND COMING OF THE SPIRIT AND DEATH 202
CHAPTER 17: SECOND DECISION FOR CHRIST 218
CHAPTER 18: SECOND ST. PETER'S WIFE 227

CHAPTER 19: THE FIRST BOOK....................................235
CHAPTER 20: THE VOICE OF GOD 249
CHAPTER 21: GIVING GOD'S WORD TO THE CHURCH 267
CHAPTER 22: THE "FAST FOR LIFE" OR DEATH........310
EPITAPH 333

INTRODUCTION

By Miguel d'Escoto, M.M.

After 2000 years of Christianity it would be fair to ask, as indeed many do ask, why there is so much violence in the world, and particularly in the so-called Christian world. Why has the Church itself used so much violence over the centuries to advance its own objectives?

I believe this to have resulted from the Church's failure to truly evangelize. It has not transmitted the message of Christ in an unadulterated fashion to the world. It has, indeed, transmitted part of the message but not the whole message, unedited, with all of its essential components. One of these essential components is the non-use of violence to redress aggression. Having failed to proclaim that the Gospels are radically non-violent and having found many ways to water down the commandment of "Thou shall not kill" by making exceptions to it, how can one say that the Church has faithfully proclaimed the full message of Christ?

One can clearly not expect to harvest what one has not sown. If the Church has not sowed the Christian seed of non-violence it cannot expect to reap a Christian, non-violent world. And because the Church has not sown this seed it has not, in fact, evangelized.

And it has done little, if anything at all, to change the culture of violence and hate that has led humankind to the point of practically destroying itself and the life-sustaining capability of our planet.

A reflection similar to this one led Tolstoy, in his *The Kingdom of God Is Within You,* to say that the Church was the greatest enemy of evangelization. Asked what church he had in mind when making such an awful assertion he responded: "Orthodox, Catholic, Anglican and Lutheran, it's all the same." He believed that the leaders of all these church organizations were placing institutional concerns over and above concerns of fidelity in the transmission of Christ's message.

For our own Catholic Church the fundamental concern of popes, over many centuries, clearly was the preservation of its earthly power status with all that involved—armies, of course, included. In 1870 the world witnessed the loss of the Papal States, but not due to the Church's voluntary and humble rectification of the anomalies that framed the basis for the old dictum: "Roma veduta, fede perduta" (When you see Rome you will loose your faith.) The political annexation of the Papal States to what is now modern Italy took place very much against the wishes of Pius IX, whose Secretary of State and Minister of War, Cardinal Giacomo Antonelli, tried right up to the end to prevent this annexation by doubling the size of the papal army. He believed this was necessary to insure, for the Vicar of Christ, the possibility of a successful pre-emptive strike.

In Mathew 20:25-28 we read: "Jesus called them to him and said: 'You know that the rulers of the Gentiles lord it over them, and their great ones are tyrants over them. It will not be so among you; but whoever wishes to be great among you must be your servant, and whoever wishes to be first among you must be slave; just as the Son of Man came not to be served but to serve." It is lamentably all too obvious that the Church opted to practically delete this extremely important guidance of Jesus for the rulers of His Church. Having done so, the Church chose to exercise its authority as power rather than service, in flagrant contradiction to the wishes of Christ.

This maddening obsession with power, and ever greater power, is what led Pacelli (later Pope Pius XII) to the horrendous Reich Concordat, making it possible for Hitler to implement his final solution. This is also what led Pope John Paul II to join Reagan in his evil scheme to destroy the Nicaraguan revolution, as Karl Bernstein has so well demonstrated. In both of these cases one sees the Pope using all his power to force religious, priests, and bishops to ignore their own consciences and blindly obey the morally reckless orders of the Pope. The fact that the German bishops, initially opposed to Hitler, eventually allowed themselves to be muzzled and, in that sense, became complicit with the genocidal persecution of Jews, does not excuse the German bishops from responsibility in the Holocaust. The same observation could be made about John Paul II's manipulation of the Church in Nicaragua by ordering Cardinal Obando and the Episcopal Conference to become complicit with the imperial aggression, including, of course, its fundamental instrument, the Contras. The Pope labeled as disloyal all priests and religious who were unwilling to commit treason against Nicaragua and were unwilling, thereby, to obey his arbitrary orders. They opted to follow their consciences instead.

It is this practical negation of the supremacy of conscience in our actions and the insistence that Christians should abdicate their personhood to become the Pope's puppets that has led to the psychologically and morally decrepit condition of the clergy worldwide, as has been amply demonstrated by Eugene Drewermann's *Clerics*. The manipulation of the Christian concept of obedience for the sake of consolidating the Pope's dream of total power must be seen as the root cause of the otherwise baffling silence of religious, clergy, theologians, and bishops in the face of the monstrous papal failure to condemn even nuclear warfare. We are obviously more afraid of the Pope's rejection than of God's holy wrath.

I have tried, though perhaps unsuccessfully, to demonstrate what I believe lies at the root of the Church's reluctance to condemn war or even genocide. I believe that this is all a result of the Church leadership's lethal addiction to power. First, it does not condemn violence and killing because it has historically found it necessary to rely on such practices in the pursuit of its own objectives. Secondly, it does not condemn violence and wars because these are essential practices of the powerful, who, for much more than a thousand years, have been the chosen allies of the Papacy. It does not want, in any way, to jeopardize its relations with the mighty of this world, even when this implies turning a deaf ear to the cry of the poor. Thirdly, I believe the Church does not condemn violence and wars in the clear, unequivocal, and categorical manner that it should because it lacks the fundamental humility necessary to rectify its traditional stands. Rectification becomes practically impossible for a Church leadership that over centuries has considered face-saving the most important commandment by which it must live.

This book is a story of an ordinary mortal, a human being who is, however, extraordinary in his immense love of God and of the Church. I believe this is clearly demonstrated in his relentless fidelity to God's Will that His Church and all His followers dedicate themselves to the creation of a non-violent world. To me, Tom Siemer is a saintly man for his untiring efforts, sparing no sacrifice in his accepted mission to move the Catholic Church officially to take at least a first step and condemn engaging in nuclear war or preparing to participate in it. His story is inspiring and worth reading.

CHAPTER 1

THE POPE'S "STAR WARS REPORT"

In January of 1985, 27 famous scientists, all members of the Pontifical Academy of Sciences, met in its quarters inside the Vatican Gardens. They gathered in this beautiful little palace of the former Pope Pius IV to study the feasibility of Antiballistic Missile (ABM) defense systems, or "Star Wars," meeting for three days with a press conference scheduled for January 25th.

Padre Enrico di Rovescenda, Director General of the Academy, a Dominican priest and my friend, had informed me of the meeting earlier because he knew I was very much concerned about the extreme danger that the ABM defenses posed. He invited me to the study summation of the Star Wars meeting. We were in Rome on January 25th at the press conference, awaiting the summation.

Di Rovescenda and I had debated nuclear weapons many times before. He appreciated my background as a nuclear weapons manager, as well as my form of naïve

Catholicism. He was the one who had told me about the Academy's scheduled "Star Wars" ABM study four months before it happened. He knew I would be very interested. He told me that in 1981 teams of scientists associated with the Pontifical Academy of Sciences were sent by Pope John Paul II to meet with the world leaders, including President Reagan and the late Soviet President Leonid Brezhnev.

The text of their message: "The conditions of life following a nuclear attack would be so severe that the only hope for humanity is the prevention of any form of nuclear war. Universal dissemination and acceptance of this knowledge would make it apparent that nuclear weapons must not be used at all in warfare and that their number should be progressively reduced, in a balanced way." "In contrast to widespread belief," the message added, "much is known about the catastrophe that would follow the use of nuclear weapons. Much is known too about the limitations of medical assistance."

The medical facilities of any nation would be inadequate to care for survivors of a nuclear war, the message continued. "An objective examination of the medical situation that would follow a nuclear war leads to one conclusion: Prevention is our only recourse."

The Academy's 1984 report on nuclear winter had noted that the large-scale use of existing nuclear weapons could trigger major and irreversible ecological genetic changes whose limits cannot be predicted. A 'nuclear winter' would follow even a limited nuclear exchange between the superpowers, resulting in the destruction of most human, animal, and plant life on the planet.

Many journalists, CIA agents, and Russian KGB agents were also anxiously awaiting the conclusions of the Pontifical Academy of Sciences Study of SDI (Space Defense Initiatives) or other defenses against nuclear ballistic missiles in space.

There were nearly 40 people at the Star Wars Press Conference on the 25th of January, 1985. Padre di Rovescenda walked to the microphone, and it finally happened.

"The following is an informal report by Dr. Carlos Chagas, our Chairman," announced Di Rovescenda, the Director.

"Gentlemen," Dr. Chagas began, "This is an informal report."

THE ANTIBALLISTIC MISSILE DEFENSE (ABM) STUDY SUMMATION.

The Pontifical Academy of Sciences has reached the following general conclusions:

1. Nuclear antiballistic missile defense systems could not stop all nuclear weapons, but would begin a new arms race in space, as well as greatly accelerate the one on earth.
2. The actual use of such systems, even on a very limited scale, would release enough nuclear radiation and fallout to endanger all life on earth.
3. Deployment of an antiballistic missile defense by the superpowers would greatly increase the probability of accidental nuclear war, to be decided in microseconds.
4. Development of such systems would be a waste of needed trillions of dollars and untold amounts of earth's natural resources, both physical and intellectual, over the estimated 15 years it would take to accomplish this task, assuming that it could be done at all.

In addition, unanticipated further dangers arising from the use of these defenses cannot be excluded. Further study is needed to determine what effect thousands of kinetic energy devices, particle beams, and X-ray-chemical lasers will have on the environment both in earth and in space.

Recent talk about defending against nuclear weapons in space, or winning a nuclear war, must reflect a failure to appreciate the same medical reality: Any nuclear war, even if only fought in space, would inevitably cause deaths, disease, and suffering of pandemic proportions and without the possibility of effective medical intervention. An objective examination of the medical situation that would follow a nuclear missile attack and an antiballistic missile defense (counter-attack) in space leads to the same conclusion: Prevention is our only recourse.

It cannot be justified when science and our natural resources are the only hope we have to feed the starving masses of a human population that will double early in the next century. In conclusion, this report embodying the study's results was given to the Pope this morning. This is an unofficial summary of that report." 1

The Doctor added, "There will be no questions taken," then he turned and walked towards the door. There was much confusion as everyone screamed questions at him at once. He shouted back: "It is the Pope's report and he can do with it what he wants! Thank you." Then Chagas walked out of the door.

1. This January 1985 meeting is noted in Volume 14, page 560, of ORIGINS, published by the Catholic News Service (CNS) in Washington, DC, as the Vatican archives' unofficial summation of this Star Wars Report.

On Sundays after Mass at Santa Susanna, the English speaking church on Piazza Santa Susanna, I always talked to fellow American Catholic parishioners from the US Embassy, the State Department, and the CIA who go to Mass together every week.

I began to attack President Reagan's Star Wars plans as usual, however, this time with Jim Grass, an old friend who was attending the Lumen Christi Charismatic Prayer Conference in Rome. Like most of the Americans, he was in support of Star Wars. Jim and I had worked together in management at Rockwell International, Inc., a giant defense contractor. Jim was defending Star Wars because it created work for engineers.

"Jim," I told him, "you know that if Rockwell was out of work they would have all the engineers there design bigger and better gas chambers and crematoriums, if you give them the money and the scientific challenge. Look at Von Braun, who is heading the Apollo Program. He worked frantically for Hitler to the very end to perfect the German missiles that killed thousands of innocent people in England. Do you think his conscience bothers him? He is proud of his unique accomplishments. He certainly does not care what his missiles do.... And what about that crazy Edward Teller, who developed the hydrogen bomb? He is absolutely mad. He wants to build thousands more. Bigger and better bombs, when all his colleagues have already repented, including Einstein and Oppenheimer. Why is it that only the most brilliant minds can design and make nuclear missiles, but they always seem to lack morals and common sense?"

"But, they say that if they do not build them somebody else will," Jim countered, and continued: "Tom, did you know that I was assigned to the engineering preliminary study for the Space Shuttle way back in 1969? The Space Shuttle has created a lot of jobs for engineers since then."

I rebutted. "Jim, you and I both know the Rockwell Space Shuttle will be totally military, as it was planned to be, after 12 or more flights for NASA, or after they get it perfected. We all know it is too expensive for any civilian company to use to launch its communication satellites and such. The military planned to use it for nuclear laser and particle beam weapons to destroy or steal Russian spy satellites and those that guide Soviet nuclear ICBM missiles in space. The Space Shuttle will service nuclear weapons platforms in space to destroy satellites, thereby blinding Soviet spying and nuclear ICBM missiles. This was the last phase of the old ABM Star Wars defenses, destroying satellites."

"Tom, you cannot stop progress."

"You call that progress, when science can put a man on the moon but can't find a way to feed 40 million people who starve to death each year?" I replied.

My friend remained silent for a long time before he exclaimed, "That's a helluva statement. So sad! What are you doing now?"

"Oh, I'm still appealing to the Pope here in Rome."

"What ever happened to your Vatican campaign for peace?" he asked.

"They should be meeting me here any minute now. They went to the Vatican Pressroom to see if there is any more information about the Pontifical Academy of Sciences' Star Wars Report. The Pope has been holding the report in secrecy since January. Today is April 11, over 10 weeks now! He doesn't want to screw Reagan at the Geneva Disarmament Conference. We got an unofficial summary of the SDI Study and I talked about it on national TV."

"What do you mean, 'in secrecy'?" Jim asked.

"I mean he won't release the scientific report, Jim, because you and I both know that 27 distinguished scientists from all over the world, including the USA and USSR, if speaking honestly, would condemn Reagan's Star Wars space weapons program. Remember when the scientists condemned our Antiballistic Missile defense system (ABM) in the early 1970s, and Congress canceled it?"

Jim asked, "What was the ABM defense system called back then, Tom? Sprint or Sprite or something? It was worth billions! Boy! Was it wild!"

I replied, "Jim, I remember the name Sprint. And it was cancelled by the 1972 treaty with Russia banning Antiballistic

Missile defense systems. It almost cost me my job at North American Rockwell in 1972."

At that moment my Italian friend Cristina walked up to us and said hello to Jim. Then she turned to me and said, "I was able to talk to Padre di Rovescenda, and I will tell you what he said if you will stay calm and not get us thrown out of here."

I turned to Jim and explained, "The Pontifical Academy of Sciences gave us great hope when they told us way back in October that the Academy would meet in January to discuss the dangers of Star Wars. Well, what happened, Cris?"

Cris replied seriously, "I'll tell you if you promise not to have another breakdown! Promise?"

"I bet it's the same old crap Professor Carlos Chagas said on the 25th of January!"

"Yes, but Padre di Rovescenda is pretty mad at you now. He almost shouted. "The Pope called the Pontifical Academy of Sciences together, so it's his report, to do whatever he wants with."

I didn't stay calm. In fact, I shouted. "I think he called them together because the Pope thought it was a good thing to have a 'Nuclear Missile Umbrella' to protect us from the Soviet missiles. Jim will tell you that an ABM defense system is worthless—and dangerous! People are completely ignorant about an ABM space defense!"

"Hey! Don't get me involved!" exclaimed Jim.

"Cris, did you get our article to the Corriere della Sera?" I asked.

"Yes; our friend Purgatori said he would print it—but probably in the form of a letter to the editor. The newspaper doesn't want the responsibility of taking on the Vatican."

Louder I shouted, "Damn! Damn! Damn! Space weapons on top of the Cruise and Pershing missiles will compound the danger of an accidental nuclear war a thousand times! The guy in UPI sympathized with me, but he said, 'Anything like this about the Pope is too touchy!'"

"Please, Tom, be quiet," she cautioned me.

"How can I keep quiet? The Pope not only doesn't pay attention to the Prophecy, he suppresses scientific information that would condemn Reagan's Star Wars space policies. It would sway the Geneva arms talks tremendously. Remember what the scientists told us in the '60s when they proved the disastrous consequences of using laser or particle beams to melt down a small number of incoming nuclear missiles, or to cause the explosions of just a few nuclear warheads in space? The result would be a catastrophic fallout of deadly plutonium and the destruction of the ozone layer so as to compromise any kind of existence on earth."

Jim added, "I remember the Colonel saying the 300 Cruise missiles launched from submarines or low-flying aircraft would undermine the whole ABM defense system and destroy America." "See!" I cried. "While 40 million human beings starve to death each year, we waste $500 billion perfecting a system that won't work!"

Then I added, "It is not only a question of the death by hunger of 40 million humans each year—it is also the greatly increased danger of nuclear extermination by a simple mistake of the warning system computer. With all those warning satellites and nuclear weapons orbiting the earth, in the end a supercomputer must decide in less than 30 seconds to destroy the earth or not. I can't get anybody to print the numerous articles we wrote about it, not even the opposition. There's a damn newspaper blackout in Italy on the subject, just like in the US!"

"What do you mean," asked Jim. "I'm sure the communists would print this story in a minute!"

Cris explained. "When the right wing newspapers didn't print it (for obvious reasons) I took Tom to the Communist Party headquarters and he gave our articles to a party executive for international affairs. At first he said he would be happy to get it to the leftist journalists and newspapers. However, two weeks later, when we called him, he said it was impossible."

"For heaven's sake, why?" asked Jim.

"He talked to me," said Cris, "and explained that the Party had decided not to print anything because there was opposition forming in the Vatican hierarchy against the Pope's position of keeping the Star Wars report secret. Any outside pressure might consolidate them with the Pope again and nip the opposition movement in the bud, the party member said. He also said that Thomas wouldn't understand—and he didn't!"

"Are you kidding, Cris?" Jim was amazed.

"No, I'm not! That's why Thomas has been in a rage of frustration ever since."

"I personally took it to all the newspapers," I explained. "United Press, Associated Press, and the International News Service. If we wait too long the Pope might try to change the scientists' conclusions, like they tried with Galileo's. We were told the scientists would keep quiet because it is a great honor to be in the Academy."

"In the meantime," Cris said, "I got Thomas on national TV shows twice to make his appeal to the people. At least that's live; they can't stop you once you are on the air. Thomas feels we must use the mass media now because there isn't enough time for conference organizing. He was on Maurizio Costanzo's TV show."

I added, "We even went to the Italian Bishops Conference in Loreto, and held up signs all day. Cristina invaded the first news conference and asked if the bishops would make a formal appeal to the Pope to release the "Stars Wars" report of

January. All the journalists turned to her in shocked unison. The politicians and the Pope will still be fiddling when Rome burns. I'm going to break this blackout if it kills me! Remember how the U.S. Catholic Bishops ran hot and cold the two and a half years before their Pastoral letter against nuclear weapons? Only public pressure and proven hypocrisy will make the Pope go against Reagan. I used to worry about Cruise missiles—now I have got new nuclear space weapons."

"Tom, have you given up trying to see the Pope?"

"No, Jim, I have not given up trying to see the Pope. I have never missed a regular Wednesday audience in the Paul VI Auditorium or St. Peter's Square. I obtained passes from the English speaking church of Santa Susanna. I always dress in black cloth like a priest to be able to get as near as possible to the Pope, even though I never wear a white collar."

Jim questioned, "How could you get close to him?"

"At every Wednesday audience I knew that the Pope would come to greet the musicians of the band, whether they were Polish or otherwise. So I moved up through the different sections in the audience one by one. I finally succeeded in reaching the musicians. I pretended to be one of them. The security service members, always on watch at the beginning of each audience, were loosening their attention towards the end, when the Pope greeted the bands. Besides, nobody thought it was necessary to stop a priest."

"Then what happened?" Jim asked with interest.

"The Pope came over to the Polish band and stopped in surprise when he recognized me."

'Thomas, musician?" he asked. "Polish?"

"No! But Papa Giovanni Paul II, please ban nuclear weapons!"

"Si, si, Thomas, I bless you in your work!"

"Another time I took advantage of the German band. Once I pretended I was sick so they took me to the first aid station on the left of St. Peter's Square. I had noticed that the Pope always went there to greet the invalids at the end of the audience. At the right moment I lined up with the doctors."

"Thomas, medico?"

"No alle arme nucleare!" I shouted as I grabbed and held his arm.

"Si, Thomas, si, Thomas, si, Thomas. Patience, patience!"
"Beginning on January 16, 1980, I succeeded in having 20 informal audiences thanks to these tricks, yet the Pope always refused to give me a full audience."

This gave me infinite sadness. Suddenly I began to weep uncontrollably before Jim and Cristina.

I sobbed, "Star Wars is not my real concern! It has always been 'The Missing Piece,' the Church's failure to teach all the teachings of Jesus Christ. My work has always been about this prophecy I received in Mexico: to get the Pope and the Church to ban justification for nuclear war."

I finally stopped crying and said, "I am sorry I became so emotional, Cristina and Jim."

"We had better leave the church courtyard, Thomas. People are staring at us," said Cris.

Nervously, Jim said, "Goodbye, Tom," and quickly left out of the side door.

Just then Fr. Ed Petruka, the pastor of Santa Susanna Church, came over to us and cornered me before softly saying, "Your wife Dorothy just telephoned me and asked me to tell you to come home. She is very sick and in the hospital."

I was shocked, but managed to thank Fr. Petruka. He allowed me to make a call to the United States, although I could not reach anyone in my family by telephone. I told Cristina about my wife and asked her if she could lend me money to get home to America, and she graciously agreed to buy me an airline ticket. I gratefully hugged her goodbye before I boarded the airplane and left Italy on August 10th, 1985.

My dear wife Dorothy recovered quickly. I really felt that she just wanted to get me home. However, it worked, and I continued to love her dearly. I realized how much I had missed her and my seven beautiful children.

On August 17, 1985, I received by mail an "official" copy in Italian of the Summation of the Pope's Star Wars Study Report from a Cesare Politi. A translation of this summary report showed it to be the same as the "unofficial" oral summary given by Dr. Carlos Chagas at the press conference on January 25th, 1985, reprinted above. Cesare said that he had been allowed to make a copy of this "official summary."

It was now six months since the Pontifical Academy of Sciences meeting, and the Pope had still not officially released the Star Wars Report. President Reagan was going on with his Star Wars defense. The Vatican again was suppressing scientific data. It was Galileo all over again. I pondered how I could get the Pope to officially release this report to the world. I had already tried to write a book and had not been successful. I could only relate to my own experience.

The years went by fast, and all I could do was send letters and copies of the prophecy I received in 1979 to the Pope, and all the archbishops of the Catholic Church, asking them to ban the justification for nuclear war. I made a mailing of a letter and the prophecy every six months.

In November of 2000 AD, George W. Bush was erroneously and almost illegally elected President of the United States. President Bush was totally committed to the Star Wars ABM defenses. Bush also seemed entirely consumed with building up all the military requirements for an empire... an evil empire with nuclear weapons in space.

I had to try to write again, at least about the dangers of Star Wars and the Pope's suppression of the report, his report, that condemned Star Wars. I also had to tell about the prophecy banning nuclear weapons and war. What else could I do?

The Pope and other religious leaders must finally commit their religious followers to accept peace. The Pentagon or other militaries will never give up war unless they are made to by the vote of all the good people. After all, most religious people believe in the one God.

I immediately began to collect all of my past writings, and with the help of a friend, Rita Clark, I wrote about my past experiences with God, the Pope, the Bishops, and building nuclear weapons for 23 years.

I will begin from the very beginning. Something happened to me during my military experience in Europe. It was seeing the total devastation in Europe after WWII and being on an aircraft carrier in Istanbul, Turkey, on the way to bomb Russia in 1949 with the two nuclear bombs we had on board... or at least to threaten them while on our way to the Black Sea.

Meanwhile, back in 2002, President Bush's ABM decision to commit the nation unilaterally to a new military course moves misguided policies to the level of public immorality. Aside from the dubious effectiveness... most scientist think it is a stupid venture... the ABM defense shield, with all the trillions of dollars it will cost, represents a crowning moment of US unilateralism and arrogance. But the obvious reason for building the ABM defenses is a form of corporate welfare for defense contractors.

Do you need evidence of Washington's contempt for the hopes and desires of 95% of humanity? Consider that the Bush Administration has announced its unilateral withdrawal from the ABM Treaty of 1972, single-handedly brought the Biological Weapons Convention (BWC) Review Conference to a halt, renounced international efforts to negotiate a verification protocol to the BWC, abandoned the Kyoto Global Warming Accord, refused to reconsider the Comprehensive Test Ban Treaty, rejected the International Criminal Court, disregarded the Convention on the Prohibition of Land Mines, gutted the UN Conference on Small Arms, dismissed the UN Convention on the Rights of the Child, boycotted the Comprehensive Test Ban Treaty Review Conference in New York, supported a unilateral embargo on Cuba, and now plans to place nuclear weapons in space. President Bush even advocates first-strike nuclear war.

Then in the fall of 2002 Bush announced that Iraq was threatening the world with weapons of mass destruction. It was obvious to most nations that Bush's claims were not true. Bush, however insisted that the U.S military would attack Iraq with or without United Nations support to bring down Saddam Hussein.

The U.N. was then pushed to pass a resolution (No 1441) to first send arms inspectors into Iraq and if this failed they would support a U.S. war. Bush has been preparing for war ever since while the U.N. inspectors had found no such weapons. U.S. aircraft have flown spy flights over Iraq and have bombed targets for over 10 years in the no—fly zones.

In January of 2003 Bush stated the U.S. military would attack Iraq regardless of what the U.N. inspectors found, without U.N. backing. For the first time since the collapse of the Soviet Union the possibility of nuclear war exploded in my mind. Bush is going to create enough hatred to cause the collapse of the moderate Muslim Pakistan regime of Musharaf and other moderate Muslim governments. If or when Musharaf falls the most extremist Muslim will have

Pakistan's nuclear bombs and eventually the other radical Muslim countries will get them.

The radical Muslims probably would blow up Haifa (close to Valley of Armageddon) and threaten to blow up another Israel city if the Palestinians are not given the West Bank. Israel could retaliate with a nuclear attack on Karachi, Baghdad, and Tehran. The nuclear fall-out from these cities alone would ruin our world from cancer and radiation. There are worse scenarios.

Suddenly it became an emergency for me to write about the missing piece of Christian history and its terrible effect on Jewish and Muslim religions. I began to write in a panic from the very beginning.

To add to my urgency, my dear friend, the great peace activist Phil Berrigan, had written to me, "These are hair-trigger times- with well manicured barbarians at the wheel, and our nuclear strike force poised and ready.". He added, "The American people will prevail, so will all thoughtful and decent people throughout the world. 'Then Jesus told them a parable about the necessity of praying always and never losing hope'" (Luke 18:1).

Phil went on, "It appears that I've graduated from chemotherapy. As a substitute for this toxin, I'll now rely on a homeopathic remedy, massive use of vitamin therapy. Thank you both for your love and prayers. Gandhi used to claim that prayer is more important than action. What is certain is that neither is a substitute for the other."

It sounded like Phil had no further use for modern medicine.

He died a week later.

"I did not mean to skip over the terrible events of September 11, 2001 and I do talk about them later on in the book. But initially they did not seem to add to the danger of nuclear war which is what I was writing about. Now they do, because of the great hatred generated by President Bush's response to 9/11.

President Bush, without any proof of who the 9/11 terrorists were, launched a war of revenge on October 7, 2001 against Afghanistan with hundreds of U.S. military bombers killing untold thousands of civilians while invading their country. Bush said it was because their Taliban government sheltered the 9/11terrorist leader known as Osama Bin Laden and his few Al-Queda Network members who turned out to be mostly Saudi Arabian Muslim extremists. Much later, years after the war had begun, the official White House position was the bush administration it had become known that 9/11 had no connection with the Iraqi War.

Now I would like to go to on with the beginning of my story."

CHAPTER 2

CHRISTIANS KILLING CHRISTIANS

God first tried to speak to me in Europe after I saw the complete destruction of Christian (and Catholic) cities in Germany and Italy caused by the United States Christian military and after I witnessed the great suffering of the people. God spoke to me through the Gospels.

I think it all began as I sat in the brig on the aircraft carrier Midway in Naples Harbor, contemplating for the first time the great mystery of life, and why men, who are all brothers, cannot live in peaceful harmony. The Italian police had arrested me for fighting that night. I defended my friend, Stankovan, and I was lying in deep meditation on the events of the past and the recent fight when the chaplain came to see me. His visit consisted merely of tossing me a paperback copy of the Bible and telling me to read the New Testament. Since I had plenty of time for the next 15 days, I began to read, and the more I read, the more interesting and enlightening the contents came to be. I read most of the Bible except for those "begotten by, who begot" passages of the Old Testament. Soon I realized that one theme was completely woven throughout the entire Bible.

I realized that God really loved all humanity and did not want us to hate each other or fight wars. However, it was always through human wickedness and not the will of the one Universal Supreme God that people fought wars from the time Cain killed Abel. I realized that all of humanity are kindred in Christ and the varied paths of Christianity are as the fingers of the loving hand of the Supreme Being—extended to all—offering completeness of spirit to all—and anxious to receive all. We could blend together like the fragrance of flowers and become one whole and eternal truth, perpetuating and living in the eternity of love, of brotherhood and sisterhood.

Aboard the aircraft carrier, I could see that the night was spreading its black garment upon the waters in the harbor. The tempest was shrieking dizzily and the rain became even stronger. As I gazed through the porthole, it seemed as though the Biblical flood was coming again to abolish life and wash our violence from God's earth. It seemed that the revolution of elements had created a deep tranquility in my heart, which often comes as a reaction to contemplation and converts aloneness into deep thought. I thought of another storm approaching: Russia and the United States were about to engage in another war over Berlin. We were on our way to the Black Sea to bomb Russia with our two nuclear weapons.

My mind could not elude the things that I had read, especially in the New Testament, where Christ said, "My command to you is love your enemy,—pray for your persecutors;—this will prove that you are sons of your heavenly Father . . . " (Matt. 5:45). He also said, "Do not offer resistance to injury" (Matt. 5:39). The scripture passages bore heavily upon me, for just a few weeks before I had witnessed the terrible aftermath of total war and had began to lose my belief in the one God who had created all nations. I had begun to think that if there were one God, He could only be a sadist, for He was again allowing His children to plan and prepare for the total destruction of each other.

The Christians, in the name of Christ, were preparing for horrible total nuclear war to save the so-called Christian capitalist free world from communism. But, didn't we just save communist Russia from the capitalist countries of Germany and Italy? Did this horrible war that had just ended solve anything? Wherever we anchored, there was complete destruction, misery, and inhumane conditions, both materially and spiritually. These were all Christian countries that we had helped to destroy to save atheistic Russia.

Therefore, I perceived that war could not be the answer; and Christ's clear command to love our enemies was not being obeyed by His Christian followers with its full intensity and dignity. If the justice of my religion did not support love for all of humanity, regardless of the country or nation, then my church is a deceiver, concealing the ugliness of hypocrisy behind shining outer garments, pretending love by total silence.

In the past, the Catholic Church had always interpreted the Bible for me. However, while searching for an answer to peace in the Bible, I found that the Christian teachings were vague in regard to war, and also vague in regard to who were our enemies that we were supposed to love. We were not taught this in our catechism, and it was never mentioned during my Catholic education. There was a missing piece. I also knew from experience that the Catholic Church did not teach us to love our enemies. In fact, just the day before, I believed that Christ was on our side and I looked forward to becoming a flyer and killing the enemies of Christ; I was truly fascinated by war. I did not begin to comprehend

Christ's command of "offer no resistance to injury" and "turn the other cheek" until I realized how futile war had become. After reading the New Testament, I realized that the ultimate and final goal for a Christian is to love the enemy, and by painful example, convert enemies to Christ through love.

Was not then Christ a successful failure? He succeeded in showing us how we must love our enemies by the example of His life and death, but He failed to convince anyone, even His church. Christians are rejecting Christ for the same reason they have condemned the Jews for, because they too wanted a great Messiah to conquer their enemies and protect them. So why did the Catholic Church, the guardian of Christian doctrine, also reject this great teaching of Christ's life and example?

I could find nowhere in the Acts of the Apostles a passage in which the early Christians advocated purchasing weapons and preparing for war in order to protect themselves. In fact, there was not one word of defending themselves. Their defense consisted of going underground and avoiding the evils of a pagan Roman Empire... and praying. Why, then, did the Catholic Church so completely ignore this command of Christ? Maybe it was because Christians never accomplished more than just loving their friends.

History proves that Christ first established the Catholic Church years before the New Testament was written down. Various monks in monasteries for centuries collected, translated, and reproduced the New Testament. During that time the church could easily have dropped those passages about "loving your enemy" and "offering no resistance to injury." But rather than tamper with the word of God, the Church retained the words, but misinterpreted them. This would somehow allow us to participate in wars, and left it up to the individual's conscience whether to kill enemies or not.

Those days and nights I spent in the brig had me torn between two forces. One force lifted me up and showed me the wonders of creation and the beauty of Christian love; the other forced me down with memories of a horrible war and devastating nightmares of the unjust works of humanity.

After leaving the brig, I told my bunk buddy, Stankovan, that I wanted to be alone with my thoughts and ideas that I needed solitude to ponder this great mystery which we had discussed constantly while in the brig. I think I almost drove him nuts. He stared at me for a moment, and I noticed a change in his expression, as if my few simple words had revealed to him a different image of the man who had befriended him and defended him in a barroom brawl. He looked straight through my eyes in a strange manner, as if he thought I had been hit on the head too hard. Then his lips started to say something, but he said nothing before he turned and started for the door.

That strange look followed me; the meaning of it I could not understand until I grew up in the world of experience, where friends understand each other without saying a word or offering an explanation. He respected my views, but he had no comprehension of how to love his enemies or what I had been talking about.

Then he stopped suddenly, and with his big Polish grin he said, "You drive me crazy. One day you love war and you can't wait to be a Navy fighter pilot. Then the next day you can't even understand why we fight wars. I ought to start calling you Warlove the Hypocrite. You even love barroom fighting until someone gets hurt, then you're always sorry. Tom, tell me the truth, are you trying for a Section-8 discharge? If you keep talking like this, you're going to need a headshrinker!"

He turned and slipped through the bulkhead hatch. I guess he was right, but I kept remembering the horrible suffering and the material and moral devastation I had seen in every country we visited. I remembered clearly the thousands of orphans living in the bombed-out streets; thousands of people starving and sick, frightened into submission by my Christian friends who were praying to the same Catholic God our enemy prayed to for protection against us. I remembered the 11-and 12-year-old boys selling the bodies of their 14-year-old sisters for a can of rations to keep their family barely alive.

By train, I had taken a three-day tour to Rome from my ship at Naples Harbor. My friend George had an uncle in the State Department who had planned to entertain us during our stay. After we checked into the Excelsior Hotel, we were given directions by George's uncle to dine in the main ballroom. We found two beautiful girls at our table who introduced themselves as Uncle Charlie's friends. As soon as I saw Gina, I immediately forced my way to her side. I knew if there was going to be a choice, she was going to be my girl. She moved likewise in my direction; and when our eyes met and our hands touched I knew that this would be forever.

Gina was a sweet child of 16 and I an old veteran of 19 when we met in war-torn Italy. She was an innocent girl torn between love and hatred. Hatred for the Americans who killed her father, mother, and brother in one of those senseless incidents which occur so often in war; and love for the attachment which existed between her soul and my soul after such a first meeting.

Gina's beauty was both earthly and spiritual. Her beauty was not in her hair, but in the way she wore it; her beauty was not in her eyes, but in the light which shone from them; and neither was her beauty of an earthly manifestation, but rather from the nobility of her spirit.

I say these things in the highest respect, but still they reflect my passionate love for her. Love, not only as a lover, but love as I have it for the sun, the spring after a cold winter, a baby's smile, or just life itself. Some lovers experience perfect compatibility in mind, body, and spirit, and their nearness necessitates and creates an unexplainable explosive chemistry. This chemistry causes unique emotions and passions never before experienced. Maybe it's the sharing of these secrets that produces a little smile within us when we realize it is unknown to the people who surround us. Even if physical love is not realized, the feeling of knowing how deeply you love another is all that you need. Some people are so beautiful in spirit that what is lacking in body makes them even more beautiful. Sometimes, love is only the fascination and joy of beholding or adoring a woman of perfect physical beauty and spirit. Gina was a combination of all these things; she created within me a tremendous desire to love, to enjoy, and to give all in a unification of complete oneness.

The day was spent talking, and I tried to eliminate the great hatred she had for Americans; but who could blame her? She had stood there helplessly, begging the American officer not to destroy their apartment building. But he didn't want to take a chance on losing one American life, so he killed 15 innocent people. They had destroyed her whole family to kill one German sniper in the top of the apartment building.

After that most remarkable weekend was over, I put in for my leave at once. Instead of taking a scheduled tour to Switzerland, I spent my leave with Gina. We went back to Naples for a week and stayed in a villa overlooking the sea.

Our first day was beautiful, and spent on the Isle of Capri. That night she told me how the American soldiers had taken advantage of other girls she knew; sometimes, only for candy bars or rations. Her hatred for Americans would not let her fully trust me. I tried hard to gain her confidence and love; I went out of the way to do Christian things that I would not normally have done.

I remember when I first met Gina she was half starved, and later she showed me where she had slept in a shelled-out building. Afterwards, to gain her deepest confidence and love, I swore that I would not have sexual relations with her until we were married to prove that not all Americans were that way. I loved her so dearly that it didn't matter. We visited her friends and relatives, and they all lived under deplorable conditions. It made me sick; I tried to help all I could, particularly with the children. I wondered at that time why the church didn't allow these people the means of birth control, since they allowed us to kill each other in war.

I remember Sunday very well, and how I forced her to go with me to Mass. One-third of the congregation were American military, and in the midst of the services, she ran out and cried. Later, she asked me how Catholics who were mortal enemies could pretend to be Christians, killing each other and continuing to pray to the same God who made us all—as though the killings and hatred had never happened.

I explained to Gina that she was right, and I even promised her that I would get out of the Navy as soon as possible, and would never have anything to do with the military again. But, she, in turn, would have to go to confession and ask forgiveness for all her hate. She wept in the confessional, and when she came out her face was as radiant as an angel. The next three days were the happiest of my life, and I never touched her—except to kiss and hug her. I went back to the carrier and sailed sorrowfully to Livorno, Italy.

I shall never forget those days in Naples with Gina, being so very happy for the first time in love.

I remember Livorno, Italy. That was the first time I failed God on war…after having been enlightened about loving my enemies and promising Gina to get out of the military. I remember when my orders were given to me on shipboard, when I learned that I had been accepted as a Naval Aviation Cadet and was to return to the States. I was happy, and I accepted them, because I had loved flying for as long as I could remember. I rationalized and said that I would just learn to fly and then I would resign my commission. Only three days before, I had promised never to have anything to do with the military. Now I was about to sign up for four more years in the Navy. I remember how drunk I got that night at the party in my honor in Livorno. That was my first step toward alcoholism and hypocrisy.

The next day I caught an Italian plane from Pisa to Rome to make a connection with a U.S. MATS aircraft for the States. At the airport I learned that the MATS aircraft was going to make its leg to Istanbul, Turkey, before it came back to Rome and then to the States. Since I had just come from Turkey, I obtained permission to stay in Rome until the plane came back the next morning. I stayed at the same Albergo Milano Hotel where I had previously stayed.

I tried to contact Gina in Naples, but no luck. She seemed so close and yet so far away. The next morning I went back to the Champino Airport and waited. It was afternoon before I was told that the plane from Istanbul was delayed. Finally, they got word that the plane had lost an engine and they would have to get one before they could fly back. They estimated it would take three days.

I immediately asked if I could go back to the hotel and call in every morning for arrival information. Permission was granted. I thought, what the hell, if I miss it, I can always catch another plane. I went back to the Albergo, since it was close to the train station, picked up my bags, and caught a train to Naples.

Fortunately, I found Gina at her apartment. She threw her arms around me and smothered me with kisses. Gina told me she had thought I would never come back, and I had renewed her faith. Her relatives had been telling her that GIs never came back, and they had many proofs.

Then she began to worry that I had deserted. I was forced to tell her why I was able to come back. I should never have mentioned that I was going to become a Navy pilot and an officer. I tried to explain that I was going to resign after I got my wings, but it didn't make any difference. There was not much to talk about for a long time as we ate our pasta. In fact, she didn't say a word. She just sat there and looked at me. Finally, she broke the silence by telling me that I would never come back for her, and she kept shaking her head slowly as I justified my actions and restated my broken promises.

After several days I began to worry about what to do. Gina could sense it and tried to force me to go back to Rome. She did not want to be married to a deserter. But I began to really not care. Finally, I said I would go back if she would wait for me until I got out of Flight School—then I would resign my commission.

Morning came, after a night of deep thoughts and love, and I bade a tearful farewell to Gina. The sky was clear and the mountains were bathing in the warm rays of the sun. On my way back to Rome, I felt again that spiritual awakening that had become a great part of me, and it was raging through every fiber of my being as I looked out the window at each destroyed village. I must get out of the Navy as soon as possible—right after I learn to fly.

At noonday, I boarded a plane for Port Lyady, Morocco, remembering my renewed promises to God and Gina. For the next six days, I waited for a trans-Atlantic hop, trying each morning to get on the daily passenger flight list. Only an ordinary enlisted man, I kept getting bumped off flights by officers' wives and their dogs. After the second day, I started to spend most of my time at Benny's Bazaar in Rabat, telephoning to check the daily flight list. I never could stand being in limbo. I was literally down to my last two cents, having sold all of my valuable belongings for food, when a "Connie" (a Lockheed Constellation) came in with a run-away propeller. The propeller's governor had failed. I proposed to the plane's maintenance chief that I would help to fix it if he would guarantee passage for me on his next flight out. He said that he would. Then I noticed that most of his passengers had left to catch a more reliable plane.

I landed in the Azores, Argentina, Newfoundland, and finally Westover Field AFB, still with two pennies in my pocket. I told the Sergeant about my plight, and he said that all he could do was give me extra meal tickets for the train. (Two years after I was discharged, I received a bill from the Navy for the 25 extra meal tickets I had used in just two days on the train to Pensacola, Florida.) To be precise, I used the extra meal tickets to buy drinks. They seemed to help me forget Gina.

I'm sorry for that too; how can I tell people now to be true Christians, when I can't cast the plank out of my own eye? I thought to myself, the only thing in my favor is that I've never discriminated against anyone because of their race. I guess it's because I remember my relatives telling me how no-good those "Negroes" were when I was very young. They did not even allow them in our town after dark.

We were late one day for Sunday mass, and I was pushed into the crowded back seat, which was reserved for one Negro family from another town close by. The little black boy who sat next to me prayed out loud, and at the communion offering, I could hear him clearly ask the Lord to protect him from the white people.

I decided right then and there that since God made all of us, and we have only one Heavenly Father, He did not want us to hurt each other, but rather love each and every one of humanity. I could not believe that He made a mistake when He created black people, Polish, and other different races and nationalities. However, I must admit that for a while I was prejudiced against Protestant Christians, but I was taught that by my religion, the same as not eating meat on Friday. Later I realized that just as the Lord had made Catholics, He also must have made Protestants.

CHAPTER 3

FLIGHT SCHOOL AND LOST LOVE

I finally made it to Pensacola Naval Flight School to be inducted into the flight program. I tell this story because God tried to speak to me again about war.

When I was discharged from the regular Navy I was immediately given my enlistment papers for Officer's School. I hesitated for a long time, reflecting on the consequences for my conscience. A sickness came over me as I began to realize that I might be giving my whole life to the military by signing up for four more years. I probably never would have the guts to get out, once I got my pilot's wings; my whole life would then be dedicated to war and hypocrisy. I also realized that I would probably lose Gina, but I couldn't get out of the Navy anyway.

The officer shook me back to reality by saying that if I did not want to sign up, he could still put me back into the regular Navy, which I dreaded. I took up the pen and failed you again, Lord.

While I was in pre-flight school at Mainside Naval Training, I met a fellow classmate named Al Toomey, who felt about the immorality of war as I did. But that's all Al felt immoral about.

One day I asked him, "Tell me, Al, why did you accept flight school, feeling the way you do about war?"

He answered, "Oh, I'm just here for kicks, man. I'm gonna have me a real good time. I love flying."

Again I inquired, "But what about war? You plainly said that you did not believe in it."

Slowly he replied, "War? Me? Oh yeah, well, let the rest of those gung-ho fools do the fighting, because Al just wants to enjoy himself."

"Well, I don't know, Al," I said. "A man with your deep intellect should have a much broader outlook on life."

He turned and looked straight at me, and said, "What's the matter, Tom? Sometimes I just don't understand you. One day you're all fired up to climb up in one of those planes and spray bullets all over the Communist world. Then the next day you've calmed down, with the intentions of a saint. You know what you are? You're a hypocrite, ole buddy. Sure, you can bet your life I'm going to avoid going to war, but I'm not going to avoid the enjoyment flying will bring. If you're serious about this, then you better get out of the Navy, and soon."

What he said was true. I was a hypocrite. Stankovan was right, I thought, when he called me "Warlove the Hypocrite."

Al was, if not a genius, a very near genius; he was a graduate of MIT with an aeronautical engineering degree. He had been kicked out of medical school, not to mention various other schools, but learning came naturally to him. He also had a private pilot's license and would have been a millionaire if his father could have trusted him with his inheritance.

Anyway, his dad had given him his old car to use at flight school, an elongated Cadillac Special which Al always kept loaded with iced beer. Al was addicted to the brew.

In the meantime, Gina and I wrote love letters across the Atlantic almost every day. She was the only thing in my life that I was still dedicated to. With this newfound passionate emotion, along with my love for God, I began to feel out of place in the military.

I wrote my Christian mother and father and told them that I was at Officers Flight School, and one day they brought the whole family down to visit me. They were so proud of me in my officer's dress uniform, and so were all of my brothers: Paul, Ray, Jim, Dick, Mike, and Phil, and even my little sister Maryanne. Once I tried to tell them that I really didn't believe in the military or fighting wars, and that I might quit. I even told them about the devastation and terrible suffering I had seen in Europe as the result of the war, and that our relatives over here in this country had killed our relatives over there in that country while we all were praying to the same Catholic God. I expected my father to be shocked, but I didn't expect my Christian brothers' attitude. They both told me what a chance this would be for me to get a free education, and at the same time a career that I could be proud of, by fighting for our country.

My father said, "Somebody has got to kill the communists or they will take over the Catholic world."

I tried to explain to them by saying, "The ordinary people in all countries are just like us; they are forced to fight wars by their unchristian leaders. Christ said 'Love your enemies and do good to those that hate you.'"

My father replied, "Christian countries have been fighting wars for centuries. Why would the Catholics have chaplains in all the militaries if war was wrong? If the Catholic

Church upholds it, then it must be right. There must be something else that's bothering you, boy. Are you afraid?"

"No!" I answered. "I love flying."

Quickly Dad replied, "Then go to it, son, and make us proud of you."

My mother reminded me that I would not fight for my rights even as a child, and that I always wanted to be a priest, and that I never believed that fighting was the right thing to do. However, now I was convinced otherwise, especially when dad came over and hugged me. I knew I was committed.

Pre-flight school was not too difficult, except for the half hour of calisthenics at six in the morning. Being that the Admiral's limousine was of the same make and color as Al Toomey's car, Toomey had made replicas of the Admiral's pennants, and could install them on his car within a matter of minutes. He loved to drive back and forth through the Main Gate and watch the Marines snap to attention and salute him, knowing that the Marines were trained to kill on command and think later. One day I realized that we were not any better than the Marines, since they were our drill instructors.

Since we could go off and on the base almost anytime we chose to in Toomey's car, we were constantly in trouble. For every five demerits you received, you had to march an hour on Saturdays. We, Toomey and I, had marched so much and become so experienced that they made us drill instructors on Saturday.

One of our roommates finally turned us in for all the AWOLs after being made acting company commander. But by chance I was paired with him the very next day in an intramural inter-team boxing match. I admit that I was not the best boxer, but I was the best slugger by far, all over the base—probably because I was raised with six brothers.

We usually just sparred with the guys in our own company and team, and particularly with roommates. I remember him saying to me, "Just take it easy and fake it, OK?" I replied, "Oh, sure! You bet I will!"

He had a worried look in his eyes because of the way I repeated those words to him, and at the ringing of the bell, I went out as if to touch gloves and I knocked him to his knees. All the other matches stopped to watch our bout, as I took great delight in beating him to a bloody pulp. The next day I was truly sorry when I saw his face; I also remembered all the devastating body punches that didn't show. However, we both shook hands and became the best of friends... He was killed in Korea. When I first learned of this tragedy, I again pondered to myself, "So you see, Lord, I don't even have the temperament to love my personal enemies; I certainly didn't turn the other cheek." I think my problem is that I don't think. Maybe that's why we fight wars; we don't stop to think first.

With all this activity, I began finding less and less time to write to Gina; in turn, her letters also began arriving more infrequently. Finally her letter came one Thursday morning, and it read:

April 11, 1950

My Dearest Tom,

In one day, in one hour, in one moment of time, the spirit of affection looked at me with your heart's eye; and from that instant my true love was born and found a dwelling place within my heart. This great love turned my sorrow into joy, my hatred into blissful love, and healed the scars of my tattered heart.

> You know that I love you as much as any heart can ever love, and I will continue to do so for the rest of my days; but time, distance, and separateness have caused me to consider an offer of marriage from another. I know you will understand this message, for you are a good man with gentleness in your heart, and you wish not to see me suffer.
>
> Oh, Tom, I tried. I really tried; but did I not wait in doubtful silence for so long for you to return to me and deliver me from this bondage and evil time? You came into my life and freed me of all hatred for others, no matter who they may be, but you also created a great loneliness. Time has now finally made me accept the fact that you will never come back, so I am accepting this offer of marriage to a dear friend next week.
>
> May heaven bless you, Tom, and through God, may someone give you the rapture that you have enfolded within the heart of mine.
>
> Love forever,
> Gina

As I finished reading her letter, tears began to form in my eyes. Gina was a sweet girl, and she had expressed so beautifully that I had made her happier than she had ever hoped to be, and that she loved me. She had revealed in so many words the great loneliness I had caused her and that she wanted to try to replace this loneliness with children and marriage. Then the shock that I was going to lose her overwhelmed me.

Gina was to be married the next week, and the letter was already eight days old. I jumped up and started throwing my things in a bag. I first reached Toomey by phone. "Toomey! Hey! I've got to see you right away! It's urgent!"

Al Toomey quickly answered, "Hey! Slow down, ole buddy;

you sound as though you're about to face a firing squad!" "It's worse than that!" I exclaimed.

In ten minutes flat, Toomey was at the room, asking, "What's happening?"

"Well, to tell the truth, I'm going over the hill and back to Italy, and I need some money," I answered.

"Whatttttt? Tom, do you know what you're saying? You're going to desert?"

Then I began to shout, "Hell, Al! I know what I'm doing! I'm tired of this so-called Navy! I'm tired of being a hypocrite! I'm tired of all this bull-crap that we're suppose to be representing! And I'm damned tired of leaving behind the most precious thing in my life!!! Gina is going to get married!"

Then Toomey said, "Well, well, well. I should have known this was all about Gina; you sure have talked about her enough in your sleep and while you were brooding over beer and booze. OK, my friend, just what is it that you want me to do?"

"Well," I replied, "I need some money, and fast!" "How much?" asked Al.

My voice trailed to a whisper, "I need much more than I dare to ask you for, but if you can lend me a thousand dollars, I'll forever be grateful to you."

"Gee Tom," Al said, "I don't have that kind of money on me, but I'll get it."

I forced a smile, and then managed to say, "Thanks Al, I knew I could count on you. But don't forget, not a word about this to anyone. OK?"

Al went right to work; immediately he gave me $265 that he had in his wallet, and sent a wire to his old man who was in Miami Beach. After waiting a full day, word came back that there was no one at his father's condo.

I began to panic, and told Al that I was going to desert anyway.

He knew that I had been drinking a lot while waiting on word about the money, and he tried to talk me out of it. Toomey tried to bring me to my senses, and gave me all the standard reasons for not going over the hill. We both had missed roll call that day, but again Al was to the rescue. He told me to have another drink while he called back to the base and tell them that we had a hospital emergency; this would buy me more time if I still decided to go AWOL.

However, in about a half hour, my two other roommates showed up, on a pretense of giving me money; they got me in the car between them and we had another drink.

When I found out they were taking me back to the base, they had all they could do to restrain me. Finally they made me realize that it was much too late. The letter was eight days old. The marriage between Gina and her friend probably had already taken place, and why screw up her life? "There are many people who marry for security while love develops later," Al said. That night I gave up Gina, my naval career, and my relationship with God. I went back to the base suspended like a dead person; at least I might as well have been dead, for all my interests were dead, except for the booze.

I remember the last real chewing out I received from our Marine Captain. He finally ended by saying, "Siemer, you're the most unmilitary man I have ever met!"

"Thank you, Sir," I replied.

"What did you say?" he shot back.

I said, "Is that all, Sir?" and smiled as I stepped back and did an about face, saluted, and walked out the door.

From the day I received Gina's letter, I knew it would only be a matter of time before I would be kicked out of Flight School, or be forced to resign. I was drunk every night.

I can distinctly recall an occasion when I awakened one morning with a splitting headache. I remained in bed with my eyes focused on the ceiling, when suddenly I found myself speaking out loud, as if I were talking to God.

"Lord, have mercy on me! I cannot stand it! I am a hopeless sinner and I have failed you so many times in the past. I'm telling you all this Lord, so that You will find someone else to carry Your word against war and on loving our enemies. Of course You already know, but I wouldn't want to repeat some of the sins I have committed after coming to the point where I didn't care. But I know You must love me Lord, although I cannot understand why; for without Your love and protection my soul would already be in the pit of Hell . . ." Lord have mercy on me! And yet I realized in my heart that I would sell my soul to have Gina back.

Weeks passed. The love of Gina was my sole entertainer, singing songs of happiness for me at night and waking me at dawn to reveal the meaning of life and the secrets of peace. It was a heavenly love, free from jealousy and riches, and never harmful to the spirit. Her love was a deep affinity which bathed the soul in contentment; a deep hunger for affection; a tenderness that creates hope without agitating the soul, changing the ugly reality of life to a sweet and beautiful dream.

It was hard for me to get over Gina; in fact, it took me several years. I knew that this was one of those cruelties that one has to live with, and I must deal with it to the best of my ability. So I continued to drink a lot.

I used the cadets' lounge to write all my letters, because the paper, envelopes, and stamps were free. I had a girlfriend back home who kept writing me letters, and then occasionally

I wrote my parents. I got to know the matronly old southern belle who was the chaperone of the club, or the ACRAC (Air Cadet Recreation and Activities Center), as it was known.

One day she invited me to a party at the club for selected cadets—her selection. To my surprise, an equal number of guests would be girls from a Baptist Girls College. Since it was a weekday night, I asked to bring a friend, and I told Toomey he was invited. He didn't want to go to any social at the club, especially one put on by the Baptists. Then I told him it was being put on by a girls college, which immediately caused him to get the faith.

The party took a turn for the better, and the girls slowly loosened up. Some got so loose they could hardly keep from giggling all the time; they even interjected sex into their conversations. The hostess raved about how good her punch tasted. One of the few cute girls came up to me and asked if I wanted to steal oranges. I thought I had heard her incorrectly and asked her to repeat the question. She said again what I thought she had said, and I said, "Sure." Her name was Lisa. We snuck out and got into the 1930 rebuilt Ford her daddy had given her. It was a masterpiece of restoration and cost $5,000. We drove down a darkened lane and stopped by the fence between two far-apart houses. She was up and over the fence as quick as a cat, while I hesitated; she urged me on, so over I went. We started grabbing oranges off the trees and she put them in her dress. Dogs started barking and voices shouting as we ran for the car; she laughed so hard she wet her pants. My Lisa turned out to be the daughter of the Chief of Mainside Naval Training. A full Navy Captain.

She was as full of hypocrisy as I, and neither of us had any goals or ambitions. All we wanted to do was live for the moment, and as happily as possible. That night of the party we were told that they needed members for the base Protestant choir. We showed no interest until it was mentioned that all choir members got Saturdays off if they attended practice.

We first tried to volunteer for the Catholic choir, but they already had too many members. So we signed up for the Protestant choir. We didn't dare tell the Marine drill sergeant until we had made two practices and one service. He couldn't believe it when we showed up at Saturday drill practice with weekend passes. That's also when I found out that Protestants were Christians too—some even more so than Catholics. Of course, we only lasted in the choir until it was proven by character assassination that we were the people who spiked the punch at the party. They never would have found out that the punch had been spiked if one of the girls had not been picked up for driving while intoxicated.

"So why do you want out?" The Captain asked me. "Sir, if I told you, would you believe me?"

"Try me," he said.

"Sir, I cannot kill. I do not believe that war is necessary. The great uniqueness about Christ was that he told us to love our enemies, and that we all have one Father Creator in heaven."

He told me, "Siemer, you should be the last person in service to bring religion into your life. With your record! And as far as peace is concerned, I heard that in the past six weeks you have had barracks fights. You would have been out of here two weeks ago except that the Chief saved you over that incident about the car and his daughter. I did not want to make him unhappy, or I would have let you go."

"Sir," I said, "I can guarantee you, he wouldn't mind at all if you pressed the charges."

The Captain thought for a few moments, and said, "I will accept your resignation as grounds for failing you. I must charge you with lack of motivation, for I could never fail you because of your grades."

I replied, "I will accept that, Sir. Sir, will you be doing the same for Al Toomey?"

He answered, "Yes, Toomey will be getting kicked out this week with a conditional discharge." Within a few days we were both failed for lack of motivation.

The Admiral complicated this by ordering a psychological test to determine how we ever got into his school in the first place. The test turned out to be the same 300 questions that we had taken to get in. This time we answered all the questions in reverse order.

The Admiral still was not satisfied, and called us into his office for final questioning. All of his inquiries were directed at me. He started by saying, "There must be 2000 young men waiting to get into this school. Why on earth would you men want to get out?"

I replied, "Well, Sir, if I stay in, I know I will be forced into a war sooner or later, and if that should happen, then I also know that I would not be able to kill."

"Why not, for Christ's sake?" he exploded.

"I'd rather not go into that, Sir. But, I am a Christian."

With that remark, the Admiral rose to his feet and walked over to his smoking stand and lit a cigar. He puffed on it a few times, then stood facing me with one hand in his pocket and the other wrapped around the cigar. "So you'd rather not go into that, huh? Well, do you mind telling me why?"

"No, Sir, it's just the way I feel," I replied.

Again the Admiral exploded, "The way you feel! Hell! We ought to drop an atom bomb on every one of those commie bastards. We saved their ass in the last war, and now they're out after ours!" He realized he had gotten carried away, and said, "OK, if that's the way you feel, then we are better off without you." "Yes, Sir," I agreed.

Toomey and I were to be discharged.

That night, I met with the Captain's daughter and told her that I had been discharged for lack of motivation and that her father had tried to save me. I also told her that her father expressed a great deal of love for her, to which she replied, "Then why wasn't he ever at home?"

Well, he had his duty . . ."

"Duty! When I was a child I needed him at home, but he was always gone. What about his duty to his family?"

I answered, "Well, he probably was out fighting the 'great war.' That's another reason why I want to get out."

"What about me?" she inquired. "Don't you even love me a little bit?"

"Yes," I answered, "I love you a lot, but . . ." "But what?"

I stammered for a while trying to think of any appropriate reason to give her. Finally I surprised myself by saying, "I want to be a priest."

I expected shouts of laughter and ridicule, but the expected torrents didn't materialize. We sat there silently for several moments before she said, "I was prepared for you to tell me anything but that."

Finally, she said softly, "I always knew that you were different, but I didn't know why. Still I don't want to believe it. I wondered why you always went to Mass."

I laughed, "That's not the reason; I was bred and brainwashed a Catholic."

"No," she replied, "you really wanted to; you never did it because you were forced. I've been thinking about God myself lately, and why we're here, and that life must have some other purpose than just living."

"Those are good thoughts, and I admire you for that." "Well," she said, "I guess this thing between you and me is the most unselfish thing I have ever done. To give you my love, knowing that I won't get it back in return, is really unusual for me. That's the first time I have given anybody anything and not expected something back. However, I enjoyed giving it. Maybe Christ was right when He said giving is better than receiving . . ."

She embarrassed me with her love when she continued. "You know you've made me suffer. I have never experienced this type of suffering, because I never had strong emotions either way. I have never loved and never given. I have never appreciated receiving because I never gave. I never experienced deep feelings or emotions, and I never understood about all that bullcrap you said when you would get drunk."

She paused for a while and I could see tears in her eyes, then she continued. "When a person gets drunk, it brings out their true nature, and when you drink, you are always full of love. I have seen you give all of your money away to some dirty little poor kid, or feel sorry for me and love me just to make me happy, and say beautiful things to me that you don't even feel. Anyone who can love their enemies like you say you do either must have great love in his heart or be just plain crazy as hell. But if there is anyone on this earth who can truly love their enemies, I'm sure you can."

Seriously, I said, "Thank you very much for the inspiration. I need all I can get at this point."

"What are you going to do?" she asked.

I thought to myself that a lie can certainly get complicated, so I answered, "Well, I think I'll go out West to the desert to think things out."

CHAPTER 4

FIRST INDIFFERENCE AND NEAR DEATH

I have to tell this story to show how God can be missing in our lives and yet still bring us back to do something good, even by threats of death.

While we were in Denver, we met a bald and bearded reprobate named Klondike who convinced us that all we had to do to make a fortune was go to Alaska and shoot timber wolves. He told us that we could go out in the sticks and roast some meat, then shine a spotlight and shoot the wolves as they came for the meat. Klondike left us saying that he would meet us at the Montana border in two weeks, so he could get his dogs in shape.

We used to roam the countryside between cities and live like gypsies in the outdoors, enjoying the wonders of nature and the bounty of freedom. However, we would eventually tire of that life of roughing it; then we'd take the car to the closest river and spend a day cleaning and polishing it. It would take another day to throw out all the debris we'd accumulated and pack all our outdoor gear in the trunk. We would shave and trim each other's hair and bathe in the river. Finally, we would put on our impressive midshipmen's uniforms and race to town. Usually we would go straight to the biggest hotel, look for the schedule of special events, and pick an affair that served food or had a free bar. Weddings, particularly Greek or Italian weddings, were the best.

First of all, you had to psych yourself into believing that you really belonged. Toomey demonstrated the approach to me when we were in Pensacola. One time he bet me $10 that he could steal 100 pounds of potatoes from a supermarket by just using psych. I picked the market, and he walked in briskly as if he was mad at the world. He went up to the cash register operator and demanded, "Where in the hell is my 100 pounds of potatoes?"

"What do you mean, you don't know!" shouted Toomey. "Butt-t-t-"

"Well I'll be damned!" exclaimed Toomey, as he stormed back to the rear of the store. He picked up two 50-pound bags, marched proudly out the door, put them in the car, and drove away. It cost me $10, but he proved his point.

So we would always push past any doorman and march across to the bar while shouting and waving to "Uncle Charlie." We both figured that we weren't stealing because we always added more life to the party. Much later, while I was in the seminary, I realized that it just might be wrong.

I remember at one of those free-loading affairs, Toomey met a little rich gal who invited us to play tennis at the Denver Country Club the next day. We literally lived at that club for two complete weeks. I slept in the car at the parking lot, and Toomey slept on a blanket on the ground. Sometimes we shared special guest rooms.

We used the pool, played golf and tennis, and ate their lunches.

When there were no parties, we would talk one of the girls into charging meals and drinks to her daddy's account. We both began to tire of this eventually and decided to move on, but we had no money. That same day a letter arrived from Toomey's mother, in which she informed him that his old buddy from MIT was running a company that was building a new road through Jackson Hole, Wyoming, all the way to the South Gate of Yellowstone National Park. Toomey's buddy sent the word that he could have a job anytime he wanted one.

Well, we were down to our last quarter, so we went into a restaurant to see what it would buy. At that time, you could buy a pack of cigarettes for a quarter, and Toomey was dying for a cigarette. I didn't smoke, so I insisted that we buy a hamburger. We became very loud and the manager finally asked us to leave. Believe it or not, this was the first disagreement we ever had; and to top it all off, we even squared off to fight it out. Since I had the quarter in my pocket, and since he knew that he was no match for me, he conceded, and grudgingly went up and down the sidewalk looking for the longest discarded cigarette butts he could find. After he found several, we ordered the hamburger and split it.

Imagine the son of a millionaire having to pick up thrown- away cigarette butts like a bum on the street! The more I reminded him of it, the harder we laughed. Then I got the brilliant idea of going out to the Country Club and caddying at the golf course.

Toomey reminded me, "But Tom, most of those members already know us."

"So what, Al, we're leaving town anyway," I replied.

"Don't you think we should have a little pride about ourselves?"

asked Toomey.

"Pride!" I shouted, "Pride is one thing and being a fool is another. Here we are, completely broke, with not a dime between the two of us, nothing to eat, and not even a roof over our heads. And you stand there and tell me about pride!"

I guess Al Toomey finally got tired of hearing my mouth, because we both went down to caddy for the golfers. It did turn out to be sort of embarrassing, especially when the golfers would keep looking at us in our T-shirts and sneakers. The smartasses *would* make a big thing out of it, I thought to myself. We would push their balls into the ground with our feet every chance we got. I felt embarrassed myself, so I knew what my friend Toomey was going through. One month we were both officers in the United States Navy, and the next month we were peons not knowing where our next meal was coming from.

I once heard Toomey say, "For Christ's sake! Maybe being rich isn't so bad after all. I could have bought and sold half these guys ten times over."

It was sort of funny watching Toomey. He didn't know how to caddy anyway!

The war broke out in Korea just as we were about to leave Denver. We delayed our departure by one night to celebrate being able to miss the war, but what good were we doing by staying out of it? It was the first time Toomey had mentioned anything to me about going back home. Going back home! My God, I forgot to tell my parents that I had quit flight school!

So that night was the first time in a long time I had thoughts about my future and my conscience, as I tried to think of how to tell my parents why I had resigned from flight school. I realized that I had failed them and God, but for what? I wasn't accomplishing anything with my life, my glorious ideals didn't even exist anymore, and I felt like a worthless wino. My conscience was so flabby now that it allowed me to justify everything. I had my chance to be somebody and blew it over a cause I didn't even think about anymore. I was pretty down on myself.

When we got depressed we always moved on, and since we were going into the mountain country, I suggested we buy a case of canned food while we had the money. We also bought a Coleman stove and cooking utensils. Toomey liked spaghetti, so we bought a case of Franco-American. Later we found out that we should have bought a mixture of canned foods. To this day, I cannot bear to open a can of spaghetti. We packed away our uniforms neatly and wore our dirty old khakis as we went through Laramie, Cheyenne, and on past Medicine Bow.

One day Toomey pointed out something remarkable. "Well,

I'll be damned! Do you notice that all the cowboys are now Indians?"

"Yes," I replied, "Custer would turn over in his grave if he could see this."

From Rawlings we kept going up and up toward the mountains, which we could see in the distance. I mentioned that I had never climbed a mountain, and Toomey, who was from Vermont, suggested that we climb the one in front of us. It took us four unbelievable hours to get to the base.

We walked to the timberline and to the face of a 500-foot-high precipice. I said we might as well forget it, but Toomey said it was "a piece of cake." He found a diagonal, snow-filled crack in its face that couldn't be seen from the road. So hand over foot we climbed the 500 feet to the top. It was the Fourth of July and the snow was melting. Little rocks, some the size of bowling balls, fell past us. I asked Toomey for the second time if this was safe. I asked, "What if I get hit on the head with one of those rocks?" He assured me that if I did, I wouldn't know about it.

He made all the steps in the snow and ice, and I couldn't catch him. The crevice was snow filled at the bottom, and there wasn't anywhere you could go if something fell down—or somebody, like Toomey. I thought we'd never get to the top, but when we did, it was worth it. You could see all the mountains surrounding both sides of Jackson Hole and the azure blue colors of Jackson Lake. The Grand Tetons' Alpine peaks were to the south. The mountain was perfectly flat on top, with snow about 6 feet deep and 70 feet wide.

I asked Toomey if we might be the first to climb it. He pointed toward six piles of rocks on the crested summit. There were names scratched all over them. We walked across the summit, and I fell back to keep from falling. We were in loose snow on the edge of a 3,000-foot precipice.

As I lay in the snow, my heart started beating again. Toomey laughed as I crawled over to the edge to have another look. It was a wonderful winter scene we saw below. Being on the shady side of the mountain, it looked like Alaska in January. It was blue cold, and a little lake was frozen solid surrounded by snow-covered evergreens. I've never stood on solid land and looked so far straight down. I imagined I was flying over the Arctic, and I lay there, awed by God's creation. I wondered, after having created all this, why did He create people to screw it all up?

After that, mountains always brought me close to God. That day, it was too close for comfort. I remember Toomey had cut a couple of short sticks; now I knew why. We walked over to look at the way we had come up, and I could not believe how steep it was. When you're climbing up head first, you never have a chance to look down. Now I did. "Call the Fire Department for a ladder. I'm not going down," I shouted.

Toomey laughed and said "It'll be easy," and he showed me how. He dug in his heels and wiggled them as he leaned back on the short stick for support. He went down about 100 feet and stopped. Then he coaxed me to do the same. Before I started I remembered the 50-foot straight drop we had climbed up over the rocks at the bottom. Again I prayed, "Lord protect me!"

Fear always brings back atheists and cowards to God, and I wasn't an atheist. I dug my heels in and supported myself with my stick. I gained more confidence, wiggled my heels, and went faster. I finally relaxed and leaned back on my stick. Suddenly my feet went out from under me, and I took off like a free-falling freight train. I remember Toomey's eyes looking up in amazement before I hit him. The last time I saw him he was about 10 feet in the air over my head. After I landed, I was sliding on my belly at 60 miles an hour. As I dug my fingers into the snow, I felt my graduation watch go over my hand.

Then I remembered the drop at the bottom of the snow, and for the first time in my life, I gave up fighting. I begged God for forgiveness. "You forgave the good thief at the last moment, Lord. I beg you to forgive me." And I was at peace.

A voice kept ringing in my ears to lift up on my elbows and go like a snowplow. I did, and finally I stopped—just 50 feet short of the drop-off. I lay there thanking God for allowing me another of the thousand second chances He had already given me.

Toomey came down and asked me if I was all right. "Yes, you mother, but if I ever get off this mountain I'll never climb a step ladder!" He finally got me down off the mountain and found that I was cut to pieces. As I slid I had kept sliding into little piles of accumulated rocks. These rocks practically skinned me alive. My sleeves were ripped off from the elbows on down, and so was my skin. I was bleeding, and where I was not bleeding, I was bruised.

Toomey apologized, in his own way, when he took my shirt off. "You certainly don't know how to climb down mountains."

"You bastard, you—I tried to tell you I couldn't do it." That night he slept in the car with me for the first time, and kept the engine and heater going. I almost died of cold that night, because the dummy had parked on the highest pass in the mountains. I might have been preserved until morning, but then the bastard got out the iodine and tortured me.

We finally made it down to Moran, Wyoming, in the center of Jackson Hole. The bottom of the Hole was like desert prairie. Halfway up were old beautiful trees, then bare rocks to snow-capped peaks. Though I was miserable I couldn't help but enjoy God's country. After the fall and having been so close to death, I realized that life was short. If I had died that day or 50 years later, it still would be only a blink of an eye compared to eternity. I was only 20 years old at the time, but I felt like I had lived 100 years.

We got to the construction site, but there was no activity. In fact, there was no one at all. We were two weeks early because of the snows, and with only $10 between us. Two miles south of the South Gate of Yellowstone, the Snake River wound under the road, and across from it stood the Flagg Ranch, which at the time consisted of a country store and six half-finished tourist cabins. Since then, I have heard it has become a multi-million dollar tourist complex. The owner felt sorry for us and gave us a tarpaulin to build a tent in an aspen grove on his property back by the Snake River. Luckily, that evening, we tied the tarp between the trees. That kept a herd of moose from stepping on us. We found moose shit all around us the next morning.

We finally started with Toomey's buddy on the survey crew. When that got ahead of schedule, we were transferred to the cleaning and burning crew. This crew was under a

65-year-old fart who used to have his own road construction company but was bought out by his competition (our present employer) with a life-long job as superintendent. The first Sunday I worked for Homer Bundy I asked him for time to go to Mass. He said, "Don't you know, boy, it's 40 miles to that mission?"

I insisted, even if it cost me my job. I told him he could deduct it from my pay. He reached in his pocket and gave me two silver dollars to drop in the collection, and he never deducted the three hours double time it took me to go to Mass. When Toomey found out about it, he asked to get off for Mass too, and Homer told him to go to hell.

Every week he would ask me if I was going to church and he'd give me the two silver dollars for the collection. It must have been the inspiration of these surroundings God had created that first led me back to Him and to peace, the first peace I had experienced since my indifference. I began to think I should dedicate my life to the Lord again. Every day I would pray and wonder what He wanted me to do, and it always came back clearly: "Go tell them to love their enemies." Every time I came close to Christ, He gave me the same command. I told Jesus one day that He had failed, so why should anyone listen to me? But the message always came back loud and clear.

CHAPTER 5

CHRISTIAN SOCIALISM

I tell this story in protest of the Catholic Church always condemning any form of socialism and backing the rich, royalty, and the capitalist while preaching that it stands for the poor.

Coming back one night from Jackson, we picked up a couple of hitchhiking girls who were going to work at the Old Faithful Lodge in Yellowstone. They stayed with us that night, and my girl thought it was strange of me not to put a move on her. "What is he, a queer?" Marta asked Toomey.

"No, he's going to be a priest," Al said. "A what? You've got to be kidding me."

So Marta and I talked most of the night. We were all trying to sleep in the two beds Toomey had built, which stretched almost all the way from wall to wall. You can imagine what it was like to have four people in one 12-by-10-foot cabin.

We had torn lumber off an abandoned ranger station to build the cabin. This was after the wife of the superintendent started charging us five dollars a night to sleep on the bare floor of a camp tent.

I remember the first night we tried to sleep in that cabin. In the middle of the night, shortly after I rolled over, the darkness was pierced by a horrible scream. Because I was heavier than him, Toomey had caught his butt between the cracks. I had to jump up and down on my side of the bed to free his ass. He had a black and blue stripe for a month. After that we nailed slats across the boards so they would all go up and down at the same time.

Marta was a Burbank pinko, and this was my first personal encounter with communism. We discussed philosophy until it interfered with Toomey's sleep; then we were forced to move to the car. The next day I did not go to work; I was persuaded by her arguments. We were in agreement over many, many things. Except God.

"There is no God, dummy; that's why we have to make the state supreme," she said.

I had listened to her for a long time and now I demanded to sum up my feelings, or my rebuttal, about communism before we started discussing God. "The existence of communism during the transition period from capitalism is a theory subversive of peace and morals. The communists admit they must have violent upheavals and disturbances to spread their idea. When you take over a country, you always kill or imprison the intelligentsia and the property owners. How can you justify that?" I asked.

She shot back, "Do you know any rich people, or any wealthy neighborhoods in your city? Do you think that these people would ever voluntarily give up their big houses, cars, and money if that could keep thousands from starving in Ethiopia? No, never! You would have to kill them to make them share. Anyway, your own Christ said it was harder for a rich man to get to Heaven than for a camel to pass through the eye of a needle. Why doesn't your church stress that, instead of giving it only lip service?"

"So when you make all the people equally poor, you are working for Christ," I laughed. "But let me finish. Communism would lead to a hard slavery by forcing everyone to accept imposed labor without any choice as to its kind or condition, without any direct return for or control over the fruits of our labor, without any say in what happened to the goods we produced by our labor. It would lead to an equality of drab misery."

"Well, what does Christ teach?" she shot back. "I understand He advocates being poor, meek, and mild. Turning the other cheek and loving your enemies. Imagine what kind of misery *that* would lead to."

She stumped me for a minute, and I changed the subject back to the existence of God. "Why don't you believe in God?" I asked. "There are so many proofs. Everything around us has to be caused by something else or causing something else. There is also the argument of motion. Since everything in the world is in motion, there must be a supreme mover. And there is the argument of design. The world has a clear design. Or another reason, the argument of universal consent, which says that all people since the beginning of time have believed in a Supreme Being of some sort."

"When are you going to go to school, dummy? I was taught about causality in the first grade, and here you go thinking you invented the wheel," she said as she pushed me.

"Then, if you're so damn smart, why don't you believe in God?"

I rebutted.

Marta raised her head with a strange expression on her face, and said, "Man's inhumanity to man has proven to me that there is no God. If we were all caused by one Creator, then why aren't we all brothers and sisters? Why do

Christians kill each other? You see, I would have believed in God if Christ had not failed. His lineage goes back to the very beginning through the Hebrew religion.

If you believe in causality, then you know you must follow everything back to a beginning, or an Alpha, when there was nothing. Is-ness demands a cause. If it all started with one molecule, and the world evolved from that, then where did the one molecule come from? Don't you see, Tom, that there has to be one thing or being in the beginning that is, always was, and caused this world around us, even if it only created the first molecule that the world evolved from."

I was fascinated by her great knowledge; spellbound, in fact. "Go on," I exclaimed, because intelligence is the one thing I have the greatest respect for, except great beauty.

Then I interjected the belief I had about Christ. "I believe that God created man because of His loneliness, and His little clay toys rejected Him and God experienced further loneliness. Then He sent Christ, His only begotten Son, to redeem man again through the Blessed Virgin Mary. He begot a Son with the nature of both God and humanity. Because Christ was God, but also had a human nature, God's little clay toys were again raised in the sight of God. Christ's human nature could have again caused man to reject God. In fact, we had two chances to reject God. The Virgin Mary could have refused to be the Mother of Christ's human nature, and Christ could have refused to die on the Cross. He showed us at Gethsemane that it was very hard to do. He sweat blood, but He did His Father's will and saved man, and made up for centuries of sin."

We went outside again before Marta said, "I believed that once, but then I realized that Christ and His teachings were a failure, and therefore He could not be God or the Messiah.

Since we all have one Father, how can we not care for each other? How can we fight and kill each other when we are sons and daughters of one Father in Heaven?"

I said, "Well, that is what Christ taught. That proves that He is the Messiah!"

"But you dummy, no one followed His commandments of love, not even your church, which He established. I do not know one single Christian who is perfect as He said we must be. The Catholic Church is our bitter enemy because it has always been on the side of the imperialists and colonial capitalists. Look at South America, which we communists are about to take over. The Catholic Spanish conquered the Indians, took their gold, subjected them to slavery. Then the Church came behind the conquerors and domesticated the Indians by telling them that whether or not they had food or clothing wasn't important—what was important was to serve their masters with love and die early, for their reward would be great in heaven. All the while, the clergy lived at the expense of and in the friendship of the conquerors. The Catholic Church hates us as bitter enemies. But they are not following the teachings of Christ either. They are no better than the communists."

I rebutted, "But look at the time from Adam and Eve to Christ. How many times did the Jewish people reject God? My problem has always been with women. But look at King David, who talked with God. He looked out the window one day and saw Bathsheba taking a bath. He not only committed adultery with her, but he had her husband sent to the front, and gave orders to have him killed. What greater sin could a man commit, especially since he still refused to give her up?–Of course, I've always said a man would have a better chance of forgiveness for loving than for hating his fellow beings, even women."

We both laughed, and we both realized that we had developed a tremendous respect for each other. Every Sunday I had off that summer, I would spend with her at Yellowstone.

Marta was the only woman I ever loved purely for her intellect and deep love of humanity. One time I remember we were about to do it, but she made the mistake of calling me "King David," and then we spent most of the night discussing Christ. Lord, what a hypocrite I am! She must have been sent by the Holy Spirit, I thought, because she taught me more about God than I ever expected to know. A communist teaching me how to love God–the thought was absurd. But she really loved her fellow humans far more than any Christian I have ever met, because she was willing to sacrifice more.

She told me about the philosophy of Aristotle and Thomas Aquinas, and I could not understand why she did not believe in Christ. I am sure she was convinced that there was a God or a Supreme Creator, because she had made me even more convinced. Later, I was taught the same things in seminary.

Then she went on to explain the argument of motion. Marta told me, "The whole world is in motion. The electrons, protons, and neutrons of this table we are sitting at are in motion. Everything about us is in motion: the earth, the stars and planets. There is motion in growing, in singing, and in understanding. Motion is the transition from potentiality to actuality. Motion, then, requires a mover that is not being moved. Whatever is moved is moved by something other than itself, and everything we see is in motion. We know that from our own observation, let alone from physics.

Now, if everything moved requires a mover, it is obvious that there must be a beginning of the chain of motions. There must be a first mover which is really first, and was not moved itself. The first mover must be one, since, being the first mover, it is not subject to any other mover. It causes motion but is itself un-caused. Therefore, you would have to trace all the way back to the first motion, and it must be identified with the first cause of all things, a one and infinite being. The Creator of the universe in motion, one unmoved mover, God, the first cause of motion."

Then it was my turn to explain the argument of design. "A design is a plan." I said. "The sun does rise every day and babies are not born by chance. Nor do animals get heavy fur when winter approaches by accident or chance. We call it the law of nature when things follow a plan as large as the universe. What makes a woman's pelvis dilate when she is ready to give birth to a child? What tells her breasts to fill with milk? We can see a plan always constant all around us. If the world exhibits a most wonderful and constant order, then it must have a most wonderful and intelligent designer.

Then there is the moral order. Humans, in their free and deliberate acts, are conscious of an obligation. We know that there is a duty upon us. We know that we must do good and avoid evil. We say that conscience is what makes us aware of the moral law. All people of all times, even savages, have come to a knowledge of right and good to be done and of evil and wrong to be avoided, as they reach the age of reason. This proves there must be a supreme lawgiver, distinct and superior to human nature and will."

We talked about the conditions in Guatemala. It was totally unjust for people to live under those conditions. Marta was not right when she told me once, "The end justifies the means—to eliminate world starvation and bring peace to the world. The communists hate the methods they were forced to use to make the over-rich share with the poor. But the world's mighty wealthy would fight to the death for their right to keep their riches. That's why the communists must deport the rich and powerful when they take over a country, because these people never become used to having less. They always start a counterrevolution. It is best we let those people go."

I had to tell her, "I could never understand how the communists could die for their cause, like in Korea, and particularly in China. I have to believe in an afterlife to be able to sacrifice my life for a cause. I would have to have a chance to go to heaven when I died. But to die for atheistic communism, even if I believed in it with my whole heart, would be impossible, if I knew that would be my complete end."

"My friend," she said, "they die that the world may become a better place for their children and future generations."

"But they will never be able to enjoy it. It's a shame; they can't enjoy the hope of heaven even though they died for what they thought a worthy cause."

Then Marta said, "Well, look at the white capitalists in South Africa and Rhodesia. They'll die for their cause of white supremacy and to maintain their plantations. You can't tell me that they don't know they're doing wrong. I have heard that German troops fight long and bitterly to their death just to follow orders. Certainly they could not believe they would go to heaven if they died for the Fuehrer, who they knew was godless.

You would also have to hold a gun to the head of each capitalist in the Beverly Hills mansions to make him share his wealth with the less fortunate. He would be willing to die for his property. What is a more stupid, godless cause to give your life for than a piece of property? Yet your Church, which is supposed to be Christian, preaches that you can take a person's life to defend your property.

The history of your country is based on fighting for your right to property. Your revolution against England was fought over property rights and taxes. They did not want to pay England taxes for what they felt was already theirs. They dumped the tea in Boston Harbor in protest. They did not want to share their houses with English soldiers. They were willing to die for money and lands—even other people's lands, like Texas and California, which they stole from Mexico. The Alamo is a religious shrine to that kind of people. Our whole history is based on this premise that one should die and take lives to defend one's rights and property.

Look at the settlers. They came and took the land from the Indians. They worked the land and called it theirs. They killed the Indians when they tried to take it back, and then they brought slaves in from Africa to work the land. How were the American people different from the white South Africans and Rhodesians then? They, too, would rather die than give the land back to the people. What an unchristian cause to die for! I cannot believe that to kill for a piece of land and to die for the same piece of land would get you into heaven, as you believe.

So you ask why the Comrades went on suicide missions and sacrificed their lives for a better world for their children? They had a better cause to die for than the Americans who will die protecting a piece of land, a house, a car, and money in the bank. Even your Christ would have to agree. In fact, the little I know about Christ proves to me that he was a great man. He also despised the rich man and loved the poor man. That's why we know we will have to kill the wealthy before they will give up the big homes, cars, and boats and share with the poor in other countries. The world is getting smaller, my friend, and we will have to start sharing."

I replied, "It all sounds like a beautiful dream, but when you say you will have to kill all those people to bring it about and cause revolutions, unrest, and misery—let alone, the murder of a large segment of society—then I know it cannot be right. There must be a better way to bring it about," I said.

She rebutted. "This change cannot come about peacefully, and you can see why."

Slowly, I said, "Then you're no better than the capitalist warmongers. Only you would destroy the world to make it a better place. They would destroy it to keep it the way it is, for their selfish reasons. You would both destroy the world. We have to find a peaceful way to settle our conflicts."

"There is no other way, my friend. We are both willing to die for our cause." Then she laughed and said, "There is one way to do it peacefully. Have all the Americans become Christians, give up their riches to the poor, and surrender peacefully to us, their enemies."

That morning I had read about the President's "doomsday"

aircraft, which would allow him to remain safely aloft to direct war operations. This implies there would be no safe place on the ground. Maybe it would be better, I thought, if we surrendered to the communists and saved the world. Maybe that is what Christ meant when he said, "Do not give resistance to injury." Anyway, Lord, I am not about to preach surrender, or they'd lock me up.

I thought to myself that if everyone did love their neighbors in only their own towns, then in their cities and in their states, then in the whole country, we would soon be ready to love our enemies. I realized the futility of it all, but I remembered the parable about the mustard seed and how that tiniest of seeds grew into the biggest tree. "Well, I better find a mustard seed and get started. Lord, it will take a million years. I know you have the time, but I don't, so you better give me a lot of help."

It was so sad, I thought, that Marta, with her most logical and intelligent mind, was never yet given the gift of faith by the Holy Spirit. She could not accept Christ because He did not change the world to the way it ought to be. She admitted to me that she did believe in a God, but she would not accept Christ as the Messiah because His Christians did not follow His teaching. I prayed that she would be given the gift of faith in Christ. The last letter I received from her placed her in Guatemala, supporting the reformist regime. She must have done a good job, because the CIA coup took over the government shortly thereafter. But I had never dreamed that a socialist would be instrumental in bringing me closer to Christ. I even thought seriously again of becoming a priest. Marta was probably killed by the CIA.

CHAPTER 6

PRIESTHOOD, OR A WOMAN?

In this chapter I am protesting the Church's forbidding many good men from the priesthood just because they want to marry and have a wife and companion.

I still thought a lot about Gina, at this time in my life, and I realized I couldn't become a priest. I probably would still have sacrificed my soul to get her back if I had the chance. "So you see, Lord, why I cannot be a priest, or even preach your message of perfection? Not while I still remember Gina."

Gina's eyes sparkled like the morning sun; the deep, dark, and midnight sky must have been jealous of her eyes. Beautiful dark eyes that tell nothing and portray only the deep passage to the soul, but not the soul itself.

Even if physical love is not realized, the feeling of knowing how deeply you love another is enough, and it is a bond that can last an eternity in your mind.

Toomey and I were not the same anymore. I had lost the devil-may-care outlook that made us simpatico. After

Marta left, I used to sit down on the mountain and look out all day at the Tetons.

Sometimes I would even pray that God would make me forget Gina and commit myself to Him.

Toomey would never discuss God or religion with me, even though he was a Catholic. Usually, at that time, Catholics did not hold serious religious discussions with their own kind. They were all supposed to believe the same way, so it wouldn't be any fun. In fact, most of my friends were of a different faith.

So, Toomey didn't come my way, but eventually I went back to his. We would drive the 40 miles to Jackson, Wyoming and live it up every Friday and Saturday night. After all that overtime I still came back with only $80 for a full summer's work. I stopped preaching to people about loving their enemies—because I made too many enemies.

Our cabin burned down, and we had to move back to the line camp. All the other construction workers were Indians.

Some wore their clothes until they disintegrated, which was about every two weeks, when they were paid. Then they would go into town, buy new Levis, and take a shower. Toomey was always ribbing them in his Irish way about taking a bath. They never said anything—that is except on payday, when they spoke with their guns. We had made the mistake only once of coming back to camp early on payday. We were suddenly awakened by a drunken Indian firing a 45 through the top of the tent, the side, the bottom, and anywhere else he chose. Toomey took his knife and cut a slit in the side of the tent to get us out. The camp foreman walked up behind the Indian, hit him in the back of the head with a two by four, and walked out again. The Indian was there for two days before he stirred. Then he asked his buddies what he had drunk the night before.

For a while Toomey was being chased by a half-Indian girl whose old man owned a huge hunting lodge. Rather than say a half Indian, I should say that she was two Indians, because she weighed 300 pounds, but she was sweet.

I always knew at night when she was in the tent, because the floor would shake.

One day we were wondering what happened to Klondike. "I wonder if he is still waiting at the Canadian border for us?" I asked Toomey. We decided that day that we'd have to go home eventually. It was the first snowfall, and if Alaska was like this, we did not want any part of it.

Old Homer Bundy, our superintendent, put us on the burning crew that followed the timber cutters. He wanted to get as much cleared as possible before we were snowed in.

He bought an old fire truck and made us fire marshals. For the first two weeks all we had to do was to move the fire truck 200 feet each day. We could barely do it with that decrepit antique. Since we were in the national park, we were under the jurisdiction of the park rangers. It was a windy day, and the rangers came up and told Homer he had to stop burning because it was too dry. "Put out the fires, boys, with the dozer," Homer ordered.

As soon as the rangers were gone he raised hell with the dozer operator for doing such a good job, then started them all up again with gasoline. Toomey was up the mountain checking for sparks. For the last couple of days, we'd had all we could do to keep numerous little fires from starting up along the right of way. Homer had the fires out of hand already when a 40-mile-an-hour wind picked up and blew them up in the woods. I could see immediately what was going to happen. Toomey would be trapped against a cliff.

I heard him yell, "What in the hell is going on down there?" I raced up and around the fire smoke to where I thought he might be and called for him. The smoke was too dense. Luckily, I had two wet blankets before I left the fire truck. I yelled and yelled, but there was no answer, so I took a deep breath and ran into the smoke. Only God knows why I tripped over him lying by a tree. To this day I don't know how I picked him up like a baby and carried him 100 yards out of the smoke. I collapsed after I got past the fire.

We both woke up in the same hospital room. I remember the first voice that came to me as I opened my eyes fully: "This isn't bad duty, is it, partner?" There he was sitting in bed smiling. I was sick all day. The cliff saved the forest and Homer's job. Homer was really sorry about getting us hurt, and didn't even care whether we covered for him with the Rangers, but we did.

We were in the hospital a week, and during that time we really had fun. We goldbricked the last three days. The nurses loved us, and we loved the nurses. One day I realized what a pleasure it was to sleep on clean sheets. It had been four months since we left Denver. I became rather remorseful, and maybe even experienced my first touch of homesickness. Toomey kept reminding me that he owed me one, but also kept reminding me of the mountain climbing incident. Finally I admitted we were all even. Between nurses we had some very serious discussions in our room that week, particularly at night.

The priest had heard our confessions the second night, and he certainly got an earful from both of us. Toomey told me before he went that he realized his whole life had been a worthless waste, that he had not done one constructive thing except to have fun. He told me about his desire to have been something, that he had not done one constructive thing except to have fun. He told me about his desire to have been a doctor but he kidded that the family already had more money than they could spend.

"You know, I know what's bugging you, don't you?" he said. "It's Gina, and that is the only reason I have lived with you. I always felt partly responsible for not getting you back to Italy when I saw how much you loved her afterwards." I didn't say anything. "Well, I will tell you, fellow, she probably weighs 300 pounds. You know how fat those Italian women get. And probably she has 10 bambinos."

I laughed with him. Finally he said, "You know, being in this hospital has brought back all my ambition to be a doctor."

I told him, "It's that cute little red-headed nurse that made you realize what you've missed."

"You know, you may be right. You know how horny I always am. But, with her I feel differently. Like having sex doesn't matter. I must be getting as daffy as you."

I had seen the little red-headed nurse by the door, where he couldn't see her, while he was talking. She came in with Irish mist in her eyes and chewed him out for throwing his butts on the floor. "Why can't you be like Tom? He doesn't even smoke."

"See what I mean, see what I mean? That's what a woman will do to you," he exclaimed laughingly, while faking hurt feelings.

She walked over and kissed him on the cheek and said, "Oh, you poor little boy." He grabbed her and pulled her down to him and kissed her squarely on the lips. I could see he loved her and I told him to do the right thing about it. He would be as miserable as I was if he did not. At least I have showed someone an example.

"What are you going to do, Tom?" he asked seriously.

I looked out the window at the snow for a long time; then I turned to him and told him that I would tell him if he didn't laugh. He promised me he wouldn't. Then I replied, "I'm going home to become a priest."

"You always were different, now I guess I know why. You used to drive me crazy with that crap about loving your enemy," he said.

"Thomas, I can't even love those damn Indians. There are two kinds of people I really hate, and that is a prejudiced person and those damn niggers."

We both laughed at that old joke, but it was no joke with Toomey. He still couldn't force himself to be around blacks or the Northern Irish.

"Well, when are we leaving?" he asked. "Right now," I answered. "Then get your damned sea bag and let's go!"

Just then Susan, Toomey's girl, came back in and ordered him back to bed. He told her he was leaving with or without her. Tears came to her eyes and she could not speak; they just stood there. I finally said, "Susan, if you love him, go with him. Don't put it off, don't do what I did and regret it the rest of your life. You might have to throw the bastard out later, but that's later."

She finally said softly, "I will go with you, if you really want me to."

He told her, using only his eyes, that he really needed her and loved her. I got up and left the room.

The next day, we three went back to camp to get our final paychecks. All the Indians hugged me, but nobody said a word.

They rather ignored Toomey. "All right, you mothers. I will miss you!" he said.

We all shook hands, and when Toomey kissed Hiawatha good- bye, all the Indians shook hands with him. Homer gave us each a

$200 bonus and again apologized for getting us hurt. He said this was his last season, and we felt sorry for him. Construction was all he ever knew and loved for 50 years. We three hopped in the car and headed for Ohio.

Susan asked me if I was really going to become a priest. "I can't believe it, you ornery rascal." I was forced to say I had nothing better to do. Then she added, "Well, you should have a better reason than that to want to be a priest." I was quietly thinking of something to say when she spoke again. "The cute little nuns better watch out."

Toomey told her not to be silly or disrespectful. Susan said she was going to be a Catholic once but she just couldn't accept the confessional.

"That's because you've always been bad and didn't want to tell your sins," Toomey said laughingly.

"No, I can't see why you have to tell your sins to a man. Your sins are between you and God. He's the only one that can forgive your sins," she said.

"You answer that question, Tom; you need the practice," said Toomey.

Slowly I replied, "I can't understand it. Almost every person I've talked to that would have been a Catholic could not be because of the confessional. I think that the confessional is one of the greatest sacraments of them all. Guilt feelings are the worst hurt to mental health and happiness. If you go to a psychiatrist with guilt feelings, the first thing he'll ask you is whether you are a Catholic, and then he'll ask you how long it has been since your last confession. Then he'll tell you first to go to confession and then come back to see him; and that will be $50 please. When someone suffers from guilt feelings, they want to tell someone about it."

"Now I can understand why Catholics can go out and get drunk or whore around, then go to confession and happily go right back at it," Susan said.

"Well, when the people asked the Lord how many times they should forgive, He said '70 times 70,' which in the Hebrew language meant thousands and thousands of times."

"Well, that still doesn't answer why we have to tell our sins to a man," she said.

"Well, that's even simpler yet. But, you know we Christians have not been too bright. As Christ told St. Peter, 'Whose sins you shall forgive, they are forgiven, and whose sins you shall retain, they are retained.' Now what if a man went to the confessional and told a priest he was sorry because he stole $1,000? The priest would tell him to give the money back. If the man refused, then the priest could not give him God's forgiveness.

The same thing is true if a single girl loved a married man and was having sexual relations with him. She might tell the priest she is sorry and ask God's forgiveness. The priest would tell her that if she would swear never to see the man again he would give her God's forgiveness. What if she said she couldn't give up the man and ran out of the confessional crying? Were either one of them really sorry for their sins?" I asked.

There was silence for a while and then Susan asked, "I know the Protestants also have communion services, but why do they have to use bread and wine, and why do the Catholics make it their whole worship?"

"Go on, Father Siemer, you are doing so well," Toomey chided me.

"Well, I'm no authority, but this is my own reasoning on the subject. Since Adam and Eve, the Hebrews made sacrifices to God either in atonement for their sins or in thanksgiving.

Cain killed Abel—both Adam's children—because God liked Abel's sacrifice better than his own. The Old Testament is a history of that time to Christ, and either God was ordering them to offer a sacrifice to Him or the Jews would voluntarily offer sacrifices. They sacrificed their best lambs, cows, and other animals back to God to show their thanks or sorrow.

Then God, the Father, allowed His only Son, Jesus Christ, to sacrifice Himself on the cross in atonement for all the sins of mankind that were committed before and would be committed afterwards. At the Last Supper, Christ told us how to offer the same sacrifice, Himself to God, every time we got together for worship. Instead of all the bloody lambs and oxen, he showed us how to offer the simplest and yet the greatest sacrifice to God, His own Son. Only a divinity could have thought of using the form of bread and wine. You can make bread of almost anything. You can make wine from anything too, and because of the alcoholic content, it won't pass disease.

Imagine if the Lord had told us to make His Body and Blood out of lamb's meat and goat's milk, or even water! All the Christians would have been dead by now from "Montezuma's revenge," diarrhea. It is so clever that only God could have thought of it. In fact, if Jesus Christ had not lived, and died, and said just what He did, I could not have believed in the Creator God. And I believe the sacrifice of the Mass is the greatest instruction.

"Tom, I hate to say this, but for the first time I really believe you are going to become a priest, and you really should. You've brainwashed me." Toomey nodded his head for emphasis.

We arrived in Columbus about 8:00 in the evening. This was nice, because for some reason I didn't want Toomey to see the blighted neighborhood where my parents lived. I guess it didn't matter, though, because Toomey and I had picked up butts off the street together and used straws to steal the cream out of cream pitchers in restaurants.

We had a short but emotional farewell. I told him I was going to kiss his girl now, because I'd probably miss the wedding. "The hell you will! I'll fly down and get you."

We didn't really have much in common except we liked each other, and for some reason I was one of the few people he had ever respected.

In order to make up for six months of not writing, I told my mother, when I first saw her, that I was home to become a priest. She was happy and proud of me. I also told my parents that's why I quit flight school. She told me it had to be for a good reason, because I had always wanted to be a flier, since I was a little boy.

She said her prayers had been answered. I felt very guilty, but maybe I *would* become a priest. A lot of boys were forced into the priesthood, because at that time it was the greatest honor that a Catholic mother could be given.

All my friends came around to see me, even some from the Navy. When my mother would tell them that I was going to be a priest, I always became embarrassed and apologetic. Then each one would take me aside and ask me if I was really serious.

The way they laughed and wouldn't believe it made me feel even further embarrassed.

One of my two buddies who were with me in Italy told me that he knew it was because of Gina. He had met her a couple of times in Italy, and the Tom he knew then would certainly not have wanted to be a priest. "Tom," he told me, "lots of guys have lost their first loves. There's still plenty of fish in the sea. But for Christ's sake, you don't have to become a priest. You should not fool around with God just because you're unhappy in love." He laughed and continued, "You'll come to your senses before you walk through those iron gates." Then he asked if I had talked to Ruth, who was my old girlfriend. I said I hadn't. He said, "You mean you haven't seen that beautiful girl in the two weeks you have been home?"

Then I would half-heartedly insist that I was still going to be a priest. After I convinced a few friends, they began to treat me differently, like I was some sort of a queer or something. They withheld personal conversation and became very formal toward me. Whenever I would stop to have a beer at the local pubs, they'd all be laughing and telling jokes when I came in. Then the conversation would die, and I'd have one beer and leave.

Eventually I started to avoid people. I began to feel lonely in a crowd. That's when I first realized the great loneliness priests and nuns must experience. Mother arranged a meeting with the parish priest about the time I was going to back out. I didn't think I could become a priest because of this great loneliness I was feeling. I didn't think I could stand to live alone all my life with no wife or children—or even any grandchildren. I've always been around a lot of people. My one grandfather, whom I greatly respected, had 12 children, and I had 72 cousins.

That made me think of my grandfather on my father's side; he was a good man and I had admired him tremendously. I used to sit in his tailor shop for hours, and he would tell me how the wrongs of the world could be corrected and he had great hopes for it if we would all turn to Christ. He told me that some day his Socialist Party would see to it that a man would only have to work eight hours a day. He told me how children used to have to work in the mines at 10, like my other grandfather did, and how the women dressmakers and teenage girls were practically chained to their sewing machines for 12 hours a day, when he started cutting clothes. How he first organized a union to fight for their rights. He was fired and banned from working as a tailor in the shops because of his protests for the women and children. But he was proud, because a year later the government passed laws to limit their hours and improve their conditions.

He told me that someday the Socialists would get through the legislature a bill to create a national pension so people could grow old in dignity, and not have to live off their relatives. They'd also have free medical care until they died. Activists were now working through the unions for extra pay if you worked over eight hours, or on weekends. The unions also have a fund set up to pay people who are unemployed and eliminate the misery I read about in *The Grapes of Wrath*. He believed that if everyone had enough to eat, a good place to live, and security all over the world, then war would be eliminated.

Countries usually fight over economics, he told me. If we could meet people's needs and give them security, they wouldn't fight. If war could be eliminated, then there would be no need for people to work even half the time. Too much human effort was spent making war material to destroy other people. If we could eliminate war, then this effort could be spent improving the conditions of life all over the world. We are all international brothers and sisters because we all have one Father in heaven.

Now all these good things have become law; still the people would never elect him, even as mayor of the town, because he always ran on the Socialist Party ticket. He never said anything about it, but my father told me that he had joined the Communist Party once because he became embittered over the conditions in the mines. Then the parish priest came to our house and threatened him with excommunication if he did not leave the Party. Grandpa had become the party chairman of southern Ohio, and I remember finding records of all the members hidden in the workshop over the old garage. I was the only one he would ever allow to work there.

My grandfather was a devout Catholic and attended mass every day after his wife died, and it hurt him deeply to have to choose between his church and what he believed was right. He chose to stay with God, but he would tell me that someday the world would be socialist or communist. Yet he also told me that he could not accept their methods of creating violence, revolution, chaos, misery, and killing to bring about their world vision. But because of the godlessness of capitalism, the socialists will win by godless means.

My grandfather's only known vice was one small glass of beer every afternoon at two o'clock. You could time your watch by it. It saddened me so deeply when he suffered a stroke and was reduced to blabbering. I could see the great man still in his eyes when he would have to sit there and listen to the absurdities of selfish and ignorant people. At those times, I would go over and pat his hand and he would know that I knew. I thought then that he must have done something in his life to have his Lord make him suffer this way. Or maybe the Lord intended him to earn a higher place in heaven, as Grandfather would have said. Thinking of him made me decide to try being a priest again.

I would have become a priest happily if I had been allowed to marry.

CHAPTER 7

DECISION FOR SEMINARY

I had to include this experience to show how terrible it was to deny my sexuality in the seminary. It would have been much easier if we knew that we could marry in the future if we so desired.

I ran into Ruth Capretta, my first girlfriend, one day, and we sat in the car and talked for four hours. She said that it wasn't too difficult for her to understand why I might become a priest. We never made love in the year we had gone together in high school, but I made her remember the time at the last school picnic and how passionately I had wanted her.

"You know Tom, if you had made love to me that day, we would probably be married today. I never thought you loved me because you never got passionate—or even tried," she said softly. "I was bothered all the time, but it was wrong, couldn't you tell?" I protested.

"Well, I thought you wanted me, but you never tried. Men who are lovers at least try. You were the most loving person I ever met, but I thought there must be something wrong with you. . . . .

Tom, I want you to wait two weeks, and then I'll meet you if you want me. But in that time I want you to make up your mind about being a priest. And if you make up your mind not to become a priest, then I want you to tell everyone, including your mother and all your friends, that you aren't going to be a priest, and why. You have to choose now to live without a woman the rest of your life, because priests must have these temptations often, and this will be your first test."

There was tremendous pressure on me now, from my mother and all my relatives who thought it was a great idea to have a priest in the family. We were definitely not from the tribe of Melchizedek, and there had never been a priest in the family. If there had been one, he would have had to be prolific. I think my family was from the tribe of the "begetters" instead.

Those two weeks were the most difficult decision making time in my whole life. I wanted to be a priest, but then again, I would think of Ruth and not want to be. Not so much because I couldn't bear the loneliness that would result in only loving You, Lord, but could I give up a wife and children, mother and father, brothers and sisters, and all my friends to help bring about the reality of Christ's intentions? I went to Mass every day and prayed that one day priests could marry.

Then one evening I was by myself before the Blessed Sacrament during the Forty Hours devotion, and I finally begged the Lord to give me some sign of what I should do. I was looking deeply at the white Host, Christ's consecrated body, when everything around it slowly turned white. I thought I was going blind. In the center of all this snowy whiteness was the golden monstrance holding the white Host. I broke out in a cold sweat.

There was no sound. It was an eerie feeling of great force.

Then the perimeter of the whiteness slowly dissolved toward the center, bringing back the reality of the dark church. I looked around, embarrassed, to see if anyone was watching. I don't know why I was embarrassed. I think it was because I was such a sinner.

I tried to rationalize that it never really happened. But I kept recalling that I was begging God for a sign. I walked out of the church in awesome awareness and fear of God. As unworthy as I am, I still took it as a sign from God that I was to be a priest. I went to see the parish priest the next day.

I told the parish priest that I thought I wanted to be a priest, but I wasn't sure. He told me he had not been sure when he entered the seminary, so the only way to decide was to give it a try. He called the Prefect of St. Charles College and arranged an appointment for me with the Dean of Men, a Father O'Reilly. We could hardly get into Father's little office suite. There were books stacked in piles all over the floor and you had to walk between them in order to get to the desk.

"Well, my son, what makes you think you want to become a priest?" he asked.

"Father, I don't know really. I'm not worthy, I know, because I've sinned so much," I answered.

"Well, that's why we have personal confessors here. We're all sinners. I don't know how I ever decided to become a priest, except that I wanted to serve Christ. Something kept forcing me and it forces me every day. Being a priest is a very lonely life, but your rewards are great. You change the world a little bit each day for Christ. It seems you fail most of the time, but then occasionally something happens that makes it all worthwhile. Besides, you are always free to go. This is only a minor seminary, and you can consider it to be a college. But, you must have some reason to want to be a priest?"

I rattled on for an hour about a calling to convince people that we must not fight wars or kill our enemies. I thought the best way to go about it would be for me to be a priest. "Then maybe people would listen to me."

"Well, we'll explain all about war in the first course in ethics, which you will take at the end of the first semester. It's a good course, but I wouldn't worry about war as the big picture. They've been fighting wars since the beginning of time. Our job is to plug along each day and get Catholics to love God and their neighbors. That's difficult enough. If we worry about that, war will take care of itself."

"In a million years," I said to myself. I couldn't wait for the first class in ethics.

He went on, "Our job is to get the people to the sacraments, and God's grace will take care of the rest." I had a notion to tell him that it had not worked in the past, at least not since the third century.

"Now, your entrance fee and books will come to about $75.

Tuition will be paid by the end of each quarter. If you don't pay by the end of the quarter, we have to ask the Bishop for it, and he'll want to see you, and it's a lot of red tape. He frowns on this unless you're absolutely destitute. Can you pay the entrance fee and the book fees now?" Father O'Reilly asked.

I only had $35, but I gave it to him, and promised the rest tomorrow. My first reaction was that it seemed like some of the rich Catholics I know or *someone* should pay to educate a boy to become a priest. Now, on top of all my studies, I'll have to get a job. I'll also have to borrow the rest of the money from my father, and he has it tough enough raising his large family.

"We like our students to live at the seminary, but I see you can't afford it, so you'll have to be an out-student, living at home." He gave me a book of rules that I must memorize, and since the semester had already started two days ago, he told me to see the Dean of Studies when I reported to school in the morning. He wished me a good day, and told me to look forward to a successful career.

I wasn't too impressed by the rules either. I glanced through them as I walked to the bus stop. That's when I realized I didn't have any money to catch a bus. I had given it all to him. I didn't go back and ask him for a quarter because I didn't want him to think I was that poor.

I walked the three miles or so to home. It gave me a chance to read all the rules. First, I was not to read any secular newspapers or magazines. I guessed "secular" meant the local periodicals. Or maybe they meant sex magazines and books, since those probably would bother a seminarian. I was embarrassed when the Dean of Studies told me that "secular" meant any and all publications not published by the Church. This was so my mind wouldn't get contaminated by earthly topics.

I told my mother about the money I needed, and that I would have to get a part-time job. "You mean the church is not going to pay your way to become a priest?"

"I guess not, Mother," I replied.

She said she had always put money in the collection for vocations. She thought that would pay for a priest's training. "You mean that the church cannot afford to educate a priest? When you give your whole life to the church?" She said that she would give me the money she had hidden from my father.

I read the seminary rules again that night. They were from the Middle Ages. I thought, if seminarians lead such a sheltered life, what will happen to them when they are turned loose in the world? It will be like leading lambs to slaughter. If you had not built up resistance while you were in school, then it would tear you apart. How could you work with sinners when sin would seem so exciting to you the first time? If I had not been around beautiful, sinning women and hadn't known what they are, I would probably go ape on the first encounter.

I used to joke: "The easiest way to get rid of a temptation is to give in to it." I guess that is one of the reasons half of my class who became priests left, and usually for a woman. A lot of other priests I knew were on the verge of becoming alcoholics. Of course Vatican II was responsible for most of that, I reasoned. Vatican II implied that priests were no holier or better than the mother and the father and the rest of the faithful.

The next morning I went to see the Dean of Studies, a Father Duffey. He was my kind of priest. The elbows were out of his cassock and buttons were missing half the way down. He was a writer in some right, and taught literature and art, though he knew very little about art. Father told me that I would have to take an extra makeup class in high school Latin while I took college Latin.

So here I was taking a high school and a college course in Latin, and to complicate things I was also taking the koine Greek language of the first century. I was not too swift at English, so you can see why I had to study until two every morning. But I had made up my mind to conquer the Latin language, and I did.

I rather threatened the Lord, through the Holy Spirit. They had pushed me into this, and they would have to enlighten me.

I had only one reason for being a seminarian and a Christian, It was the sheer love of Jesus Christ. As early as I can remember I loved Jesus Christ, I loved what He said and what He did. To me He was obviously the Son of God.

No one had to tell me that. My mother used to read me the Gospel every night. She was used to it, because she had been a Protestant most of her life and only became a Catholic while she was carrying me.

I believed in Christ's nonviolence as early as I can remember. I wouldn't fight back when I was hit by the kids, although it hurt me to be called a "sissy," even by my father and my grandmother. My whole family had been very militaristic. It took many years of training before I learned to strike back.

I was an altar boy at nine years of age, and the first to learn my Latin Mass responses. My greatest joy was to serve at Mass and receive the Body of Christ in Holy Communion. Sometimes I would almost be in ecstasy.

Jesus was good, and therefore, I reasoned, God must be good and loving and kind too. I loved Jesus because I loved everything He said—and I still do. His love was so obvious. Every one of Christ's sayings was based on love and nonviolence, from those against stealing to those against adultery. The beatitudes are filled with love. They were one of the strongest reasons I loved Jesus. And the Lord's Prayer—all you had to do was "forgive others" and God would forgive you!

I would sit for hours looking at the Holy Host in the monstrance. I would talk to Him like a child to his loving Father. I never really learned to love anything else as much in my life. I believed He loved me no matter what I did. I would go to confession for the slightest thing that offended Him. He gave me a certain feeling of independence from this world. I needed nothing else but His love, and when I did anything wrong I was terribly sorry because of my love for Him, not because I would be punished.

CHAPTER 8

FIRST HOMOSEXUAL DILEMMA

I must tell of this experience to show my understanding of the dilemma of homosexual priests in the Church. It's a "don't ask and don't tell" hypocrisy.

Father Dudley took me to my home class and introduced me to my classmates. They were friendly and helpful. It did not take long, though, for me to realize that there were two homosexuals in the class. No one was aware of it, possibly not even themselves, but I knew because once I almost lost my virginity to a man. Yet, I know some fine priests who are homosexual.

It was the first day of the time I waited in Rome for the MATS aircraft to take me back to the states, before I went back to Naples and Gina. I was the only American sailor in Rome, and I was just 19 and standing on a busy corner of Via Veneta in front of the Excelsior Hotel. I had bought a map and I was trying to figure the way out of the city.

Someone shouted, "Need help, Sailor?"

I looked around and next to me stood a rather handsome man in a blue serge suit. He bubbled with pleasantries and offered to take me to lunch. It was around two o'clock in the afternoon. He knew of a fine restaurant a few blocks away, and suggested we take his car. He snapped his finger in the air and a U.S. government limousine pulled up in front of us. I thought to myself, this man must be some sort of a wheel. I found out later that he was second in charge for all of Italy at the American Embassy in Rome. He was delightfully entertaining.

I told him about the first time I was in Rome, which was the first time I had drunk wine. A fellow sailor and I went into this restaurant and found a bottle of red wine sitting on the table. The waiter showed us the bottle of wine and we nodded yes, because we didn't know the word for beer. He brought us a little cheese plate that was delicious, and we ordered our pasta.

We sat there drinking for about an hour. When we had finished the first bottle, the waiter brought us another one. We said "Wait a minute, Paisan, we would like our meal."

"Excusa," he said. "In Italia we do not serve your meal as long as you have wine in your glass."

I gulped the glass of wine down and showed it to him. Harry, the man I was with, laughed and laughed.

I told him, "I really acquired a taste for wine that day. I learned to sip it instead of drinking it like beer. Needless to say, after we drank the two bottles of our first wine we felt great. But when we went into the air outside we both started bumping into buildings. It got so bad we were going more perpendicular to our path than we were proceeding forward, laughing heartily the whole time."

"We had to go past St. Peter's Basilica to get to the Albergo, so we thought we would join our tour again. I am sorry to say I got sick on the steps of St. Peter's. We never did make the pilgrimages to the four great Basilicas, as required by the Holy Year. I swore then that I would come back the next Holy Year and make the pilgrimages like a true Catholic."

Harry was still laughing. I told him that I must visit them today, because I might leave tomorrow. He suggested we leave immediately, and he would take me to them in his car. I thought that was awfully nice of him. It certainly was a fast pilgrimage, but I made it. St. Paul's, outside the Walls, was the most beautiful of the churches; of course St. Peter's was the most spellbinding. St. Peter's looked small from a distance until you saw a man the size of an ant walk in the doors.

Everything was enormously huge, but its hugeness was diminished by the harmonious relationships of the various parts. For instance, windows were 50 feet high, doors were 100 feet high, and columns over 150 feet. The most striking thing about Rome was its life span. Some buildings were dated 100 years ago, some 300, some 1000, and some 2000 years old. The United States was not even 200 years old at that time. It made my life span appear to be no more than the bat of an eye.

That evening, Harry took me to dinner at the Excelsior hotel.

It made me sad because I remembered Gina. American colonels and even a general knew him, and would come up to speak to him. Harry was not embarrassed when he introduced me, but I was ignored by the others in conversations. Harry asked me to go up to his suite in the hotel. My God, I have never seen anything like it. It was all pale pink and white marble. It had a snow-white, deep furry rug. The bath could pass for the swimming pool at some of the motels I have stayed in. The bed was bigger than a king-sized bed, and was round.

Harry put his arm around me and said I could sleep in the bed if I wanted to. I began to wonder why this guy loved me so much. None of his friends with the State Department seemed to like me. I told him that I already had a hotel room, and the more he insisted on me moving in, the more I insisted I was going back to my own hotel. Then he told me that if I stayed he would get the most beautiful woman to sleep with me. I was so in love with Gina and religion that I refused. I told him I was trying to make a good pilgrimage and I did not want to ruin it.

We had our first disagreement when he said, "You don't really believe all that bull about religion! You are just doing it because of custom and your upbringing."

I said to him, "I am going to walk back to my hotel."

He responded, "Wait a minute while I make a phone call, and then I'll take you back in the car."

He spoke in Italian so I didn't know what he was saying or to whom he was saying it. When he was through he told me he wanted to introduce me to one of his friends. His friend turned out to be a lovely young girl. It's strange how strong you can be at times and so weak at other times. Later when I was weak I could have kicked myself, but I still protested.

The girl pulled me on the bed and wrestled with me.

She was almost as beautiful as Gina. When Harry saw he was getting nowhere he told her to leave and said he would take me back to my hotel. I was hesitant in getting into his car. But I did, and on the way he detoured. I protested. He told me he wanted to take me to a park he knew and show me the most beautiful sight in Rome at night.

We parked in front of a huge, ornate garden or park that was on a slight hill. I think he told me it was formerly owned by a Count Orsini. As we walked up through the bushes to the top, Harry would look for the longest time at every outdoor urinal that was being occupied.

Boy, was I in trouble. But I'd never had the opportunity to talk with homosexuals, so I wasn't quite sure.

Well, I thought to myself that I was a hell of a lot bigger than him and I could handle it myself. We walked over to the edge of the ornate stone wall. It was a beautiful sight. There before us was the Plaza Del Populo, the Tiber River, St. Angelo's Castle, and then St. Peter's Dome, all lit up. You could see the whole Tiber River Valley. Uh-oh! I thought as Harry put his hand on mine. "Is it as beautiful as I told you it would be?" I removed my hand as I admitted to him that it was.

Then he told me that he was an atheist because of St. Peter's and what it stood for. "Those people over there are all a bunch of politicians just like everyone else. They run the church just like we run the State Department. Their intelligence network is better than ours. I have met them all, including the Pope. You don't think the Pope was appointed by God, do you? He is a politician just like Harry Truman. When the cardinals vote for a new Pope they make deals, just like our politicians do. They have blocks of liberal and conservative politicians who make deals for power. Look around you. The Pope's bitter enemies are the communists, and they are about to take over the city by popular vote. All Italy will be a communist country someday soon. If Christ founded the church, then why is it surrounded by its enemies? Even though the people are all Catholic, they still vote for the communists."

What he said was true. I had just left Livorno, Italy and the city was 95% communist. In fact, Stankovan and I unwittingly went to a dance at the Communist Party headquarters. We were welcomed by the people until the party chief came in, then we were thrown out bodily.

I tried to prove to Harry that there was a God, but being uneducated made me no match for Harry's logic and intelligence.

He put his hand on mine once more, and I asked him point blank, "Are you a homosexual?" He was taken aback by the direct question. After the if, ands, or buts, he finally admitted that he was. I tried to get away, but he hugged me around the waist. I convinced him that if he did not let me go I was going to punch him. He told me passionately how much he loved me. "Let go of me or I will use karate."

He laughed at that and told me that he had a black belt. Now I really was worried. I knew boxing, but all I knew about karate were the yells. I gave him an elbow in the ribs a couple of times and he let me go. Then we went back to the hand-holding bit. I told him I was getting mad, and I might not know karate but I did know some dirty street fighting tricks. He told me he knew he would never see me again, and if I would spend one hour with him he would give me up. I agreed if he would unhand me. We stood and talked for a while, and then I turned and ran down the sidewalk, with Harry running after me. "What is a girl going to do?" I thought.

Everyone was laughing at us. I was really embarrassed. I stopped and said, "If you don't let me alone, I am going to call the police." He again told me how beautiful I was and how much he loved me. He offered again to drive me back to the hotel. "Are you crazy? I will never get into a car with you again. What kind of a guy do you think I am?" I screamed.

Harry began to cry and then he turned and walked off into the darkness. Now I really began to feel sorry for him, but I kept walking.

I thought many times in my youth that I would like to be a priest. But every time I did I would lock it out of my mind because I could not imagine living my life without a wife and children. I could never survive as a priest without a companion that I loved and a family.

After Harry I thought how great it would be to be a priest if you were a homosexual and a good and spiritual person. It would certainly be easier to give up women, and you would be praised for it, while living with men. Maybe someday the Pope will allow priests to be married, and I still would want to become one. There are so many wonderful priests in the Church who are lonely. They could serve Christ and His Church far better if they were able to marry. They would also better understand the problems of married couples and parents in the Church.

I tell this story to show my understanding of the fine priests and other religious who are homosexual. I understand their great yearning for love, just like a man's for a woman or a woman's for a man. They are in the same dilemma as heterosexual priests who yearn for the love of a woman but cannot be married.

Both, however, must practice celibacy. It must be far more difficult for the homosexual priest, because he has to live in houses and take showers with only other men.

The Church needs to establish orders of married priests, as well as orders for those who will not marry. Women's ordination is also something that needs to happen in our churches, especially within women's religious orders.

CHAPTER 9

SEMINARY LIFE

I must tell of my own seminary life, where I experienced a sense of affluence. We were taught and lived in very expensive buildings and dorms, surrounded by immense manicured lawns. We ate the best of food and were pampered. I felt out of place being poor.

"How am I going to go to school with those perfect 18 year olds at the seminary who have been sheltered all their little lives?" I asked myself. I will probably contaminate them, having been in the Navy and around all the ports in the Mediterranean. But we also had a worldly person teaching the college's Latin course. Father Obetz loved translating the Latin works of the Roman author Ovid.

Ovid was a sexually passionate writer who wrote some pretty horny poems for the early Romans. Father's reasoning was that his boys must learn a little about the world and women. I think he caused a little unrest among the troops. Those poems bothered me sometimes. I loved Greek, though, because we would translate the early Greek Bible as we went along. If you learned the early Greek of the second century, it gave you the opportunity to read the Bible as it was meant to be read.

There were no ambiguous words or words that have change their meaning over time, like "queer." It took us two years to translate the Greek Bible, and I enjoyed every minute of it, with Father Woltz as our teacher. My mind was satisfied beyond a doubt that Christ meant for us to love our enemies and not offer resistance to evil. It takes two parties to fight, and if we as Christians refuse, then there cannot be a fight or a war. We would probably be dead like the early Christians, but by our example we would eliminate war and convert all nations to Christ. The hitch is that nobody wants to go first.

I prayed, "Lord, this is going to be a bigger task than I am a person." Yet, I thought, St. Peter was a dumb fisherman when he started out, and there is no one more simple than a professional fisherman. Yet, I have never met a bad one. Fishermen seem close to God because their livelihood seems to directly depend on God.

The Holy Spirit will have to work day and night with me, I thought. I have to unlearn all my bad habits before I can learn good habits and reach perfection. I loved the daily prayer and meditation periods. One cannot be talking when one is listening for God's direction.

We started off every year with a full week of retreat—I guess in order to forget the summer delights and prepare ourselves for the trials of study ahead. We were not supposed to talk for a whole week, or at least only when necessary. I loved it, and came closer to Christ by it. But some of my young, innocent friends would get together in a room and talk most of the night. It was usually the 18-year-old professionals, though. I mean the ones who had gone through four years of preparatory high school for the seminary. These were the sheltered ones.

The strange thing I realized was that many of them were from wealthy Catholic families. They knew music and the arts and languages. They knew the gentle life. They never had to sell their sisters, or beg and steal to stay alive. They just asked Papa, and Papa gave. Mamma also kept them away from adversity and trials.

What is a fellow going to do when he is highly educated in music, the arts, and religion except be a priest? I thought how tough life would be for them later.

I used to sketch people a lot in boring classes, so I was asked if I would design and paint the sets for a Latin play. The professor said he wanted a Roman street scene.

He asked me if I could do it, and if I knew anything about perspective. "Oh, he certainly does," my friends said. "Have you seen his houses and castles? They have beautiful perspective!"

I had never had the occasion to use perspective on this scale before. I looked in the well-equipped little theater they had and found many canvas side panels and canvas backdrops. All I had to do was to lay out the scenes on these and start painting.

When the professor saw what my crew was doing, he ordered me to buy material and construct all new panels and backdrops.

I asked, "Why? There are plenty of good ones." He told me not to argue with him. "Just do it."

Then I said, "Father, the money we save on the scenery we can give to the poor."

A hush fell over the class, as if I had said something wrong.

Then he said, "My boy, I want you to make new ones so that the other students will gain experience."

"Father, what do they need this experience for?" I retorted,

"This has nothing to do with saving souls or helping people."

He looked me in the eye and said, "I want new scenery made, and that is an order!"

Well, I bought enough lumber and canvas for one new panel and used the old ones for the rest. I slanted some panels back, all the way to the wall, and painted fronts of houses diminishing in perspective to form a street that appeared to be three blocks long, with two corner buildings on each side of the stage. I even sloped a triangular panel from the stage floor upward to the apex, so that the road surface of the scene also appeared to run three blocks.

It was my first experience with water-based tempera paints, and I loved it. It was a master piece of perspective. Art teachers from all over the city came to see it. Then the good father told me that I would have to paint it over, because the scenery would take away from the Latin play.

I asked, "How can you take away from a Latin play?"

The Prefect of the school came around just before we would have destroyed the masterpiece. One of the other students told him what we had been ordered to do. He said to leave it alone and he would talk to the Latin professor. Then he took me aside and told me that he hated those Latin plays, and that the Church would do away with Latin someday. This scenery would give the captive audience some interest, though. Latin students from all the Catholic high schools were marched in to see this play. Now, all through the boring play, people would try to guess how far that road really went back.

After that I painted murals for churches and acted as an art adviser. This took me further away from my goals and studies. I could find only one person there at the seminary who believed my peace and nonviolence goals were important, and he was an alcoholic priest.

I came to believe that the church had rejected the most important teaching of Christ, just as the Jews did. All that the Jews wanted was a great earthly Messiah who would protect them from their enemies. The Jews also loved their countrymen but refused to love their enemies. Christ warned the Jews, and I believe that Christ has warned the Catholic Church for the same reason. He allowed the split in the Church between Roman Catholic and Eastern Orthodox in the middle ages because they preached and fought wars. He allowed the Protestants to split away from the Church and the so-called "Christians" to hate other Christians for centuries, like in Northern Ireland.

The Catholic Church's first and only justification for war is based on self-defense. Not one time did Christ say that you can kill in self-defense. He said, "Do not offer resistance to injury," which will show the pagans that we all have one Father in Heaven. The Catholic Church and other Christians have rejected Christ, and now He has warned them. He will again allow them to destroy each other in a total worldwide nuclear war, I thought.

The American Christians even believed that they should destroy their enemies, and themselves, if necessary, to protect the church in the name of Christ. How wrong they are, and what a great sin of omission it is for the Catholic Church not to speak out against war! I felt I must make them give up their security in weapons. I must speak out to the hierarchy and to the priests to convince them that this is wrong. Right is right, and if there remain only 10 Christians in the world who speak out against war, then still they must speak.

I prayed, "Lord, we must start someday to love our enemies and stand up to be counted like the early martyrs did. Lord, where do I start? Surely not as a Latin expert."

I must convince the church that war is not necessary and that forbidding it is in the realm of Church authority.

I remembered when Al Toomey and I traveled, after we resigned from the Navy in 1950. I remember the Charro Days in Brownsville, Texas, when the Mexicans and Americans joined in one great happy fiesta. It brought warmth to my soul to see the people of two countries that spoke different languages come together to celebrate brotherhood. I thought that some day soon Mexican peasants might choose communism, and then these happy friends might be killing each other. That day, there was only love for each other. All past and future differences were forgotten in love. Shortly after the grand opening in the International Friendship Garden Pavilion, they had the "Fiesta de los Ninos," the "Festival of the Children." To see beautiful little children all in costume, going hand in hand, brown, white, and black faces sparkling in love and happiness, brought tears to my eyes.

We should never fight wars to make sure children can enjoy life in love. I have seen little children all over the world together, and the beauty is that they don't discern race, creed, or color. They know by nature that we are all the same in the eyes of God. I would gladly give my life if God would eliminate war and let the children all over the world live in peace.

Children are the first to suffer from war. First, the father leaves, and many do not come back from wars; then their mothers cry and are bitterly unhappy. The children don't know why. Then the bombs hit homes and many children die. Their parents and relatives are killed, the children are homeless, they are hungry, they do not know why this happened to them. Their conquerors come and the children hate them, but the children most quickly forget and forgive. Only some do not forget. They remember because they are homeless orphans and can never forget. Through no fault of their own, they will gladly fight and die in the next war. They will never love their enemies, anymore than children do now in Palestine.

I was taught in ethics that you can never do one evil to make a thousand goods. Then how could we have dropped the atomic bomb on Hiroshima and killed all those children to save American and Japanese soldiers? The Pope didn't raise any objections or excommunicate anyone. So at the time, I thought it must have been right. I did not hear one priest condemn it from the pulpit.

The children marched hand in hand around the arena. Mexican children with American children, hand in hand. How could we kill children or teach them to hate when they are so full of love? We have killed them for a piece of land or a principle. Christ said we must be as little children. We must love each other as those little children in the parade. We must love our enemies like the little Mexican children who loved the Americans, even though their ancestors took Texas away from them.

These people of southern Texas were Indians until the Spanish conquistadors conquered them and took their land. Then the Americans came and took the whole state of Texas from them. The Mexican people were forced to forgive and forget, but finally they forgave. There are no big guns now pointing across the Rio Grande. We live in peace—but that could all change quickly if Mexico went communist. Then we would teach our children to hate each other for a cause they don't begin to understand.

I watched the parade that afternoon. It was wonderful to see people celebrating international friendship. I wondered what the children felt like at the 1936 Olympic games, when athletes from all countries, including Poland, France, England, Italy, and Germany, marched together. When just a couple of years later they were hating and killing each other.

We say it was a "just war," but the innocent children still died.

I loved to hear children's voices singing in unison. They are voices of angels. It is so tragic that we have to teach them to hate and kill. When I saw the children of two countries singing and dancing together it made me realize that there is still hope; even if they have to fight each other later, they will remember the friendship of that day.

There was a strange thing about Brownsville, Texas: Hardly anyone spoke English. Ninety percent of the people were of Mexican descent, but when you would try to speak Spanish they would switch to English as if they didn't want to admit it. They wanted to be "Americanos" with other Americans, but with the Texans they would speak in Spanish.

A disabled veteran came by limping. He was selling Rebel Flags. I thought to myself that all the guys I knew who survived a war were strong advocates of fighting another war for our rights. I think it is because they lost not only friends, but their own legs and arms. They wanted to justify their participation in war. They felt they were making up to those friends they lost by making sure everyone fights for his country at least once. This was so sad, because they believed they gave their limbs and lives in the name of Christ. Most did feel that they gave their all for their neighbor, and in so doing were working for Christ.

I suppose the thousands of German soldiers who died at Stalingrad felt the same way. The soldiers were not responsible for starting the war, so Christ would probably forgive them, but could Christ forgive his Church when it did not condemn the war or forbid Christians to participate? I thought what a shame it was to spend so much effort studying Latin. Latin had nothing at all to do with Christ's message of love for our enemies.

The Advent season had arrived, and our studies were discontinued until after Christmas so that the seminarians could serve in the ceremonies at the Cathedral. The seminarians always served the Bishop at all functions in which he participated. It was very impressive to have a hundred cassock—and surplice-clad young men march before the Bishop through the church to his throne.

Advent is a time of penance and spiritual preparation before the coming of Christ. The seminary had a full-time priest who was the protocol Master of Ceremonies at all these functions. He always gave us instructions on what we were supposed to do during each ceremony. He was a nice young priest, but several times through the year he lost patience with me.

The first time I saw Bishop Ready, he was being attended by five priests who were dressing him. Then I remembered that he was the good man who I had met when I delivered my first telegram in 1944.

We had just moved from the hills of southern Ohio, and I had started to work for Western Union that day. I was 14 years old and didn't know my way around Columbus at all. It was six o'clock in the morning, and I found the address of the house next to the Cathedral. The telegram was addressed to Bishop Ready. After I pounded on the door and rang the bell over and over, a man stuck his head out of the front upstairs window and asked me what I wanted. I said I had a telegram for the Bishop. He said he would be right down to take it.

He appeared in a white T-shirt and black pants. He said he would sign for the wire. I made him promise that the Bishop would get it. He assured me that he would, and then asked me what school I went to. I told him "The Holy Family Catholic School" and he said "That's great." He asked me what I wanted to be. I told him sheepishly that I wanted to be a priest if I could. He asked me why and I told him.

Then he asked me if I would do him the honor of kissing his ring. I looked around awkwardly and wondered what a boy had to do to deliver a telegram. He held out this big ring to me, and I looked around to see if anyone was watching before I kissed it. He blessed me, and as I was leaving, I told him to make sure the Bishop got that telegram or I'd lose my job. He assured me that he would and gave me a two-dollar tip. The people inside must have heard us, because two servants ran out half dressed and began apologizing to the man as I rode away on my bicycle, thinking that kissing a ring wasn't too bad after all, for two dollars.

That night I read that a new bishop had been installed the day before, and his picture was that of the man I had given the telegram to. I was always embarrassed around the Bishop at the ceremonies because I thought he would remember me.

What a change had come over the man, or the Bishop, who I saw standing there seven years later! Everyone was afraid of him. He had changed from a humble man to a man of perfection in both ceremony and speech. He was fussy about his dress and appearance, and sometimes used the word *damned* on the altar when someone would screw up, meaning me.

That first day the Master of Ceremonies gave me the crosier and my friend Jack the miter. Well, I couldn't remember which was the crosier and which the miter. So the Bishop called for his miter, and we looked at each other, and I took the gold staff to the Bishop's throne. The Bishop looked at me and said quietly, "No, the miter, you dummy."

The Master of Ceremonies ran across the altar and took the miter from Jack and put it on the Bishop's bowed head, and pulling me back down the steps, tripped over the crosier and fell on the floor. I felt sorry for him standing there, red faced, and I wondered to myself whether I was ever meant to be a priest.

One time, when I had to hold the missal for the Bishop to read, I accidentally flipped out all the pages and the markers came out. It took the M.C. five minutes to find all the places, while the Bishop fumed in red.

That reminded me of the first time I was an altar boy, when I was 10 years old and living in Corning, Ohio. It was Holy Saturday morning, when they bless all the new Holy Water for the year. The old priest had told me to go out and bless the bushes with the remainder of the old Holy Water. There were a lot of bushes on the church lawn, and I was at the tenth one when the priest ran out of the church, grabbed the bucket and dispenser from me and asked me what the hell I was doing. I didn't know he had wanted me to pour it all on one bush! So you can see why the Master of Ceremonies always gave me the lesser jobs thereafter.

I have never met a more articulate or more brilliant speaker than Bishop Ready. His sermons made up for all his arrogance. He used to spellbind me. I often wondered why the Holy Spirit had wasted such talent on ceremonies and administrative work.

Every year we seminarians were reviewed by the Bishop, and I was petrified before my review. He must have received 10 telephone calls while I sat in his outer room, and all of them were about business. He was involved in buying properties for schools and churches, putting up new buildings, and remodeling the Cathedral. At the same time he was assigning priests to parishes and interviewing seminarians. I thought to myself then that God gives people talent to accomplish the jobs He gives them. I suddenly had a great respect for the Bishop, and knew that I would never want his job. In fact, in the year I had been at the seminary, I couldn't understand how I could ever be a parish priest.

I ran youth programs in the Diocese and came in contact with a lot of parish priests. In order to keep schools running, teachers paid, and lights, heat, and air conditioning running in the church, they were for C.E.D. to become business administrators. They constantly had to think about raising funds and running bingos and church bazaars. A successful priest seemed to be judged by how well he ran the finances of the parish. The most holy priests were terrible financial administrators and were always in trouble with the Bishop, who was in trouble with the Cardinal if he did not run the finances of the Diocese well. We weren't being taught anything about finances in the seminary. What a waste of vocations, I thought. They should have lay people to do this work and let the priests work at saving souls.

The Bishop finally called me into his office and told the secretary not to disturb him for 10 minutes. He asked me how I was doing and went over my grades. He asked me why I wanted to be a priest. I told him about the special calling I had to try to teach Christians to love our enemies.

"Son," he said, "we must learn to love our neighbors first, and then we will love our enemies."

Then he told me he had not seen me on the altar lately and asked me why. I told him I had fouled up so many times that the M.C. was putting me in the lesser roles, far away from him. He said he thought he had known me before he saw me on the altar, and asked me where it was.

I was forced to tell him about delivering the telegram to him the day after his consecration. He reminisced about the good old days before God had placed the weight of running the Diocese around his neck. He told me about the great converts he had made in the East before he had become Bishop. Sometimes, he thought he couldn't bear to run the finances of the Diocese, but he would have to persevere until the end. As I was about to leave, he asked me to pray for him in order that God would allow him the grace to persevere.

I had great respect for that man thereafter, and he always smiled when he saw me on the altar.

I felt that all those language studies were taking me away from my goal, but I read a lot about philosophy and I loved it. We studied a great many philosophers, and at one time I asked Monsignor Woltz, a brilliant mind, "When does a person become a philosopher?"

"My boy," he told me, "the day you begin to think for yourself is when you become a philosopher."

He went on to tell me that so far I was the only philosopher in his class; the rest were still students. He knew, because of the questions I would ask. He knew I was thinking for myself and he knew I was a lot of trouble.

CHAPTER 10

FIRST JUSTIFICATION FOR WARS

The day finally came in ethics class when we were going to be taught the Catholic Church's doctrine of the justification for a Christian to fight, the theory of "just war." It was in the last chapter of the ethics textbook. "War is defined as a condition of armed and active hostility between two or more nations," Father Woltz read from *Ethics,* the textbook written by Monsignor Paul Glenn, our seminary prefect.

I put up my hand. "Yes, Siemer?" he said.

"'Then this would mean that Russia and the United States are already at war. They are armed and hostile already." It was a leading question.

"Siemer, can't you wait until I even finish the first paragraph? In fact I want you all to hold your questions until after I have discussed the conditions for a just war," he said. He went on reading. "War is distinguished from rebellion, which is an unlawful uprising of citizens against their government; from revolution, which is a justified resistance against tyranny; and from the public conflict, called civil war; for war is a conflict between nations. That is why England called our War of Independence a 'Rebellion of the Colonies,' because they deemed it illegal, and we called it the 'Revolutionary War,' because we deemed it justified resistance." Fr. Woltz continued to read from the book.

"Wars are divided into 'just' and 'unjust,' offensive and defensive.

A just war is one that fulfills the conditions necessary to make a war a lawful undertaking. The conditions necessary for a just war are the following:

1. War must be declared by competent authority, for a just cause, and it must be undertaken with an honest intention. The last named requirement warns us that a war–granted the cause is just–is rendered unjust if undertaken for revenge, lust for power, hatred of opponent, etc.
2. War must be the last recourse, undertaken only when all other means of settlement have been found unavailing."

"Wait a minute, Father," I interrupted. "Has the Christian United States tried every means of settling our basic differences with Russia to avert war except trying to build hydrogen bombs? The Church might negotiate a settlement and—"

"Hold it, Siemer. I told you to wait until the end!"

"Yes, Sir! I apologize." He went on reading.

3. The war must offer a reasonable prospect of success; else war would be a greater evil than the wrong it

seeks to right.—Now, don't open your mouth, Siemer!" he said emphatically.

4. War must be conducted in a manner approved by civilized people. Hence there must be no wanton slaughter or destruction which has no direct effect on the outcome of the war. There must be no direct killing or maltreatment of non-combatants. There must be no use of inhuman and barbarous methods, such as the poisoning of wells and streams, the use of envenomed weapons, the poisoning of the air by noxious gases (I thought of the atomic bomb fallout, but I didn't say anything.). There must be no use of means that are intrinsically evil and against the natural law, such as lies, perjury, or inciting to treason."

I laughed. Hells' bells, I thought, the CIA has been doing that for years and so have all the Catholic countries.

"There must be no continuation of hostile acts after an armistice or peace has been declared." Damn, I thought, what have the United States and Russia been doing since the end of the war? No wonder they called it the "Cold War."

He continued, "War is licit when all the conditions mentioned are met. For just as an individual has the right to repel force with force, just as a man may defend himself, under certain conditions, by the indirect slaying of his unjust aggressor, so may a nation defend itself."

This is a joke, I thought to myself. If the USA lived up to all these conditions when we fought the communists, then it would be impossible for us to win. We have broken most of these laws just during the Cold War; no wonder the church is so silent on war.

Father went on with the text. "Again, the state has the duty of self-preservation and of defending the rights of its citizens; and it is clear that there are times when this duty cannot be performed by a state without repelling unjust aggression, without waging war. Hence wars are sometimes licit."

"Are there any questions, Siemer?" he asked. "Yes, Father!" The class laughed.

"Is this the Catholic Church's official position, in regard to the conditions for fighting a just war or a nuclear war?" "Essentially and basically, yes, it is," Father answered.

"Then, why was I never taught this in catechism or in religion in high school? I never once heard these conditions described from the pulpit."

"There are a lot of things, Siemer, you don't know yet," he replied. The class laughed again.

I had already read the last two pages of the textbook, and I was ready with a list of questions on the conditions for a "just war."

"I have a list of questions, Father, that I would like to ask you. We don't have much class time left, so therefore I would like for you to answer them all in your summation."

I asked the following questions:

1. "Why is the Catholic Church so silent about immoral wars or when the conditions for a just war have not been met? Yet it makes such strong statements against abortion, birth control, divorce, etc. Is this because of the Church's past? The Catholic countries of Spain, England, France, and even Italy fought for centuries. Popes raised armies and fought wars and crusades for land. Even the conquest of the Holy Land wasn't justified.
2. Was Spain's conquest of South and Central America a "just war?" They made slaves of the natives and

took their lives and gold in the name of Christ. Why didn't the Pope say anything?

3. Why didn't the Pope forbid German Catholics to fight for Hitler? Or why didn't the Pope forbid Italian Catholics to fight to conquer Ethiopia?
4. Why didn't the Pope speak out and condemn the many known Christian unjust wars over the centuries?
5. Why is it that all the Catholic countries are the first to be taken over by communism? I think it is because of the hypocrisy of the Church in regard to wars, and its indifference to conquering or conquered people.
6. Just think how different the world would be if the Catholic Popes had never allowed Christians to fight wars! The Papacy would never have become a political tool. Even if the Popes were forbidden to fight, who of royalty would have wanted the job? It would have been far from politics as usual. The head of the Church of Christ would have always been neutral, a respected mediator. Where in the New Testament does it say Christians have the right to buy weapons and defend themselves?
7. What would happen if the Pope would forbid American Catholics to work on the nuclear bomb, or be in military service to deliver it, or if he excommunicated those Christians who advocate the use of it? We would be condemned as Christ said we would be, but we would show an example to the world. You just stated that we can't use an immoral weapon, like the nuclear bomb, that will kill everybody.
8. Why aren't we forced to come to terms with the communists at all costs? We are not even

attempting to come to terms with our enemies. We are building more and more weapons each year. Do you think that this is bound to lead to war someday? And you just said, a "just war" must offer a reasonable prospect of success; otherwise war would be a greater evil than the wrongs it seeks to right. How about hydrogen bomb warfare? It is suicidal.

9. Is communism so evil that we cannot try to come to terms with it? If the whole world became communist, would that end Christianity? Doesn't the church imply this? I couldn't believe in Christ or Christianity if I thought Christ's Church would fail and end if the whole world became communist. Yet, don't most Catholics believe this? Is it the Church's fault?
10. Isn't the pure theory of socialism more Christian in principle than so called 'Christian capitalism?'
11. I might agree that to kill in self-defense is my right, but if I stood face to face with an enemy and we both held 45- caliber pistols to our heads, then I would definitely want to come to terms, even if he didn't. That's what you just said we must do.
12. Father, when is the Catholic Church going to stand up and be counted as completely Christian? When is the Church going to educate the young Catholic boys and girls with the same doctrine you have taught us in this class? The Church has committed a serious sin of omission by remaining silent. The next war America fights may be an unjust war, a little unjust war like the Mexican-American war, when we took Mexico's land. If the youth don't know they have a moral choice of whether to fight or not, then they will still feel it's their duty to fight

> for their country–right or wrong. This is the end of my questions."

You could hear a pin drop when I sat down.

Monsignor said to me, "You certainly have a hangup on war. You make it difficult for me to sell the party line, St. Thomas Aquinas's reasoning that we can fight just wars in self-defense. The last world war proved to both of us that the conditions for a "just war" no longer exist unless we consider innocent children as combatants, like the world does now. If you consider the whole population as combatants, then you are allowed to fight a war against the whole population 'in self-defense.' Then you could allow countries to fight preventative wars in faraway places, like Asia and Africa, in the name of self-defense of the country."

"You don't believe that?" I asked. "'No," he replied, "but that is what most of the so-called Christians are being allowed to fight wars for."

"Then why don't you and the Bishop and the Pope tell them it is wrong? How will the people know they are doing wrong if they persist in this 'just war' rationalization and you don't tell them it is wrong?" I asked.

Then Father said, "The reason for this is that the Church wants to remain neutral and to minister to the faithful. The Church would be destroyed if it always demanded non-violence. The Christian world was being destroyed when St. Augustine reasoned that we must raise arms and protect ourselves."

I said, "Nowhere in the New Testament did Christ or the early Christians advocate buying arms and defending themselves against the pagans. They went underground and by their example, sometimes their deaths, they converted the pagan Romans. I have had great respect for the brilliance of

St. Augustine except when he rationalized war in the name of Christ. Then I realized that one saintly old peasant could have more knowledge from the Holy Spirit than all the great minds."

The next day Father Woltz went over what constituted a just war again and asked the class, what was it about the Second World War that condemned it as an unjust war? The class was shocked at the suggestion that the Second World War was unjust. At least we were attacked by Japan first, anyway. I told the class that I thought it was the indiscriminate bombing of populations of women and children and other non-combatants with immoral weapons.

Father said "That's a good example. Remember when I told you that a just war had to be fought between legitimate combatants? Remember that I also told you that just one evil cannot make a thousand rights? The death of one innocent child cannot justify saving a thousand lives. The nuclear bomb is a good example of this. The justification for dropping the nuclear bomb on Hiroshima was that it would save a million American and Japanese soldiers' lives and end the war. But have you seen the dead, burned, and mutilated bodies of the little children? They had no idea that a war existed, nor what it was being fought about. We did not have to invade Japan.

To win the war did not make it right. I expect some day in your lifetime the Pope will ban the use of the nuclear bomb and those who advocate it, build it, or use it will do so under pain of serious sin," said Father Woltz.

"What about the firebombing of Tokyo? More children's lives were lost during that time. Or, what about the systematic firebombing of German cities like Dresden by the Britons, and other cities by the Americans? Millions of innocent lives were lost. How can that evil create a good? It didn't even end wars."

Fr. Woltz continued, "The Americans and Russians are now preparing for a nuclear war that will again end all wars. It may end the human race! Maybe that is why St. Thomas Aquinas, shortly before his death, stopped writing and wouldn't continue. His close friend urged him on. Finally, exasperated, he said, 'I have seen something that makes all my writings as worthless as straw.' Then Thomas became a very devout, simple monk until his holy death, shortly thereafter. Maybe, with his great mind, he had missed this simple message of Christ: total nonviolence." With that Father ended his talk.

But at that moment, a choice was forming in my mind: one of the most important choices of my life! I started having a deep distrust of excessive intellectualism.

I was bitter because, listening to Father Woltz, I had experienced the clear feeling that he enjoyed himself while proving his point about "just" and "unjust" wars. He invoked the burned children of Hiroshima, but his description did not evoke the children of Hiroshima. The children remained abstract examples, exploited to prove a concept, whether correct or incorrect. I experienced a chill of horror towards any cold game of intellect. The older I grow the more I perceive the figure of the intellectual as a threat, a castration and a dispersion (by dilution) of the powerful direct force that is needed to change things in this world through the simple gospels of Jesus.

St. Augustine and Thomas Aquinas frightened me. Centuries of Christian wars proved their dangerous—their "diabolical"— ability to justify with logic one of the strongest weaknesses of mankind: Violence!

The whole of European culture is a clear example of this.

European Christians have lost the courage to be Utopian, and with it they have lost the power of indignation.

Their culture implies a certain discomfort with unadulterated goodness, and a holy terror of being labeled as "naive." Intellectual Europe, from the Renaissance on, has always been like a feast in time of plague; culture has even made the mistake of believing such a feast could end the plague! We, therefore, became used to the death—by hunger and poverty— of those born on the wrong side of the world. Now we are all in the process of even getting used to the idea of our nuclear destruction, and that of our children. In the beginning nuclear weapons frightened us, but now the shudder seems out of fashion.

From that day in the Seminary on, I clearly and deliberately chose simplicity. And I went out searching for the most elementary, undeniable truths—those truths the simplest of peasants can understand and those the intellect cannot deny. Like "If we fight a nuclear war we will all die," or "Would Jesus use a nuclear weapon?"

CHAPTER 11

THE LONELINESS OF A CELIBATE

During the first seminary summer I was overwhelmed with loneliness. I tried to make up for it with many acts of charity. I had to get a job, too, because it was so hard to study and work in the winter. North American was hiring mechanics at their new Columbus facility and they paid students well, but they also made war planes, and I couldn't be a part of it. But I couldn't get a job anywhere else, so I went out to St. Charles College to talk about it.

Monsignor Woltz had been assigned elsewhere, so I talked to Father O'Dea, and he asked me what I would be doing at North American. I told him I would be working on T-6 trainer planes. He told me that trainer planes were not an instrument of war, but it was up to my own conscience. I rationalized that he was right, so I took a job on the flight line for the summer. Lord, I think I deeply failed you again.

I thoroughly enjoyed working on the flight line and made many friends, but they kept testing me by trying to fix me up with girls. They couldn't believe I was going to become a priest.

Then I remembered what the Monsignor once told us: "As soon as you put on a Roman collar, all the dear religious girls in the world want to see what makes you tick." And they did! All the young girls in the Catholic Youth Organization seemed to like me. I would come home from work and three girls would have left messages for me. They usually pertained to meetings that they wanted me to be present at or some such thing.

It was very difficult for me to be celibate with the worldliness at work and women all around me. The hot summer nights worked on me too. My buddies from high school all came back after their three-year enlistments, and I got wrapped up with the old gang again. It seemed like there were parties every night. I began to drink more and more, and my resistance became less and less. I wanted to serve Christ, but perhaps it was not to be through the priesthood. I reasoned that I was too weak to become a priest, and therefore I must quit and get married. I couldn't stand this loneliness any longer.

I went out with the boys to a party one night and got drunk. This kid's older sister was there. Not a beautiful girl, but a pretty Irish lass. She tried to sober me up by saying that a future priest of God can't act this way. She would not let me out of the car, and I went to sleep.

The next morning when I woke up she was gone. She had walked all the way home in the night. I only see her once a year on St. Patrick's Day, but I still have a great respect for her. She made a decision that night not to become a nun. She soon married a Greek fellow, and now has a beautiful family.

I received a letter from one of my former classmates at Pensacola, then from several others. They invited me to my class's graduation, and urged me to come. They were receiving their commissions as ensigns in the Navy. I thought about those wild days at flight school, and about the Captain's daughter.

I realized I needed to get away from home and this would be a golden opportunity. So I proceeded to pack my bags and get my old car ready for the week-long trip.

I went to confession the day after I got drunk. I confessed that I had been intoxicated and desired a woman. I didn't do it, but I wanted to, and that's just as bad. The priest asked me if I planned to marry the girl. When I said no he told me that I was really bad. I had a notion to ask him what the difference was, but I didn't. I prayed for an hour before the altar of the Blessed Virgin, asking for the strength to be pure. I felt good again. I always felt good after going to confession and after I committed myself.

On the way to Pensacola my car broke down in Nashville. As I was sitting at the garage in gloom and disgust, a young woman who was sitting across the shop in front of me said that when her car was ready she would be glad to give me a ride.

"There was such gentleness in your eyes. I hope you will forgive me?" she said. "You'll have to forgive me because I… I am married. My husband, whom I love very much, is in Korea. He has been gone for a year. I was so lonely that I couldn't stand it, and when I looked into your eyes I knew that you were lonely too."

What could I say? How could this happen to me? I think I could have loved this girl very deeply, and now she tells me she is married. Damn, why couldn't she have been single? Since she told me about her husband, I thought it only right to tell her that I was studying to become a priest.

She told me how much she loved her husband, and she cried when she said she didn't think their marriage could work. They had loved each other in high school, and they had run away to get married. After high school, he got a job as a busboy. They had no money and had to live with her parents, so one day her husband just picked up and joined the Navy.

She told me she became very angry after he left, went out with some girlfriends, slept with a man, and got pregnant. She felt compelled by love to tell her husband when he came home three months later from boot camp. His pride hated her, and he left without even making love to her. She had the baby and got a job as a nurse's aid. She didn't know whether he would ever come back to her, but she would wait to see.

I told her all about Gina, and we talked for hours. I felt so sorry for her, and yet I couldn't love her. I thought of how one incident with Gina had ruined my life and how one incident had ruined her life.

"I am a Catholic and a marriage to a Catholic is forever," she went on. "I've thought of getting an annulment, because we do have grounds, and turning him free. I know he loved me once, and if I turn him free he may choose freely to love me again. But then I might have to explain my reasons for an annulment, and that would ruin my baby's life."

Things were so complicated now that for the first time I became very uneasy. I hopped up suddenly and said I had to go. She picked up her year-old baby and drove me to Montgomery, Alabama, that day. I intended to go on to Pensacola from there.

"We cannot have each other. We must go to confession this afternoon and really be sorry for our sin."

It was Saturday and we found a Catholic Church that heard confessions at four o'clock. We were both lighthearted and happy afterwards, and we both had to promise to stop seeing each other forever. I told the priest about riding back to Nashville with her, and he said it was O.K. if we never did anything and left each other at Nashville.

That night we slept in separate beds with our clothes on. When we got back to Nashville the next night there was a letter from her husband in the mailbox. He said that he had learned in Korea that he must forgive everyone everything. No matter how much he tried, he still couldn't forget that, so he had forgiven her. He also admitted that it was mostly his fault. He said he was stationed in San Diego now and he would come back to her in four weeks.

She cried and cried with joy. I insisted that she fly out to see him immediately, and I gave her the $200 Toomey had given me. I had to buy the plane ticket for her. We got my car back, and after she had dropped the baby and her car off at her mother's, I drove her to the airport.

We loved each other deeply, but not as lovers. She kissed me goodbye and begged me for my address. She wrote to me secretly for many years after that. "God be with you," "And with you," were the words we said to each other as we parted. I drove out of Nashville wondering when I would ever find that kind of happiness again.

I never did make it to that graduation. Two weeks later, I was back in the seminary. I didn't have the guts to tell my mother I wanted to quit. I also reasoned that since I didn't have a girl anyway, I might as well continue. I could so easily have become a priest if I had been able to marry!

The second year was interesting from a studies point of view. I took psychology, logic, and apologetics. I also became worldlier and organized a billiards tournament in the basement recreation room. I figured that the boys should get away from their studies now and again and relax. They had hardly ever used the billiard table before I came there.

My brothers and I were always taught that the most important thing was to win and better the next guy. Later on in life, I realized that was unChristian, even though it made things interesting, but I thought it was great at the time. All men seem to have this same instinct of competition. I remembered many fellows I met who loved to fight in wars for the same reason. I also met many people with inferiority complexes who always loved to better someone, even at the simplest things.

I had given up wanting to become a priest, but I had not given up trying to serve the Lord. I got the brilliant idea that I would organize a Christmas fund at the seminary to help the poor people. I felt that the seminarians shouldn't just give their money to a Catholic charity for distribution. They should participate in the distribution and see how the people live.

I wrote a crazy barroom play to raise money. Most of the cast invented their own lines, and it was funnier than heck. We raised $500 the first night and were asked to put it on again the next weekend. We had a packed house, and cleared a thousand dollars after expenses.

We formed a committee that bought food, toys, and candy. I was voted to be Santa Claus. I was also given a lecture about how Santa Claus takes away from Christ. I said that a little child can understand the goodness of Santa Claus, with the help of the department stores, long before he or she will understand the love that Christ stood for.

We went into the poorest slum area in town. The little shirtless, dirty kids were bewildered as I rang my sleigh bells, yelled "Whoa" to my imaginary reindeer, and banged on their doors. In almost every apartment there was a little child. I would ask them whose birthday was coming, and hardly anyone knew. Then I'd tell them it was Baby Jesus's birthday and He gave me these toys to give to them. I would tell them how Baby Jesus loved them and wanted them to be happy, and also to mind their mothers and fathers.

Half the time the fathers would be drunk. Many times tears would come to the parents' eyes–and to mine and those of the other seminarians.

Once we went into an old shack on the back of a brick tenement. It was very cold, and everybody was crying. A young Mexican couple stood there in total defeat. The woman was holding a baby in a blanket, rocking it from side to side. I told the children it was Baby Jesus's birthday, and that I was Santa Claus, here to bring them presents.

"No," the father said, "Baby dead! Baby dead! Jesus dead, too! Go! Go!"

We stood there for a few minutes crying with them. We realized that the baby in the woman's arms was indeed dead. We all reached into our pockets and collected what money we had to give them. "No money! No money!" the father said, "Go! Go!" We left the baskets and the money.

We were a sad bunch as we walked back to the car. "Lord," one of the other seminarians said, "I didn't know people lived like this in America. I thought we had welfare and unemployment."

I told them. "These people were probably not educated enough to know how to apply."

Another said, "Well, they must be Catholics, because they had the Sacred Heart picture and a crucifix on the wall. What about the Catholic charities we donate to?"

The next day, three of us went to the Catholic Charities headquarters and told them about the family.

"Oh, yes, the Gonzalez family. Yeah, we've been giving them $15 or $20 a week."

We looked at each other and said, "Fifteen or twenty dollars a week for a family of five?"

I said, "Now only four, because the baby died last night." "Oh, that is too bad," the administrator said. "Did you call the emergency squad?"

We looked at each other. We had thought of it, but the baby was already dead.

"You should have called the emergency squad anyway, then the county would have to pay the expenses of burying it. I'll look up their address and call the squad," he said. He called the squad and told them there was a very sick baby at the Gonzalez's address. We waited around to see what would happen. In about a half-hour the squad called back and said they had gone to the Gonzalez home but there was no sick baby. Two children there did look to be in bad shape.

On Christmas Day I walked down the alley in front of the Gonzalez's shack. The two other children were happily playing in the snow. I talked to the child who was about seven years old and she told me that her two-week-old baby brother had been taken to heaven. The baby had been born in the shack.

As I looked through the wooden fence, I saw a little mound of snow with fresh dirt mixed in it. A small white board had been nailed across the pickets. I leaned over the fence and tried to read what had been scribbled on the board with a pencil. All it said was "Pedro Gonzalez." A soul had been created, probably baptized, and died, unknown to the world, in just two weeks. He is probably in heaven, I thought; maybe it was a blessing in disguise for him.

We three adopted the Gonzalez family after that and brought them back to Christ. The biggest problem was that they were "wetbacks." The adults had swum the Rio Grande, and the one child they had at that time had been carried on his father's back. Mrs. Gonzalez nearly drowned, and is petrified now when she goes near deep water. After the Gonzalez's got to Texas, they were swallowed up in the cheapest labor force: illegal aliens who had no rights. They were practically slaves of the landowner who covered for them. The immigration authorities nearly found them when they moved to the north with the seasonal workers. They ended up working around Findley, Ohio.

I got the family real social security cards with false birth certificates, and through a friend of mine, helped get the father a job. We found them a house in the bottoms and they began to do really well. I co-signed for them to buy a small stove. They paid it off quickly. They were American citizens now, because they had established credit.

Dolores, the mother, would always cry when we talked about the Christmas we met. She studied English, and one day she told us that she couldn't sleep because her little Pedro's body was not buried in sacred ground. "He spirit would not be able to rest."

Nothing we said could ease her mind. So one day, Charlie and I went to the Catholic cemetery and found a big, granite grave marker with the name "Gonzalez" on it. I carved on the side of it, with a chisel, the name "Pedro" and the year "1952." That night we exhumed Pedro's little body, which had been buried in a five- gallon can, and placed it in a steel box that we had made. We all went down to the cemetery and buried the angel Pedro in holy ground. Dolores was at peace, and Pedro was happy in heaven.

I met Dorothy Jessberger, a cute little German girl, one night at a party, and we had a very enjoyable time. I stayed late and took her home. We made a dinner and dance date for the following Friday. I will never forget that night. I stopped my old beat-up '37 Pontiac in front of her house. I must have cared for her, because that day I had painted the inside of the car to impress her. It was the first time I had tried to impress a girl in ages. It looked cleaner than it had ever looked before, but it was not very neat.

Dorothy had two adorable little sisters, who were born late in her parents' lives. Dorothy was 19, and Anton, her oldest brother, was 21. He was in Korea at the time. Her youngest and most beautiful sister, Susan, the blonde one, was four years old and pleasantly bashful. Lillian, a beautiful redhead, was six. Another brother was named Robert. Dorothy's hair and eyes were very dark, and she never sunburned. Her deep tan made her look like a beautiful Sicilian Italian.

Getting back to the evening in question, Dorothy came to the door, and we proceeded to the car. Only the car would not start. So her entire family got out and pushed us down the street. It was a good beginning.

We drove shakily down the hill on Broad Street and made it across the city to within half a mile of Valleydale Hall, where the party was. The lights dimmed to off and the motor came to a stop. We coasted to a garage at the intersection. My battery had gone completely dead. They couldn't charge it but they said they could get me another one in an hour. I called a cab and the driver took us to the dance. That wasn't all; the big dinner dance was the next night, and there was no one there. I hadn't tried to impress a girl in ages, and this was disastrous.

The hell with it; we must not be meant for each other, I thought. We took the cab back to the garage. I didn't say a word all the way back until I saw St. Charles Seminary across the creek. I proceeded to give her cab money to get home, and told her I was going to stay there until the car was ready. She asked me what I was going to do then. I told her I was going to go to the bar next door and get drunk. She insisted on going with me.

She wouldn't drink anything, and just sat there sadly listening to me, and by the time the battery came I was bombed. She drove me back to her house and we sat in the car. I thought to myself, I have no money, clothes, car, or future, and I want to end this thing with her. I wasn't ready to be tied down to anyone, but she still persisted in being with me. I told her I was already tied down to someone.

That was all I could think of at the time, and it was sinful, but she wouldn't leave me for the next two months, and I became attached to her. She never really believed me, but she loved me. When I told her for the first time that I was a seminarian, she cried and told me that she could never see me again.

As I look back, I was certainly a free soul then. I never owned anything except for two pairs of slacks, shorts, a shirt, and a jacket. I always believed that it was harder for a rich man to get to heaven then for a camel to pass through the eye of a needle. The girls I knew must not have cared if I went to heaven, because they all seemed to want money, sharp clothes, and a new car. That was, except for Dorothy, and she didn't seem to care about those things. So I began to love her, and I couldn't go a day without seeing her. It was a slow process, but I was truly falling in love with her. Without her, life wasn't interesting. She was such a good girl, and so loveable that everyone who knew her seemed to love her.

Father O'Dea, my confessor, called me early in September and asked why he hadn't heard from me. I told him that I didn't think I would be coming back. He asked me if I would see him before I made a decision. I went to see him that day, the 12th of September. I remember the date because it was the day I had initially entered the seminary. Earlier, I had joined the Navy on that same date.

He tried to persuade me to stay. He told me I was a red-blooded man, but I could overcome the weaknesses of the flesh. He believed that I had a special calling to serve Christ. I told him how bad I was and that I couldn't be a parish priest anyway. He said he knew some preaching orders that would be glad to have me. I told him I wanted to wait for a while before I did anything.

He told me he knew a man, a contractor, who had no sons and wanted to adopt a young man and teach him the business; in time he would turn over the business and retire. The man built a lot of Catholic churches. Well, I thought that was a great idea. It would bring me closer to Christ. He also told me in confidence that the Bishop had assigned him as my guardian for two years, until I adjusted.

It seems that, and i know it to be true, when a man quits the seminary he sees himself as being a complete failure. He wouldn't be at the seminary unless he had some sort of a calling from God, so when he decides not to become a priest, it is like rejecting God, deciding to go the way of the world and ending up in hell. I never completely got over that feeling of failing God. Despair sets in, and it's dangerous. I was told that Hitler and Stalin were both once seminarians.

Father told me that if I did not want to become a priest, I should get married and have lots of children. Being a father and raising good children is almost as important as being a priest. He made it sound so simple: one way or the other.

I bade farewell to Father and to the seminary, and went out looking for Dorothy to marry. Now that I had made the choice, I wanted to act like everyone else. It was the beginning of an acting career that carried me through the next 20 years. I loved Dorothy deeply, but I had to act the part of really belonging to our great society.

I don't think I was ever truly a part of the society around me. I had to act like money was important, or winning a card game or a ball game. I had to act as if owning a new car or home or boat was pre-eminently important. Lord, I had to act like a husband and a father, a capitalist, and the Joneses. It took me a long time to realize that I was a misfit. I had to act out my life as if I were on a stage to please everyone else.

Every time I became my real self I would begin to drink heavily. It was always so much easier to act and forget God's calling then, but I loved to play-act the pleasant parts. I loved to act the part of a true lover, a Romeo, or a poet, or an artist, or a scholar. I guess my experience with Gina caused me to be in love with the thought of being in love rather than with really loving. I didn't understand what that meant then, but later in life I did. I was told by three different people that I would never love, but I loved the joy of being in love. They also called me a romanticist many times for that reason. I would create in my mind a perfect woman, my wife. When I looked at my wife, I saw the greatest beauty, and then I made her a perfectly sensuous, witty, charming, and lovable person.

Father O'Dea got me the job with the old contractor. That was a move I soon regretted. The contractor promised me the business, and he gave it to me. It was mostly my fault though; I wasn't really tough enough to be a capitalist. He tried to teach me every possible way to get the most out of a dollar. However, he would step over a dollar to save a nickel. I think we both knew that I would not work out after the first month.

He also had a stone company, and I spent all my free time carving art objects out of scrap stone with his air hammers. I eventually did all the complicated designs, but he had hired me for the General Contracting Division where the big money was. I was rather interested in the stone works, but the worst sin I could commit in his scheme of things was not being profit-conscious. "I am in business to make money, not to make beautiful stones and buildings," he used to say. "If I built the Taj Mahal and lost money, I would be a failure as a contractor."

I realized what he was trying to say later when I had my own business. Then, though, I thought quality and beauty were the most important things and most of all, honesty.

He used to love to have someone come in the shop and say they wanted a certain type of house stone or marble sill, no matter what it cost. If he would even overhear this remark, he would take over the sale.

One day I found out that he had a daughter, because her husband came to work in the office. I was told to train him as best I could. That was the beginning of the end. I liked the old fart, but he couldn't make a businessman out of me.

I will always remember the grand finale. I felt that I could design anything from aircraft to outhouses. The Bishop called one day and asked him to cut a niche high in the stone wall at the rear of the cathedral. He wanted us to design a base stone, so the job was given to me. I designed a flat face-stone to sit flush with the wall and the base for the statue; it looked like a quarter of an orange with the round part showing. The stone weighed over 300 pounds. We only had wooden scaffolding. I asked to rent new scaffolding, but he said they had been using those wooden ones for ages and they'd never had an accident. He refused, so we left with the old wooden scaffolding. I forgot to mention that he had a deaf and dumb Negro man who worked for him and had worked for his father before him.

On the way to the job, I looked at the back of the truck just as the handle of our expensive concrete machine became embedded in the side of a U.S. Postal truck. "The dummy," as he was known to all, had wanted to tie it down, but I had said to let it go. "Oh well; win one, lose one," I said.

When we got to the cathedral, I went in and got the other two men to help us carry in the stone. It took three men to lift it comfortably. We had cut the niche in the wall the previous day. I told the stone-setter to double up the planks and each scaffold section. Two of us were below and two above. We finally got it up to the top section. The cut that the base stone sat in was about three feet higher. Again, I said to double the scaffolding, and was told to go to hell by the stonemason. Three of us proceeded to lift the stone up into place. "The dummy" was beneath us. The two men put all their weight on the board near the wall to hunch it up. There was a resounding crack, and stone and men disappeared through the scaffolding.

When the stone fell, it took out the remaining cross-bracing support that we had not removed to get the stone in. I swayed to the right and then to the left, and the scaffold tipped, throwing me across the church. It is a good thing I took tumbling in the Navy, because it was all I could do to keep from breaking a leg.

I finally ended up against the wall, on my back with my feet in the air. I limped up and ran over to the site of the debris. A head and one hand were sticking out of the middle. "The dummy" was rubbing his round head and grunting. When I found that no one was hurt, I sat there and laughed until my sides ached. When I called into the office I still couldn't stop laughing. That was a mistake, and it was a bigger mistake when the boss arrived. All the worshipers in the church thought I had gone nuts, but it struck me so funny that I couldn't stop.

The next day I left to accept an offer of a job at Columbus North American Aviation. The "dummy" had written the boss a complete and most legible resume of what had happened the previous day. I knew he couldn't talk, but I didn't know he could write.

The contractor told me that I had great talent and that someday he hoped I would learn to apply it. We parted as friends, and his son-in-law took over. He turned out to be worse than I was, but the contractor couldn't fire him.

North American Aviation, Inc. gave me a job in the Experimental Structural Test Lab in the Engineering Flight Test Hangar.

They received a contract to modify 200 old North American T-6 Air Force or SNJ Navy trainer aircraft into fighter-bombers for the French to use in a place called Indochina. I was experienced with the SNJ from my time in the Navy.

I told them I was going to transfer my credentials from the St. Charles Fine Arts College to Ohio State University to study engineering. They said they would be glad to pay my way through Ohio State University. The planes had to be readied for flight test at night and flown in the daytime. This meant I could take regular courses at OSU during the day.

This was an offer even a pacifist could not refuse. It was the only job offer I had during the cold month of February 1953. I accepted because I wanted to walk away from religion and pacifism for a while to think about marrying beautiful sweet Dorothy.

I still wish I could have become a priest and married Dorothy too . . .

CHAPTER 12

MY DEAR WIFE AND WORK

I must include this chapter to show how I have always regretted not being able to become a priest. I felt like a misfit in every job I had except serving God.

I realized that I had grown deeply attached to Dorothy. When I wasn't with her I was lonely, so I spent all my free time with her. She was so naive and sweet; her soul and spirit were even more lovely than Gina's. She was a model of pure goodness.

Just before Christmas, I talked to Dorothy about marriage. I had no credit whatsoever, so I had to buy a $100 ring for $350 on credit through the "Friendly Jewelry Store." Before we got engaged, I had told Dorothy that I would never get married unless we owned at least a lot for a house. I had always wanted to design and build a house. I designed a beautiful split-level Spanish house. Then I said I would never get married until we had a loan to start the house, so she got a loan from some dear friends of her family, Mr. & Mrs. Joseph and Anna Hofbauer of Plain City, Ohio. He had come to this country from Germany with Dorothy's father and had prospered as a butcher. They were both wonderful people.

So then I asked Dorothy's father if I could marry her, and he asked me how much money I had saved. I told him I hadn't a cent, but I was going to save some. He asked me if I owed on my car. I told him I still owed $200 and the car was only worth $100. He gave me a flat "No." Also No and No. In fact, he never did say yes, but he helped me build my house. He insisted that we dig the half-basement by hand like they did in Germany. So, two months later, we laid the footer, and I broke some of my brothers' backs in the process. My father helped a lot too. From then on, the neighbors called me "Digger O'Dell."

When I first met Dorothy's Dad he had a huge wine cellar and two 50-gallon kegs, but in a few years all that was gone and he couldn't make it fast enough. I will say, in the deepest respect for him, that he had been forced to retire at an early age because he had silicosis from inhaling stone dust. He had been a master stone cutter. He carved some of the most notable monuments around the city, but he could never work with stone again. The pain in his chest was unbearable, and the only relief he got was through alcohol. He had an old quack doctor who was a famous alcoholic from the Bottoms, and he used to give my father-in-law 90 proof cough medicine. The doctor made it himself.

Once when I was going hunting with Pop, I had caught a cold from the rain, and he gave me a bottle of his medicine to take along. When I came out of the woods my cough was cured, but I was dead drunk.

It was a ritual with Pop to go to the old doctor's office every Wednesday. He would visit all his old friends all over town and get back early Thursday morning. One morning in 1965, he didn't come home. A high school boy coming back from a party had killed him. We just happened to know his family, and my sweet mother-in-law, Anna, wouldn't sue because she said that she knew it would happen to Pop someday. She said that anybody could have hit him that night. This may not have a bearing on it, but the boy later became a priest. My sweet mother-in-law had prayed for him constantly. I know Pop is in heaven, because he always served God in his own way. He was the most colorful figure on the West Side, and everybody missed him.

That all happened years later. Back in 1953, the months rolled around, and the two-story part of the house was almost completed. When we set the wedding date, a Saturday in September, we didn't know it would fall on the twelfth, but it did. I was so busy working nights at the plant and building the house that I could hardly believe it when the time came to get dressed for the wedding.

I looked at my body and laughed when I saw I was red from neck to toes. My buddies had dyed me in a tub at our temporary apartment the night before the wedding. (We were paying $40 a month for that apartment, and it wasn't worth a penny more.) I laughed harder when I remembered trying to retrieve my clothes off the neon sign of the Rainbow Grill the night before. My buddies had dyed me red, taken my clothes, and hung them on the sign before they left.

A lady standing below tried to ignore me at first, but it was impossible. She gazed upward and caught me in my nakedness, standing there on the pipes to the sign. I will never forget the look on that little old lady's face, down on the street waiting for the bus. I saw her running down the street, just as I got to my clothes.

I had never really had time to think about marriage until I was dressing for the wedding; that was when I realized that I shouldn't get married. I had not planned it—it had just happened. How can I get out of it now? I talked to my Best Man, and he told me I was crazy. My dear mother told me that I couldn't change my mind now; I couldn't hurt sweet Dorothy.

I remembered Father's words as I left the seminary, "Don't look back or you will be miserable." I had stopped looking back, but the future made me nervous. I was ready to back out until I saw Dorothy coming down the aisle. Then I was glad.

Her father had rented the big Knights of Columbus Hall downtown, and the reception was fabulous. My relatives numbered in the hundreds, and the patriarchs got loaded. It was the first of the great weddings. I think that was where most of Pop's wine went, come to think of it. The wedding reception was the only time in my life with Dorothy that she didn't want to leave a party early. She had no relatives in this country, and she was fascinated by mine. All my aunts and uncles on my father's side were musicians, singers, and dancers, at least until they got drunk, and then they still thought they were.

My father always sang children's songs or cute little ornery songs, and everyone loved him if he didn't talk about money. He started his career just as the Depression hit. Because he was so full of ambition, he never got over his own depression during those years. I was the first child born and suffered with him. He and my mother, Naomi, had three children right off, and things were tough. My parents, reluctantly, had to farm me off to my mother's parents. My mother cried and cried about it.

Later I thought it was great out on the farm every summer with Grandma Mary and Grandpa Tom Blower. He came from England, where he had worked in the mines at the age of 10. He married my grandmother at the early age of 15. She was half Cherokee Indian, and the contrast was tremendous. She was a strong woman, and he was as soft as

English pudding. Grandpa did not know that she was half Indian, only that she was beautiful.

The Blowers were all at the wedding that night, and watched in Protestant dismay as my Catholic relatives caroused. They sang and we all laughed and Pop's wine flowed. My Aunts Emma and Cecelia were the life of the party.

I finally begged Dorothy to leave at one o'clock, and an hour later, I got her away. We made it 40 miles to Mt. Vernon, Ohio and collapsed, but we made up for it the next day, and I was happy. I was really married and I liked it—belonging to someone and to each other and not like a celibate priest.

I had one great fear, though. The doctor had told me that I was sterile because I had the mumps when I was a senior in high school. I worried for about two months and then my wife became pregnant. We named our first daughter Maria, and she was always a most lovely child.

I could always tell after that. When Dorothy became pregnant her body temperature would rise and it would be unbearable to sleep next to her. This was the only time I couldn't sleep next to her; she would be like a blast furnace.

The years went by fast, working and loving, and we had six children before I ever knew where they came from. We talked about practicing birth control once, but my wife wouldn't hear of it. I thought if the Church said it was up to an individual's conscience to kill their enemies, then it would be all right to limit your family, because Christ did not say anything about birth control.

The good Mother Church was there to interpret the Bible for us, and we both had the faith deeply. I always believed that Christ established the Catholic Church first; He did not order anyone to write the New Testament. It was written down a couple of generations afterwards. He gave Peter the keys of the kingdom of heaven and the Catholic Church kept this word through 19 centuries. I often wondered why they never changed the part about loving our enemies. They could have at any time during that period.

In the third year of our marriage we had a son, and I called him Thomas, egotistically, after me. He was a beautiful child and I loved him very much. Thomas was a different child from the others, not because he was a boy, but because he was so emotional. I often regretted the fact that because I was so busy during those days, I never gave him the attention he needed. He was such a sensitive child. I always loved him dearly.

Dorothy insisted, after Thomas was born, that we wait a full eight weeks. No matter what, our beautiful daughter Tina was born nine months later. Babies need lots of love, and I think that Tommy needed more time to bond with his parents than he got. We had three in diapers at the same time. Sometimes a baby needs the undivided attention of the mother most of all, even though the Church might not agree.

When Dorothy would get that "up to here" look, I would drop everything and take her off someplace for a couple of days.

When Marcia came, we were in the middle of building our second house. The money I made at North American wasn't enough, so I had to build houses during the summer to supplement our income. We were blessed by the Lord and always had plenty. I felt that I could earn as much money as I wanted by just applying myself, but I hated applying myself to an unworthy cause.

I was doing well at North American Aviation that winter and summer, and the company was working around the clock, stockpiling planes and parts ahead of schedule. I was making $400 to $500 a week with overtime, and I was getting a lot done on the house with the money, but I hardly had a chance to say my morning and evening prayers.

The company was preparing ahead of schedule for a union-busting strike that happened soon after. I spent the 11 weeks we were on strike rapidly building my house. I actually made more money while we were on strike than I did working.

One night I was working in the engineering flight structures lab hangar when my old friend John Bernard came up to me. He was a plumber supervisor on the night shift. Somehow he was also a union executive.

The union was more than ready to forget the strike, because most of the workers, including John, had come back early, before the end of the strike.

John was a great guy. We had been halfbacks together in high school. We didn't join the Navy together, but we ended up in the same squadron at the Jacksonville Naval Air Base. We always liked to recall those carefree and uncomplicated good old days.

I had walked into the barracks one day and there was this hairy Italian sleeping in the next bunk. "John!" I yelled, and he jumped up and we hugged each other. I was going to St. Augustine that weekend with some buddies, so I invited John to go with us. John said he couldn't go because our captain was personally going to fly him home to Columbus, Ohio, to get his golf clubs. John had been the National Caddy Golf Champion when we graduated from high school in 1948. Our squadron captain was a real golf nut who was also captain of the base team.

We lived it up for about six months at Jacksonville before I volunteered myself and my other buddies for sea duty. That is how I ended up on the carrier *Midway* in the Mediterranean. John played golf for the rest of his military career; it was the only thing he did in the Navy.

That night in the hangar, John told me that the union elections were coming up, and asked me if I would help his slate beat the incumbents. He asked me where I stood on seniority, and I told him, "At the very bottom." I also told him that I did not want to get involved with the union because I was too busy.

John said, "My slate needs some brains, and you are the only man I could think of. The rest are all uneducated, and most of them are hillbillies." He also told me that if his slate got elected they would give me a job with executive union seniority, and that the company could not lay me off. I thought about starving for awhile without a job, and then I agreed to do it.

The election was three months away, and I would have to start immediately. The incumbents were going to be tough to beat. If he saw, at the end, that we couldn't beat them, he would shift to the incumbents and salvage something for himself—and for me if possible.

That night he took me over to the man who was running for president. Bob Kopp looked like a boy, but he was a bright politician. He also had high ideals about unionism. We got along fine, and are still the best of friends today.

I began to put out a one-page scandal sheet called the *Old Peeper*. All our committeemen and their stewards would gather information and gossip from around the plant; any bad deals between the incumbent members and the company were brought to light. To liven it up, we would run a gossip column, usually about the immoral acts committed by the incumbent members in the past, particularly their lives at the National and State Conventions.

I justified my bad actions at the time by convincing myself that we were doing the best thing for the union. I ignored the fact that I was doing it for job security. In fact, at that time, all the candidates were doing it for job security, but of course I rationalized that my reason was a worthy cause.

Bob Kopp, our candidate, easily won the election, and I was the hero of the union administration. He wanted to place me immediately on his executive board, and asked me if I would take the Directorship of the Committee for Education, Publicity, and Welfare. This would mean that I would also be the editor of the union newspaper.

He expressed surprise that the International congratulated him warmly and that there were no reprisals. "To the victor go the spoils." Two days after I went back to work I was notified that I was going to be laid off. The new president and the International protested that, as a member of the union executive board, I was exempt from the law of seniority. I really wasn't a member of the executive board until Bob was sworn in as president, but the outgoing president graciously and immediately appointed me to his board for the rest of his term. I always had great respect for the man and he had proven his worth by this act. That is what has made American's system of democracy so great and effective. No matter how bad the party behind the candidate is, the political system requires that the party put the best man out front in order to win. It may be selfish reasoning on the part of the politicians, but it works for the betterment of the country.

That day I understood for the first time what makes political workers get out there and work so hard. I had always suspected that most of them didn't love their candidates as much as they put on. It was for a job or for job security.

Politics, I found out, was a tough 24-hour-a-day job. You always had to watch what you said and who you said it to. Everything that you did had to have a political motive and a subsequent reward. Realizing this, I became a very successful politician, and actually took over running the union behind the scenes.

The old president once told me, "Nobody does nothing for nobody for nothing." It sounded harsh until he went on to explain. "Missionaries give all their lives in Africa helping the poor and the sick. Would they do it if they were told they would go to hell when they finished? Certainly not! They would not. They are working for life everlasting, the greatest reward of all.

It's the same with a mother loving her child and caring for it. She gets her reward and joy in sacrificing for the child. She enjoys it, and she hopes that the child will reward her someday with love in return." "Only crazy people do something for nothing," he would say.

Politics is like a business, and the only power a politician knows is the power of getting votes. He will buy that power or trade it for something of equal value, like the promise of a job. Precinct workers are always expecting some gratuity, even if it is only the power to get a parking ticket canceled. The old president helped me tremendously with the newspaper. He had once been the editor, so he graciously showed me a lot of shortcuts.

My first executive board meeting was a dramatic experience. All the opposition I had torn down with my editorials were present. By now they all knew the part I had played in their defeat. Some had been on the executive board for years and had worked hard. Some would lose their jobs because of me. They realized that this was only the second union meeting I had ever attended, and I had cut them down with my pen in a very unchristian manner, ruthlessly and unfairly. I hadn't even known these people. I could not tell the difference between them and our candidates.

The next night, I asked Bob Kopp to keep three of these people on union seniority for a while as a favor to me.

"Are you crazy?" was his reaction. "I must have a list of 50 people who I have promised seniority."

I told him, "I have to keep these three people because I promised them. It will soften the opposition so we can get things done. If I can't keep this promise, then I can't take a job with the union."

"But you would be laid off if you didn't!" he exclaimed.

"I don't care," I replied. He said I would be responsible, but he reluctantly agreed. He created three new union jobs for them.

Being the editor of the paper was a trying experience at first. Each officer and each committee chairman was supposed to write columns for the paper. I soon found out that the editor's job was to ghost-write all those columns. In fact, it was my job to write the entire paper, and I wasn't the world's best writer.

The news releases we received from the International were way over the heads of the membership, and most of the time they were two months late. I made up my mind to make this paper the most enjoyable union paper ever written. I felt I could use it to expound my socialist Grandfather's great ideas. I made it a contrast of union idealism and humor. I included a couple of my own cartoons, and I kept the "Old Peeper" column in a humorous vein, but still politically powerful.

After two or three months the whole plant, including the supervision, would rather read the union paper than the company's publication. I didn't mention any names in the paper, but I did identify departments and sections. "A certain supervisor in Department 35, Section 8, has just promoted his brother to foreman out of the line of seniority. Now that is what I call real brotherly love, since he probably could get in trouble over it."

Although those in the know knew I was the "Old Peeper," his identity was officially a secret. I started writing for other union publications around the city. I was never in the plant anymore, and I was having a ball. I had organized a fantastic Educational Committee of trusted workers throughout the plant who also served as my spies. I knew everything that was going on in the plant. The president gave me a free hand because I was one of the few people he could trust. In his absence, everything had to go through me for approval.

The big day came, in 1961, when I was sent to Atlantic City for the National United Auto and Aircraft Workers Convention. I was given $400 expense money and travel expenses for 10 days. I used to get legitimate travel expenses for traveling from the plant to the union hall, at $7.98 each trip. It was a half a mile to the hall. Union officers didn't make much money, but we loved those expenses.

We were paid so much a mile to Atlantic City, so I formed a car pool with three other delegates and we saved a lot of money. It was all so new to me and so exciting! Our International Region had reserved a whole hotel on the boardwalk. From my room on the seventh floor I could look out over the ocean and the swimming pool. It was beautiful, and I had a pocket full of money. I wasn't a delegate, but I was an editor for the state of Ohio.

My job was to report back to the union membership through the newspaper about the activities of the week. I was reminded before I left that I was to expound the great virtues of our President and slate of officers.

In addition, I was given the $500 Graflex camera that the union owned and was told that I was also the official photographer for the region of Ohio. That was the one thing that made me a bit nervous. I had never taken pictures with this type of camera before.

President Kennedy, Mrs. Roosevelt, and Arthur Goldberg were going to address the union convention. I couldn't get the stupid camera to work, so I spent the first day at a camera shop. Finally, the owner loaned me a similar camera, with my camera as collateral, but I had to agree to get all my pictures developed through him. That day, I must have taken 30 pictures, which all had to be developed, before I could get the right light and distance settings for the convention hall.

There were hospitality bars all over the place, and it was difficult for a man not to get drunk. The Regional Directors and staff paid for it all. Walter Reuther paid for many parties at the higher level. He and the other UAW Officers had rented the Carlton Hotel with all the ballrooms. Each Regional UAW Director under Reuther, I found, was also a vice president of something or other. I remember Leonard Woodcock as being the most appealing.

Each director and all of his staff went to great lengths to cater to the delegates in the next five days before the election. Their opposition was always kept disorganized at the local and regional levels. I realized after a few days that Walter Reuther's men had complete control of the convention. That is, except for a few leftover

"Red Shirts." They were the remnants of the communists, who I was told he had beaten out four years earlier.

At that earlier convention, the communists had come out strong within the union to take it over, and I guess the election was a terrible battle. There were fist fights and beatings all over the boardwalk.

Reuther had barely beaten them then, but had broken their backs in the years that followed. All but a very few were kicked out of the union. The handful of protesters were always booed down. People thought that Ruether had done the union and the nation a great service. I was now a part of that history, though that night I didn't know it.

The next day Arthur Goldberg spoke before us, and I got some practice taking good pictures. He told us what a great man Walter Reuther was. Walter Reuther's publicity staff had a cocktail dinner at the Carlton with all the union editors and newsmen. They also told us what a great man he was. I didn't like their pre-printed press releases, though, so

I wrote my own stuff. I met the chief of Reuther's publicity department that day, and he liked me. He tried to help me later on.

That day and the next, all opposition to Reuther's slate was gently crushed. The regional staff members never left their delegates. They searched for the opposition at all levels. The process was a quick and valuable education in politics.

The big day finally arrived when President John F. Kennedy was going to speak. Probably it was planned that he would speak the day before the general election for the President of' the UAW, to give Reuther a plug.

Out of the 20 pictures I took of the President, two were better than good. It could not have been staged more perfectly. President Kennedy was in the middle with an exuberant smile and waving. Walter Reuther was on the right, clapping, and Leonard Woodcock was with him. Emil Mazey, the old vice president of the union, was on the left, perfectly balanced.

I rushed back to the photo shop, and as I went, I wondered whether I could sell these pictures to the convention members as souvenirs. The photo shop worked all that night, and in the morning before the election, I had 1,000 pictures for $500. Bob Kopp said the local would take what I didn't sell. I made $5,000 in two hours, and they were crying for more.

Walter Reuther personally signed five for me and asked me if I would give him five for President Kennedy to sign. He promised me he would get President Kennedy to sign one for me. I gave him the five pictures, but someone at the union hall stole the picture President Kennedy had signed, and I have always been remorseful over it. I still have the pictures of President Kennedy that Reuther signed.

That day, I was contacted by Reuther's publicity chief, who offered me $200 for the negative. I told him I would give him a copy of the negative free of charge, but not the original. He was insistent, but I wouldn't give in, though I did give him the copy negative. He sent me $200 later for the best picture taken at the convention. It was used all across the country in union publications, but they cut off Emil Mazey and Leonard Woodcock.

Naturally, Reuther and fellow officers won the election, except for the region of California. I can't remember that young director's name, and I don't know how he pulled it off, but he beat one of Reuther's men. You never know. I was very much impressed by Reuther, even if his methods seemed to be undemocratic. I always hated committee rule.

That evening, Mrs. Eleanor Roosevelt was his special guest at the victory banquet. I tried to get close but they would not allow me. Reuther saw me standing with the press, motioned me over, and introduced me to Mrs. Roosevelt as his favorite photographer. She was a gracious lady, but I could not understand her at all when she talked. She was very old by this time and she spoke very softly.

THE AUTHOR APPEALING TO POPE

My wife always hated my union activities because of my prolonged absences. I kept plugging away, though. I really hurt the company during negotiations with my editorials and cartoons based on their profit and loss statement. Their profits had increased 30% in the last four years, and our wages had only increased 6%.

I wrote an open letter to the corporation's vice president of labor relations and published it in the newspaper. It told how we, the union, should share in the increased profits because it was our blood, sweat, and tears that had primarily produced the profit. I was congratulated many times on that article.

Bob Kopp was in negotiations in California, and during his absence I was in charge, politically, that is. I was the power instead of the union vice president, and I had to attend meetings day and night. My wife must have thought I was living it up in Atlantic City and heady with the fame I had gained over President Kennedy's picture, because she began to distrust me.

President Kennedy had been happy and confident at the UAW Convention in Atlantic City in 1961. However, just one year later, in November of 1962, U.S. military spy planes spotted Soviet ships with intercontinental nuclear missiles on board sailing towards Cuba.

Immediately the hawks in Congress demanded a blockade of Cuba and war, even nuclear war if necessary, to stop the missiles from being deployed so close to our own boundaries. I noticed that Kennedy's countenance had changed to worry and insecurity.

President Kennedy ordered the U.S. nuclear bombers and missiles to strike Cuba within three days if the ships with the missiles did not turn back to Russia.

Nikita Kruschev said he would not back down and nuclear missiles would be launched if Cuba were attacked.

He pointed out that U.S. nuclear missiles surrounded the borders of Russia, so why not Soviet missiles close to the United States? I gathered my wife and children around me and we prayed and went to Mass every day. I knew what could happen, because I had built nuclear weapons.

Maria, my daughter, asked me, "What's wrong, Daddy?"

"My dear Maria, two macho world leaders would rather destroy our world than back down for peace," I replied. "And daddy is responsible too. Daddy helped to design and build the first all- jet-carrier-launched nuclear bomber, the A-5C Vigilante. I have worked on this nuclear bomber off and on for eight years in the engineering structure test lab, perfecting it for carrier landings. The bomber carries five nuclear bombs that could destroy five cities and kill five million people. Later, from the A-5C bomber, we made the RA-5C spy plane that took the pictures of the Cuban missiles."

"Why did you do it, Daddy?" she asked.

"For the money, honey. For the money for you and mommy." My children lost some respect for me that day.

Most fortunately, Nikita Kruschev backed down first and turned the missile ships back to Russia. I lost much respect for President Kennedy because the U.S. did not back down to save the world. Finally President Kennedy agreed never to allow the U.S. to invade Cuba, which is what the whole thing was about.

President John F. Kennedy was assassinated one year later on November 22, 1963. The former vice-president, Lyndon B. Johnson, became president and immediately accelerated the war in Vietnam, which I would also become a part of.

CHAPTER 13

FIRST CAPITALIST EXPERIENCE

Christ said, "You cannot serve God and money." A capitalist is totally about making money. I was a capitalist once–one of the worst kind.

One day the company offered me a management position. They contacted my wife first. She forced me to go to the company and find out about the job. Labor Relations told me that anyone who had the talent I had should be working for the company, not wasting my time on the union rabble. They told me that I would be the Shop Support Authorization Manager for Manufacturing. Since all this work was done in the Experimental Department, but for Engineering, I would know what was going on. They must have known that the current chief of the Experimental Department was ripping them off for the sake of the employees. But Engineering, which was getting ripped off, and then Manufacturing had both agreed on me as the man. I was really working for Engineering.

I stalled taking the job by saying the salary was not equal to the responsibility, and I refused until my wife said she would divorce me if I didn't leave the union. I wasn't a brilliant writer, but I loved what I was doing for the union. I also enjoyed working for a cause, not for a profit.

The following day I went to see the Chief of Experimental, Mr. Krallman, and he took me to his boss, Mr. Al Leonard, who was the director of all manufacturing. They called him "Black Al," but he must have mellowed in his old age. I guess during the war production years he had been sheer hell to work for. He had a devoted staff, and was a clean-desk type of manager. By that I mean that he hired the right people and stood behind them 100%. He let you do your job freely, but you had better not bother him with your problems, and you had better produce results. He allowed you 10% error. If you exceeded that you were out and he got another man.

He asked me if I was going to give up all the union writing he had been shown. I told him I would if I took the job, but I wanted to discuss the pay. We bargained and he began to like me. We agreed on a price increase and I reluctantly took the job. I say reluctantly because I always hated business, and I also hated to be around purely business-oriented people, especially those who made nuclear weapons.

I was a Bohemian at heart, and now I had to fake being a businessman. I trained myself to think like one, but it was difficult for me to put profit before all else.

In the meantime, we had another beautiful baby girl, whom we named Monica. One morning when she was a year old and I was sitting at the table reading the morning paper she recited the Pledge of Allegiance from start to finish. I looked around the room and over at the TV to see where the sound was coming from. I about flipped when she started to repeat it.

"D—Dorothy!," I screamed, "come here!" We couldn't believe our ears listening to her as she sat in her high chair. She was always a brilliant child and could mimic anything and anyone. From that day on, she never stopped talking. She could draw anything at a very early age. Her sense of color and composition was near genius.

In fact, all my children inherited my limited art abilities and expanded on them. They were all the most beautiful and handsome children. They had taken after their mother.

Tommy always was a most loving child. He had to have his tonsils out when he was 10 months old, and I think he thought we had deserted him in the hospital. His throat had been hurting him since he was born. When he went to school he needed glasses and we didn't know it. It didn't help matters that at the time I was too busy to play with him. He eventually grew into a great inner peace and I am very proud of him. He became a Christian lay minister and evangelist.

I would never allow my children to be in competition with each other. I always told them that the only thing I wanted them to do to make me proud of them was to go to heaven. If they did not go to heaven then I would wish they had never been born.

Maria, the oldest, had to be perfect, and as a child she was. I felt sorry for her at times. I knew what it was like to be the oldest of eight children. I was responsible for setting an example for all the rest and so was she. She used to cry a lot, but she never complained or talked back.

Tina, the next daughter, was all woman from the day she was born. She always dressed perfectly and would never allow her hands to get dirty. She would roll those big eyes at you and use every womanly trick to get her own way. She was always a beautiful woman.

Marcia was the "tomboy," and could run faster and fight better than most boys. She also had an emotional problem for a while because she couldn't learn. She couldn't master any studies easily, but she could excel in any sport immediately. Later on I found out that she was just lazy with studies, because she caught up a whole year that she failed just so she could stay with her classmates. Marcia was also beautiful.

Lisa was the ham, the theatrical one of the crowd. She loved to be around adults and intrigue them with her theatrics and her knowledge. They loved her, and I did too. She was smitten by the Holy Spirit at an early age and developed a beautiful religious character. Lisa was a brilliant child and also a beautiful person.

Maria was first to set the religious example, and the rest followed. I always said that you can set a good example in two ways. You can either be very good or very bad. For example, most of the people that I know who won't drink a drop had an alcoholic parent. I always used this example when I was bad in their eyes, because I was definitely not a saint. I am greatly proud of all my children, and I thank my wife for setting such a good example.

My wife was the type who adopted stray dogs and other animals. You know, the type who will drop everything to help a stranger. I remember when we owned a day care center for children. We bought an old farmhouse to start the day nursery.

It was a mistake profit-wise, because Dorothy would always feel sorry for the needy parents who had to work. If the parents mistreated their children she would reprimand them. The majority of the children were from broken homes, and there were many emotional problems. Almost every night when I came home there would be children sleeping on the living room floor. She would adopt the most disturbed children until they were straightened out.

Once we kept five little brothers for two weeks while the father tried to find his wife, who had run away. I thought of my sweet mother then. She had seven boys and never complained.

I was totally unhappy with my occupation in those days and drank a lot. I always hated to be a businessman, but I was forced to be a good one. I used to build houses on the side each summer because it took away from weapons making. I always had a project going to create interest and make extra money.

I started a recreational land project south of Lancaster, Ohio, in the first foothills of the Appalachian Mountains. It was a beautiful spot until I started selling lots to too many people—that is, to the non-Bohemians who wanted everything perfect and always complained.

The corporation I had formed to sell lots did become very profitable later on. I neglected to file income tax for three years once, until the government finally sent me a notice. I went to H&R Block and they recommended that I find an independent expert. He had a most difficult time trying to show that I did not make a profit.

When I finally got all the papers together I wrote the government a longhand letter, explaining the whole situation. I used "ain't" and misspelled words throughout the entire text. I was writing contracts for the company at the time, and our director put it on the bulletin board as an example of the last resort in dealing with the government.

"Plead ignorance and prove it!" he said.

I broke him up once when he warned me that alcohol destroys the brain. I told him that it was true. "Would you believe that I was a genius just a year ago?"

I adapted to the business world because I had to make a living. Sometimes I used to think it would be better living under communism. Then you only had to do one job to survive, and your wife and kids wouldn't have to keep up with Jones. Everyone would be a Jones. I wondered if they allowed moonlighting in Russia.

I had worked for the company about a month when Bob Kopp, the president of the local, called me and told me that Walter Reuther had offered me $25,000 a year if I would come to Detroit and join his publicity staff. Bob had the painful job of telling the International that I had left the union. They could not believe it. He also told me that he was leaving the local and taking a job with the International Union. That was what he couldn't tell me before, until it came about. Twenty-five thousand dollars was big money in 1963.

Bob was going to be the director of political action for the AFL-CIO in Ohio. This would put him in charge of all union political expenditures in the state of Ohio. He was planning to get the International to appoint me president of the local in his absence until elections, which he was sure I would win.

"You certainly screwed up when you left the union. You are just a number at the plant, and they'll dump you the first chance they get." I told him I had to keep my promise to my wife and I hated it. In fact, I wanted to drink more now than before. He thanked me for all I had done for him and told me if I ever needed help to call him. That was the end of my good union days.

Now at work I had the authority to approve all expenditures to the experimental department that I used to be in. The monkey was on my back, and I had to prove myself. I began to get two estimates whenever Engineering would send me a job, something no-one had done before. I would send one copy of the drawing to Experimental and another to the Production Department for a counter-estimate.

I quickly made the Experimental Department honest by giving their work to Production at half the price.

Soon Experimental prices came down, and I saved the company thousands of dollars. Charlie Krallman, the head of Experimental who got me the job, hadn't contemplated this, or else he didn't know that his estimators were making a gravy train out of his department.

As a result of my actions the group of six SSA Coordinators in Engineering was disbanded and four were laid off. I took over their functions with only two men and a secretary. The Experimental Department went from 375 people down to 190. I did a great job, but I put a lot of people out of work, the capitalist way. Yet all the people who got laid off thought they were good capitalists!

As Administrator, I was responsible for the status of all experimental projects in Manufacturing. When Engineering or Manufacturing was late or delaying a project, I began sending copies of my status reports all the way to the Vice Presidents, and once to the President. I would address them to my immediate supervisor, Bill Johnson, and then I would under-handedly send copies all the way up the line.

The time I sent a letter to the President was on a multimillion-dollar Navy "Condor" Cruise Missile Program. The corporation had previously developed the Red Head Road Runner Target Missile, which was designed to fly by computer control over the White Sands, New Mexico, anti-aircraft target range at low altitude.

For two years no anti-aircraft system, either projectile or missile, was able to destroy the target missile. It was an Army target missile program, but the Navy became interested in using the missile to develop a low-flying guided "cruise missile," a slow-flying offensive weapon that could fly 1500 miles undetected by radar.

The Navy wanted the missile pre-programmed to be launched from naval aircrafts or ships and to strike targets inland with precision without the danger of being shot down or risk to aircrafts and pilots. We accepted the contract with some doubts about our ability to meet the performance requirements.

We created a super-secret area in Engineering Building No. 6 at the Columbus division. On the floor of that same area we simulated a scale model of all the terrain in the China Lake Missile Range. It was huge.

Over this simulated terrain we passed vidicon (TV) cameras and radio altimeters on booms and rails to program a guidance system into the missile's computer memory.

The Road Runner Missile was too small (12" in diameter and 22 feet long) to accommodate the computer, warhead, vidicon, electronics, and altimeters. So in the middle of the project, engineering decided to completely redesign the missile shell. About this time many new and advanced miniaturized electronics were flooding the market, and we were using them for the new Hellfire Missile design.

The Condor Missile had limited engineering study funds. However, I estimated that we were not going to meet the schedule requirements we had to meet for a Preliminary Design Review (a PDR), which was critical to getting millions of dollars more. It was going to be a disaster.

The physical work was being done in Krallman's Engineering Experimental Department and authorized by me, so I had a real handle on it. Not even the first engineering drawings were available for the PDR review, there was no way to build a mock-up of the missile, and everything was due to be completed within one month. This was flat out impossible.

All the chiefs were telling everyone how splendidly the program was coming along. When my report proved to them that Engineering was flat on their ass and would miss schedule by three months, all hell broke loose.

The president of the Division called all the VPs into his office, and they could not deny anything to his satisfaction. I put the burden of guilt on Engineering early instead of waiting until the project got to Manufacturing. Good old Bill Johnson sweat blood, but Pappy Leonard loved it. That same afternoon the VPs of Engineering and Manufacturing called a general meeting to work things out. The Engineering VPs criticized me three times, but I was right and they knew it. I had really calculated the program as being five months behind schedule, and with all their special efforts it still ended up three months behind schedule like I had predicted.

I was now well known by all the management in the plant, and Mr. Leonard loved it. Bill Johnson warned me once that I had better be right when I made waves, or else both our heads would roll.

The Navy Condor Cruise Missile Guidance and Propulsion System was very crude, but it was the first birth of all the cruise missiles. The simulated terrain of the China Lake Test Center we had created was expanded into an enlarged secret area to simulate all the terrain in Europe around Russia and the targets in Russia.

The Pentagon planned to flood the Russian defenses with thousands of these cheap little Cruise missiles flying at treetop level under Russian radar. They planned to destroy the Soviet missile fields and missile command centers in a first-strike sneak attack. Then big, new, super-accurate missiles would be launched from close submarines and from western European countries. My friend Joe McLaughlin was responsible for coordinating the specifications.

Later this primitive cruise missile guidance system was replaced by a TERCON grid system. As the missile moved from grid to grid it always knew its position in relation to the target and corrected itself.

Much later the cruise missiles and all the guided weapons would be totally guided by satellite positioning, as in the Norstar Guidance System. Three satellite-coordinate guidance systems would easily guide the missiles to their target areas. Of course we were also planning, and would soon be making, the Rockwell space shuttle and other space weapons to steal or destroy the satellites that our enemies intended to guide *their* nuclear missiles and other weapons. I found out later that this action was a scheduled phase of the ABM Defense System.

One day, to my surprise, Charlie Krallman called and told me that he had just been promoted to Manufacturing Manager of the new OV-10 "Bronco" Aircraft Development Contract. I congratulated him. Then he asked me if I would become his Manufacturing Administrator. He said it would be quite a jump up in salary. I would be in charge of all schedules, budgets, and so forth. I needed a higher position like a hole in the head, but if you turn down a promotion in industry, that's it. You never go any further. In fact, you are lucky to keep your job. I hate business, but I had a family, so I said yes. I called my wife and told her, and she was happy.

It only took me a couple of days on the program to realize that we were in trouble. First of all, I found that the VP and the President had cut the initial contract estimate by 10%, in order to buy into the business of FAC light-recognizant aircraft. Then the contracts department withheld another 10% as a kicker, to force better production.

Therefore, Manufacturing's budget had been cut by 20% of their initial estimate. That was out of a best-effort-ever estimate to begin with. Based on the AMPR weight of the aircraft (the base weight of the hollow plane minus the propulsion system) and compared to past histories, this overall estimate was lower per plane than for any plane North

American built during the war. Now this rock bottom price was cut 20%.

The first drawings that came out were unfinished, but we built the first plane anyway, and on schedule. We had the Assistant Secretary of the Navy there for the big rollout. He congratulated us on our efforts. As soon as his limousine had pulled away we rolled the plane back into the hangar and tore it apart to make necessary changes.

I began first to make charts for the real world which showed we would over-expend our budget by so much. These would be unacceptable to the VP. Then I would make a set that would show best efforts for about half that overrun. These would also be unacceptable. Then I would make a set showing us within the budget, and the VP would force Charlie to sign it and send it to the corporate office.

It was the day before Christmas, and we still had two planes to complete, but we were out of money. We were in the office getting drunk when I finally convinced Charlie that there was no way we could come out of this winners. He admitted I had been right from the beginning. We made up our minds then that we were going to enjoy our job and ride it out to the end. I would lie like a capitalist CEO to cover us. We did enjoy those last six months.

One day as I was sitting in my office with my feet on the desk, looking at the real-world charts, a pleasant little man appeared and took my charts away from me. He then took all the other information I had and led me into Charlie's office.

Charlie was finally frank with him and admitted everything. This gentle, smiling man was the hatchetman for the Corporate V.P. of Manufacturing from California. The next week the Corporate V.P. came to town to review the program. The next day when I came into the office the girls were crying. They quickly told me that the whole organization was disbanded and that no one had jobs.

I was rather relieved. At one time, I had 255 people working in our own departments, and I was responsible for all the other supporting departments too. I had expended 20 or 30 free hours of overtime every week. Now we were being blamed for the fiasco. I couldn't see why, because Engineering had spent all the money.

The Columbus Division was bitter with Charlie and me because Charlie had committed a grievous sin. He had hurt the integrity of the Division by telling the truth to the corporate office.

Now the Division made us the fall guys and blamed us for everything. Charlie was able to retain a job as foreman with one of his best friends. We were being blamed for a $12-million-dollar loss, when Manufacturing had only lost $2 million of it. That's a matter of record.

I tried to stop Charlie that day when he admitted everything. As I've said before, my golden rule is never to admit anything. Bill Johnson saved me for about a month before I went out the door. It was a great experience for an ex-union official.

The V.P. was forced to retire a short time later, and we heard he was in a mental institution. All chief executives have to have at least one nervous breakdown before they are successful, but the great ones eventually become alcoholics.

I could never have a nervous breakdown because I could never remember my worries. I had acquired a nasty habit of drinking four martinis every night after work. I loved to drink, and it was my downfall. I found that I liked everyone when I drank and very few people in business when I was sober. But I was always glad to be with my family.

I spent the last four weeks before I left the company diligently designing the plans for a new addition to our day care space. I finished the plans and got them approved by the state. During that time, I also co-authored and cast a theatrical play. My wife was excited about the day nursery, and I was hopeful that she would make some money.

My dear brother Ray got me a laborer's job with my uncle Henry Justice's construction company. However, the job was in Pendleton, Indiana, on the Post Office. We were building a large addition to it. I left early Monday morning and came back each Friday afternoon. Every weekend was like a honeymoon, and the other nights I was as free as a bird. It was wonderful not to have to take my work home with me. I painted pictures and carved wood at night. I joined an art class on Tuesday and Thursday nights. There were 15 in the class with me, and we had a ball.

A couple of weeks later, my uncle showed up on the job and asked me if I wanted to be superintendent of another Post Office job he had in Wappakoneta, Ohio, now that I had a union card. I really worked hard to make an impression and finished the job two weeks early.

My uncle then sent me to Wadsworth, Ohio, to run a Post Office remodeling job. During that time the manufacturing Vice- President, my old boss, was fired and committed to a sanitarium, where I understand he lived happily ever after.

My friends at Rockwell repeatedly contacted me about coming back, but I was enjoying the freedom from hypocrisy and I refused. However, my wife was getting tired of my leaving on Monday mornings and coming back Friday evenings.

The party was over one day when my wife called me and told me that I was officially called back to Rockwell. My old friend, Bill Johnson, had gotten in touch with her instead of me. She had mentioned to him that she wanted to get me back in town. Well, he told her that he could get me a job, and I cursed him out for it later.

I told my wife that day that I didn't want to go back, but she said she would leave me if I didn't. She couldn't stand the lonely nights with six children. I called my Uncle Henry that day and told him I had to go back to Rockwell. He told me that if stayed with the company a while longer, I could take the place of an estimator and V.P. who was about to retire. This fellow had been threatening to retire for years, so I told my uncle that my wife was forcing me to leave, but when his V.P. retired he could call me and I would work for him. He never did call me.

On the morning of the day that a new superintendent replaced me, the Union Business Agent came around. I had worked the job for four weeks without having contacted the local union hall, a must in the Canton, Ohio, area. He roared at me and asked me who was the superintendent. I pointed over to my replacement. While he was threatening the new superintendent with a fine, I slipped out of the Post Office and went back to Columbus. That was the end of my construction superintendent career.

CHAPTER 14

MY CALLING AND VIETNAM

I was offered a job in Rockwell's Contract Division because of my management skills. I was surprised to find out that I would make slightly more than in Engineering. At the interview with my future manager, I held out for still more money. After I had started working, the personnel division cut my pay back to the original figure, so I cut my working hours to compensate. I had put 20 or 30 hours a week in unpaid overtime into the previous program, so I felt the company owed me a lot.

My new manager was a southerner, with a German accent. He had been sent to Germany for most of his Air Force career. I loved to listen to him. When he had a few martinis, he would inevitably slip back into his South Carolina drawl. He was a bright and overeducated country boy.

He loved the outdoors and to hunt all kinds of game; we had a lot in common in the hills. He always liked me most of all his team, even though I caused him the most trouble. I was a country boy too and I understood him.

Since I didn't have much experience in Navy contracts, I was named coordinator and data manager of all the small Air Force contracts that Rockwell had. No one else knew Air Force contracts or data, since 90% of all their contracts were Navy. This made sense because the facility was owned by the Navy. Being assigned to the Air Force contracts was a business break for me.

Because at the time I started there was no expertise on Air Force contracts, I soon became the only expert in that field. I started with the Air Force T-28 Aircraft Modification Programs. These were old trainer planes modified, updated, and equipped with guns and bomb racks for Vietnam.

I began to think about my Christian pacifist commitments every time I delivered a plane. Would it be used to kill women and children? Lord, once I even remembered my commitment to you, that I had made so long ago. I drank a lot and hardly ever remembered that I had promised to devote my life to world peace. I needed my job to support my wife and children; I was told they must come first, and that was my vocation now. Lord, you have your Pope and your bishops and priests to demand the end of war and the beginning of the Christian era. Besides, every time I mentioned this calling in confession, I was told it was up to the individual's conscience whether working in a war plant or fighting in a war was right. I killed my conscience by conditioning.

The priests always seemed more concerned about the times I wanted to practice birth control. I rationalized that maybe it was more important to create a soul than it was to worry about destroying bodies. After all, the soul really was more important than the body.

Deep in my own soul, though, I couldn't convince myself to forget about the third unique principle of Christianity, loving your enemy. I told myself that trying to love God and my neighbor as myself was enough to occupy most lifetimes. I reasoned that if I conquered those two items, then I would work on loving my enemy or the Viet Cong.

One morning I was walking from the parking entrance through the huge open clerical area beneath the corporate executive offices. I had taken the East Security Entrance as a shortcut to my office.

Suddenly a young man came running down the center aisle shouting, "You murderers are killing millions of farmers in Vietnam."

When I turned around this young man looked me straight in the eye and said, "Why do you kill for money?" He quickly passed me and continued running and shouting as he entered the private office area.

I turned back around as two police officers ran up to me with their guns drawn and shouted, "Which way did that pacifist go?" I shall always remember that pacifist. He was my conscience looking into my soul, with such peaceful eyes! I continued, however, to be a hypocrite for the money and my family.

One of the proofs that God exists is based on universal consent. That is, all races and people from the beginning of time have reasoned that there is a Supreme Being who created us all. By the same reasoning, all races and people from the beginning have justified the practice of war. None of the good Christians I worked with could see anything wrong in selling arms to kill the Vietnamese "to protect themselves" or fighting, in "self-defense," 10,000 miles from our shores. After all, we were protecting their country from the enemy of Christians, the communist. So what if we were killing a few million Vietnamese in the process?

I rationalized that war was always a part of our Bible. The Old Testament is a total history of wars fought by "God's chosen people," the Jews. How could God say it is right for them and not for us? God even helped them destroy their enemies. Yet God told them "Thou shalt not kill." Maybe it was because the Assyrians, the Babylonians, and the Egyptians were not created by God? Maybe God did not create the North Vietnamese, Chinese, or Russians either. Maybe people don't count if they are not circumcised or baptized.

When I would try to understand these mysteries I would eventually get drunk. Then the world would seem like a wonderful place again. It was easy for me then. I would joyously love everyone around me and wish everyone well. I would think that maybe all my Christian friends were right. Love the people around you, and if you get sucked into a war then fight, because it really wasn't your fault. Our leaders will be responsible. Our Church never preached against the Vietnam War.

I kept on working and I kept on drinking and I enjoyed my job. It was a challenge. I could hold my own with the best Air Force administrators. Finally, when a new Air Force program popped up, the T-28 Aircraft Program was coming to a close.

I was called into the office and told that I would be assigned to a little $750,000 Wright-Patterson Air Force Base contract. It seemed as though some top Missile Guidance System engineers had gotten together and wanted to submit a formal contract proposal and substantiation drawings to the Air Force Research Center at Wright-Patterson.

I had to go to Wright-Patterson, in Dayton, Ohio, to negotiate the requirements. This program turned out to be the birth of the 2,000-pound "Smart Bomb." The engineers had taken an existing electro-optical (TV) guidance system, put it on the front of an MK-84-2000 bomb, and added an electro-hydraulic control section on the rear end of the bomb. They called it the Hobos GBU-15 Guided Bomb.

The control section would also make a glide bomb out of it, thereby increasing the range. The TV guidance system could be locked onto a target by a TV monitor in the aircraft, then dropped, and it would hit the predetermined locked on target.

The Air Force was crazy about it. They hadn't been able to knock out the railroad bridges to China, where all the Russian supplies were coming into North Vietnam, because the bridges were too heavily fortified. The pilot could drop this bomb out of anti-aircraft range and run for home while the bomb glided to its target.

In three weeks time, we sold the Air Force on a million-dollar further study program, and within a month they raised the ante to $7 million, which included test models. The Electro Optical System was an edge tracker. That is, it followed the contrast on the edge shadow of the target or bridge it locked onto.

The one significant problem this method created was that the seeker would slip down a vertical contrast, or highway, because there was no intersecting shadow. So in our drop test plans, which I had to submit to Eglin Air Force Base, we specifically designated the type of targets that would be constructed, the type we could hit.

I had no concept of the nomenclature of a smart bomb in my initial meetings. I didn't know the vidicon from the gyro platform, or a seeker from a control unit. I had not the slightest idea of how an Electro Optical (EO) Seeker performed, and because I was an administrator, I had to ask the questions.

I got the job because I was the only one who had worked on Air Force contracts before. I was completely lost in the position until I remembered Toomey's advice: "Act like you own the place and you can get by with anything.".

I soon found out that half the people in the organization were doing the same thing. They were faking it just like I was. I soon learned who the bullshitters were and began to deal with or trust only the knowledgeable people. Because I wasn't knowledgeable enough about the engineering, I picked the few brilliant engineers on the program for friends.

I bought a lot of drinks and dinners before I was able to carry on an intelligent conversation about engineering. I quickly found out all the problems with the system, and would ask about these problems during meetings. That's the only time I would speak up in the meetings. That took care of the Engineering Division.

One day, as I was sitting in a meeting, an engineer was telling us about an Air Force proposal to use our EO guidance system on an anti-personnel bomb. This bomb would destroy any living thing within a quarter-mile radius of impact. When it exploded, it would horizontally shower thousands of small metal projectiles in every direction. It would be very useful both to destroy V.C. villages and in the jungle against hidden personnel.

As the engineer stood there in his white coat, I realized that he was the same person who had invited me to a Christian Bible meeting that day. He was a most happy fellow, and always seemed full of life, with love for everyone.

He went on to explain how those commie "Chinks" were winning the ground war in Vietnam. He said, "And I tell you, gentlemen, this is a critical stage and a most notable crisis. It makes everything so difficult, especially when we can't even trust the South Vietnamese. Hell, we'll probably have to destroy most of them in order to protect South East Asia from being taken over by the communists."

As I listened to him, I realized that I had lost my soul. I considered myself more of a hypocrite then he was; at least he didn't know any better. I did know better; that's the unforgettable sin of rejected enlightenment.

That morning I had read about Father Dan Berrigan and his brother, Father Phil Berrigan, being arrested again for their protest against the Vietnam War. After saying our morning prayers and reading about the two pacifist Catholic priests, my day turned sour at the breakfast table. I hated to have my conscience aroused so early. They were the first Catholic religious war protesters in my time, and being a loyal Catholic, I was deeply bothered. I always expected the Church at any time to condemn the U.S. slaughter in Vietnam, but it never happened.

The engineer went on to say, "Don't you think it is the right thing to do, to protect our loved ones? The first law of nature is self-preservation. Therefore, I say to all of you that it is much better to kill the communists over there than to wait until we have to fight in the streets of San Francisco, in order to protect our Christian country . . ."

That did it! I laughed, and said, "Christian country! I wouldn't use the word 'Christian' in regard to this bomb or Vietnam. Christ taught us not to kill women and children or plan to kill civilians." There was a brief period of dead silence, and all eyes in the meeting turned towards me. Finally, an Air Force officer said, "You mean to protect our women and children from the terrors of communism isn't a Christian act? We've got boys over there dying everyday so that you and people like you can be safe and live in peaceful harmony. Now here you sit, safely on your ass, selling us weapons for exorbitant prices while many men are dying delivering them; then half the time they don't even work! You have a hell of a right to say anything! In fact, none of you bastards have a right to say one single word! What in the hell have you got to complain about, anyway? I'm the one who should be complaining if there is any complaining to be done... I just lost two very close friends over Hanoi last month!"

Silence again hovered in the room as the officer sat down on the edge of his chair, pulled a handkerchief from his pocket, and began to wipe the tears from his eyes. The eyes of the observers were staring at me as though they were daggers.

With my lips trembling a little, I stood up and spoke softly.

"S-s-sir–I apologize for the statement I made. I know that I have the least right to say anything. I was addressing my comments to my friend John. This is a very inopportune time to discuss the ethics of war, and as you say, I am the least of us who has the right to discuss it at all. I make my living at it, and you give your lives for what you believe in, so you're not the hypocrite that I am. What you're doing, you are doing for the good of the country in your own conscience. So again, I can only say that I am sorry . . ." The meeting broke off after that episode, and afterwards I was really chewed out by the program manager. He was shouting. "Have you been on that joy juice again?" I answered, "No, I haven't had a drink for four months; maybe that's my problem."

"Then, by God, you had better start drinking again. You've really got those guys burned up and turned off. I want you to take them all out and have a good time tonight! Charge it off to the company. And when they come in here tomorrow, I want them ready to approve this proposal, and our last progress payment request on the basic program contract, or else."

He turned and stormed out of the door. I sat there for a while in the empty room before I realized that I really was an A-1 number one hypocrite, thanks again to the Berrigan brothers. I left and looked for the captain who had chewed me out. When I found him I again apologized and told him that I had too many martinis for lunch, but I was sober now.

I invited him to the DCSC Officers Club for the party we had planned there.

Now I was faced with another situation. I had denied Christ three times in five minutes, and I really felt like my whole life had been wasted. I couldn't stand it any longer, and before I realized it, I was drinking martinis at the Officers Club.

When I looked up, I saw the same officer come into the club with his superior officer, the Colonel, who was supposed to approve my payment request and also the new program. After a few drinks, the Colonel told me that he understood what I was trying to say during the meeting. He said that he had fought in two major wars, and had grown sour on war and all of its aspects. He had been shot down during World War II and was taken prisoner. He didn't mind fighting wars to save his country, but he also hated those so-called Christians who hypocritically preached that they were fighting in Vietnam in the name of Christ.

He even said, "When I was in that POW camp, I read the New Testament over and over, and it was then that I began to realize that Christ never advocated war. He preached loving our enemies and was the greatest pacifist of them all. However, since the military and fighting wars was all that I knew, I had to continue with my chosen profession . . ."

He continued meekly, "I remember reading where Christ said that those who live by the sword shall die by the sword. And if a man like me chooses to live by the sword, then he will eventually die by the sword. But I never once read where he said that the man would go to hell. If he did, he may as well have said that if the United States continues to live by the sword, then this country would eventually be conquered by the sword, like all the other countries of the past."

After the party that night, all three of us got so smashed that we ran out of money somewhere around three in the morning. However, I had a Bank Twenty-Four credit card and could get some cash out of the City National Bank.

We drove to the bank and parked near the computer-operated payment window. I had memorized the secret number before I got out of the car, but when I got to the computer window, I simply forgot it. So the next time we all memorized the number and marched up to the computer. I inserted the card and then we all argued about which was the correct number. Then we repeated the same process of going back to the car, memorizing the number, and returning to the computer window, only to have the same thing happen again. Suddenly, the Colonel came up with the brilliant idea of writing the number down on a piece of paper. Why hadn't we thought of that earlier? I really don't know. So we three drunks marched to the window again, and I inserted the credit card. When I punched the numbers, the machine chewed up my credit card. "Wrong again," the Colonel said.

Then the Captain noticed a Bank Americard sticker on the computer and asked me if I had one of those cards. Great idea, huh? We checked the secret numbers, punched them correctly, and the machine promptly swallowed up that card too. Now that we had run out of booze, we began to sober up and decided to go back to their motel.

The Colonel woke me up about 8:30 a.m. when he tripped over me while en route to the bathroom. He was about to pee on me when I protested and directed him to the bathroom. He was really out of it, and so was I. I was always able to snap back the morning after a drunk, but barely this time only enough to keep dry.

Suddenly the telephone rang. I was the only one capable of answering it. I heard a voice on the other end say, "Good morning, Sir! We are waiting at the plant for you to start the meeting."

My God! I thought to myself. I looked at my watch and it was 8:30. I was already a half-hour late, because I was due at the plant at eight sharp. I tried to revive the Colonel, but to no avail, so I told the caller in a stern voice, "Tell those V.I.P.s to go on with the meeting! I am having a preliminary meeting with Tom Siemer in regards to approval of the program and progress payments. We will be at the one o'clock conference without fail."

I hung up and complimented myself on having mocked the Colonel. I then went and pulled him out of bed; having finally put him on his feet, I pushed the Colonel into the shower and turned on the cold water. He didn't stop yelling until he had adjusted the temperature.

I called my wife and told her that I was with the Colonel; that we had worked all night at the motel on the proposal. She said she hoped I hadn't been drinking and that she and the children had prayed for me. She thought I was in jail again until the Colonel grabbed the phone and explained the critical meeting we were conducting. I called room service and we sat in the middle of the floor laughing and shaking our heads as we drank our coffee.

It was the Colonel who broke the silence when he asked for a battle plan from the Captain, who was in the worst shape of us all. I began to think fast, because after yesterday, I knew that I'd probably be fired. I can usually think my best when my back is to the wall. These are the times when thoughts flow through my head as smooth and steady as a mountain stream of bullshit.

"Colonel," I asked, "Does the Air Force plan to approve the new weapon systems program?"

He said, "Hell, yes! The Air Force program director has instructed me to approve anything within reason as far as the cost is concerned. We need this program badly."

"Great! That's our way out!" I replied. "You basically reviewed the program yesterday. If it's within range, then I will call contracts and get the paperwork prepared, and we'll take it into the meeting." He thought for a minute, then said, "You know something, Siemer, you're not such a bad guy after all; in fact, this sounds like a good idea."

"That's great!" I said. "If I don't get a progress payment on the basic contract, my job will be in jeopardy. My entire division has been having cash flow problems that the corporate office doesn't seem to understand."

The Colonel retorted, "How much was the company asking for?"

"$11.8 million," I answered.

He rubbed his fingers back and forth and pondered my words for a few moments, then he bellowed, "Why don't you make it an even $12 million? That sounds better."

I smiled and almost jumped in my shoes; then *I* picked up the phone and called contracts. "This is Tom Siemer. Would you please finalize the copies of the proposal contract for the new weapons program? The Colonel will be ready to sign. We all laughed and walked out of the door.

Instead of going home, I stopped at J.C. Penney's and bought a new shirt and fresh underwear before going to the plant. I went into the company's recreation center and took a shower and changed while the Colonel and the Captain waited for me in the lobby. But while I was in the shower, I heard women's voices in the dressing room. I remembered then that this was Thursday, and that this day was set aside for ladies' day at the facility. I hid my nakedness in the corner until I heard their voices trailing off. Then I put on my shorts and pants and sneaked out of the workout room and on into the lobby, carrying the rest of my things in my hands into the men's toilet.

Women were seated in the lounge chairs with their backs to me when I tiptoed into the men's restroom. The Colonel almost gave me away as he went into hysterical laughter. The women looked around, but I was already in the restroom. However, when I came out, the Colonel asked me, "Tom, tell me something; is this one of your typical unfortunate days?"

Then I replied, "What can I say, Colonel? What in the hell can I say?"

Again, the laughter echoed through the lobby. "Tom, I must confess, at first I had my doubts about you, but even I can be wrong in trying to judge character. You're going to be all right, and we're going to get along just fine. Yes-sir, you're all right, guy. Maybe it's because we're so much alike . . ."

On the way to the meeting, I picked up the contract documents. The Chief of Contracts congratulated me for an outstanding piece of work, and said that he would surely pass the word on my behalf to the higher-ups in the firm.

The Colonel opened the meeting by saying that I had sold him on the new program and that he would order the contracting officer to sign the appropriate contract documentation.

The Colonel also added that he had approved a $12-million progress payment on the basic program. I had to spend the rest of the day with the Air Force contracting officer, but it was well worth it, because we got everything signed.

The president of the division called me up later in the same afternoon and congratulated me. He said that the division would not have shown a profit that month without my help; so as it turned out, I was a hero.

The Colonel understood my actions and me very well from that day on, and would help me out of the damnedest jams. In turn, I would do him favors, and I remained his loyal drinking partner. I would always tell him the truth on matters concerning the program, even if it hurt the company.

From that day on, I realized that the only way I was to ever enjoy being a hypocrite was to keep on drinking. And believe me, I did just that; and everyone loved me—for just being me.

The guided bomb program eventually grew into an $800- million project. I continued to do what I pleased, because no one in the division could touch me; nevertheless, my drinking increased, and my dear family suffered, without my being aware of it.

A few months later they showed us the results of our tests on villages in Vietnam. The films and photographs showed whole Viet Cong villages covered with bodies. The canister bomb had killed every man, woman, child, and dog within a quarter of a mile radius.

Later, the Israelis used the same weapons against villages in Lebanon after they had promised not to do it.

Was I responsible? I only did it for my wife and children and for the money!

The old Catholic chaplain at Eglin AFB was going to give me communion. I told him I was unworthy to receive it unless I went to confession. He stopped and heard my confession. I said: "Father, bless me, for I have helped to kill hundreds of thousands of people in Vietnam with anti-personnel guided cluster bombs. Also, I helped to build the first guidance system for the cruise missiles that will most likely cause an accidental nuclear war in the future, which might kill my own wife and children. I have been the worst sinner for 25 years, because I believe that Jesus was a pacifist and Jesus would not want me to fight a nuclear war. Please forgive me." There was a long silence.

Finally the priest said, "Remember, my son, you need the job. Your wife and your children come first. You must support them in your chosen field. Peace be with you!"

CHAPTER 15

MY CAPITALIST VENTURE

One day in early 1970 Rockwell unexpectedly announced that the Columbus Division was being closed and moved to California in a consolidation move. Things were very slow, business-wise. I had been assigned to an antiballistic missile defense study and proposal. The government was thinking about canceling this antiballistic missile (ABM) space defense study and proposal due to a great outcry against it by the scientific community.

Four hundred famous scientists signed a full-page ad in the *New York Times* condemning the ABM Space Defense Program as dangerous and overpriced. Many of the moral and religious leaders of the country were crying out against the ABM Space System.

I had been assigned to work on all the overall proposal schedules for the entire program. As a result, I was given information about all its phases. It was so far out and absurd that at the time I could not believe our country would spend $5 trillion over an estimated 15 years to complete it. It would give me and my friends many years of job security. It would not, however, give any form of protection against ICBM incoming nuclear missiles.

Later, in 1972, President Richard Nixon and the Soviet signed the ABM Treaty banning space defense systems. It was time for me to find another line of work.

I began to plan for my future. I took the rest of the day off and went down to my cabin to ponder the situation. I finally reached a solution. I would go into the government contracting business like my uncle, Henry Justice, and bid on government post office remodeling and repair contracts. I had gained a thorough knowledge of federal contracts at Rockwell, so why not use it?

I also had built houses during the summers for extra money, and I had been a superintendent on three USPO jobs while I worked for my uncle Henry. In fact, I had an old specification in the trunk of my car. It gave me the address of the General Ser vices Administration (GSA) in Chicago, and I knew some of the inspectors there. The idea appealed to me. I could use these various sources of contracting to better my life and that of my family.

I felt rather guilty at times, but I reasoned that I had to have my alcohol if I wanted to work at Rockwell; otherwise I couldn't stand the hypocrisy. Every time I mentioned to my family that I wanted to quit I was given the usual lecture, "You're crazy! You have a wife and six children to support . . ."

But not only was I thinking of them, I was really thinking about my soul during those critical times. I knew that the weapons I helped produce and sell were being used in Vietnam, and I did not believe that the war we were fighting in that country was right. Still, I knew I had to live, so the next day I called the GSA inspector in Chicago and told him what I wanted to do. He said that he would send me the bidder's application form; he also told me that I would have to have a financial statement with my assets equaling the total price of the job for which I was to bid. I received the forms a few days later.

The bank agreed to loan me $17,000 on my little cabin. I over-stated the value of the lake and land in Hocking County, which was already in the name of the corporation. My wife had some AT&T stock that she had bought when she worked for the telephone company, so I took the stock to the Rockwell Credit Union and borrowed on it. I even mortgaged my house. We were approved.

One night I got the brilliant idea to ask my brother Raymond, who ran different post office jobs for my uncle, if he wanted to go to work with me. He had become dissatisfied with my uncle because he had made another nephew his vice-president instead of him. Ray had worked for him for 15 years, and the other nephew was just recently brought into the firm, had been a small contractor, and was very sharp in whatever he undertook.

My brother Ray knew all the ins and outs of remodeling construction, but he was inept at business and the legalities of government contracting procedures. In addition, he was practically uneducated. He'd had a hard time getting through high school. He had to learn everything the hard way, but he had learned construction through many years in the school of hard knocks. He was an expert in that field.

My father also was uneducated, and he made up for this by applying superhuman effort to get a job done. Because of my father's lack of education, education was never stressed in our family; however, everyone had a great basic intelligence. I often wondered how successful we would all have been if we had applied ourselves toward getting college degrees first. Yet, we were all successful builders and businessmen.

Many times I experienced frustration because I did not yet have a college degree. However, after marriage I went to classes for seven years while working my job. Even though I could never decide just what I wanted to be or what I wanted to do, taken all together, my piecemeal formal education would have added up to a masters degree.

One thing was certain, and that was that I did not want to be a businessman. I loathed the cold indifference of capitalistic profit and loss statements and quarterly dividends. It seemed to me that a businessman's profit usually came at the expense of someone getting used or stepped on. But my family of eight had to eat, so I had to proceed against my will.

I offered my brother Ray 50% of the net profit on each job that he ran, after overhead and salaries. I planned to eventually have a number of happy superintendents. Ray accepted. Then we started to estimate our first job, which was to remodel the USPO at Kent, Ohio. The total job had a limit, so we cut and shaved our original estimate until it was barely under that figure. I was so nervous when I called GSA for the bid results that I could hardly talk.

I was told that some new company, by the name of Abbeyhills, Inc., was the apparent low bidder, by a bare $2,000. That was my firm. My happiness was short lived, however, because they told me that they had never heard of my company before and it wasn't on the approved bidders list. I told them that we had submitted our application two weeks ago, and to please contact the Inspector we knew in Chicago. He OK'd us. We were awarded the contract!

Nevertheless, I was informed the next day that they had indeed received my application, but my assets were low. I told them that since I had filed that application a sufficient amount of capital had been placed into the monetary fund of the corporation. They continued to be reluctant to award me the contract, but they said they might, pending a complete resume of previous experience, backed by substantial character references, more financial backing, and complete bonding and insurance approval. In the end, they approved us. On May 4,

1970, at the beginning of our contract, Ray met with the engineering inspector of the General Services Administration (GSA) and the postmaster at the post office in Kent, Ohio. It was our first post office contract, and we were excited.

Suddenly a postman broke into the meeting and told everyone there was a riot taking place at the Kent University campus, and that the "commie students" were chasing the Ohio National Guard soldiers, who had rifles.

The postmaster thanked him and went on with the meeting.

They were going through the post office, reviewing everything that had to be done, when some postmen came in and said that several students had been shot and killed on campus by the Ohio National Guard.

When I heard the sad news I began to weep. The postmaster also wept. The GSA inspectors' reaction was to immediately approve a contract change. We were to provide a new steel door and a security lock system to replace the old unlocked wooden door on the post office roof, so the radicals couldn't get in. It was beginning of the end of the Vietnam War.

My corporation kept on growing in structure and in capital. It became increasingly difficult to work at Rockwell and also run my company, Abbeyhills. What complicated things was that Rockwell had decided not to move the Division from Columbus, because they had found, or I should say my department had found, $80 million worth of accounts out receivable assets in the Columbus Division, mostly in the category of not billable for some reason.

Some of these accounts went all the way back to the Korean War. We found that numerous study and test programs had not been billed to the Navy because someone didn't send in a final test report or never followed up to get Navy approval of the final payment. We found hardware deliveries that had been made but never billed because there was no government receivable record. With the help of our accounting firm, Haskins & Sells, old man Rockwell decided to stay in Columbus until the whole $80 million was collected. That would allow us to continue bidding on contracts until we failed.

On the day of the announcement, the controller of the Division was fired for being too lax in the field of accounts receivable. He and I were the only ones on the executive staff who were unhappy when Rockwell made the decision to stay.

I was making money hand over fist, but my conscience was killing me as I continued to work for war. My only escape was to get dead drunk on Thursday night and enjoy a peaceful day of mental oblivion on Friday. Friday was the day I could stop and smell the flowers and bathe in the contentment of stupidity. My computer mind would be completely relaxed, and I would be full of blissful serenity and happiness. If I had any problems, I couldn't remember them, although it took at least 10 martinis contract to Hughes. I expressed my deep disappointment along with the rest, but every time I did, George, my assistant, would laugh, and I couldn't keep a straight face. Everyone thought we had cracked up. I reasoned that after all, that contract had been assigned to me as a side task, because I was running the Hobos Guided Bomb program.

But needless to say, Hobos was in trouble, too. The original program director had been moved up to director of all guided ordnance and had to relinquish his total hold on the program. For the first time in his life, he had to delegate his managerial authority to someone else. I could see the handwriting on the wall. This program was going to hell because of company policy and procedures, and I really didn't care enough to tell him. There were times when I bothered to fight with him over things like that, and somehow, he seemed to really appreciate it.

Right now, though, I had enough problems running my own corporation. For every level-headed, practical government man, you'll find 100 bureaucrats. And bureaucrats lie. For example, Abbeyhills contracts had all the same standard government procurement clauses that Rockwell contracts had: Equal Employment Opportunity, non-segregated facilities, Davis-Bacon weekly reports, OSHA safety, Hire the Handicapped, and so on. But how in the hell are you going to use handicapped people in the construction business? OSHA probably wouldn't let you have them on the job. Besides, it was enough to keep your own able- bodied men from getting hurt. I was always signing certifications that we were black, or Indian, or crippled, or something to that effect. I always said, "What the hell! We'll just lie if we have to." It's not that we didn't try to comply with all their impossible regulations. It's just that CEOs almost have to lie.

My corporation was getting many new military contracts. My secretaries at Rockwell began to complain about taking my outside business calls, which were getting more frequent as the business grew. All my new contracts were military.

We were doing business with the Corps of Engineers, Rickenbacker Air Force Base in Ohio, VA Hospitals, the State of Ohio, and the Defense Construction Supply Center (DCSC), which was next door to Rockwell. I would coordinate the jobs at DCSC before I went to Rockwell and I would stop by twice during the day to see how things were going.

My bank and bonding company still would not allow me to quit Rockwell International, even though my own corporation was doing wonderfully. They wanted a feeling of security, so that if I screwed up I could work the rest of my life paying them.

I talked my wife into going to Spain on a company-sponsored tour. We took a side trip to Tangier and toured the Casbah during the heat of the day. We were so hot and dry when we reached the beautiful Riff Hotel for lunch that Dorothy had four goblets of sweet French wine. As I sat there with my brother Jim and his wife, Sylvia, someone in the back started throwing pieces of orange at the belly dancer.

When I looked to see who was doing it, I saw my wife winding up. "Dorothy, don't do that!" I protested. The sweet French wine had gone to her head. She had never had so much to drink before.

"Ah, I can dance better than that!" she boasted.

I asked my sister-in-law to escort Dorothy to the powder room. A few minutes later, she ran back, exclaiming, "She is in the men's restroom!"

When I arrived, I found her with Jim. As I pulled her out of the room, she ran through the lobby to the outside and jumped into a beautiful grotto swimming pool. When I tried to pull her out of the pool, she tried to drag me in. Three busboys finally were able to bring her up on dry land. Then she tried to throw an old, monocled fellow in, along with his oriental mistress. As waiters and bellboys came running, I faded into the crowd. I laughed and laughed as they chased her through the lobby. She unwound turbans and hugged and kissed everyone. She entertained everybody on the bus back to the airport.

I think it was that night, after 11 long years, that Dorothy conceived again. The doctor thought it was impossible, but little Susanna arrived Christmas Eve. She was almost dead. She had her at the children's hospital, where she was placed on oxygen. I was informed that there was not much hope.

I really prayed to God for the first time in ages. I could never ask God for anything that I could get for myself, such as money, houses, cars, and boats, but now I begged him to cure the baby. I know now that this had happened for a purpose. I had gotten away from God; I did not even know how to pray. I prayed that my wife would be able to accept the outcome if Susanna should die. She loved children so much that she wanted a dozen. My other daughters also prayed. Some even swore that if she recovered, they would never eat chocolate again.

After two weeks, Susanna was able to breathe normally, and we brought her home. Every night we would all pray that she would wake up alive the next morning. Each morning I would thank God for her life. At the age of six months, she had severe heart failure, so she had to take strong heart medicine twice a day. If she had not been in the hospital when it happened she would have died. I prayed, "Lord, my daughter is dead, but if you will come and lay your hands on her, she will be alive."

I would read the New Testament every night. After nine months and five trips to the hospital, we were told that she had two heart murmurs, one of which was caused by the huge hole in her heart. We were at wits' end.

CHAPTER 16

SECOND COMING OF THE SPIRIT AND DEATH

Maria, my oldest daughter, begged us to join a new Christian prayer movement in the Catholic Church called the Charismatic Movement. She said, "They have worked miracles through prayer and healing groups. They may be able to help Susanna."

"The Holy Spirit is working closely with us now," Maria would say. "Hallelujah! Praise the Lord!" She had been smitten by the Holy Spirit, and I had witnessed a remarkable change in her life. She was now dedicating her life to Christ. She took my wife to a Charismatic prayer meeting at St. Cecelia's parish one night. A great change came over my wife as well, but she still worried about the baby. All my other daughters and even my son started going, and again I witnessed a great change in their lives. It was as if they came out of the dark and into the daylight. They begged me to go also.

I would say, "I am too big of a hypocrite now to become a greater one." They still would not understand. The baby's condition worsened, and I became desperate. One evening, I attended a prayer service with my family at Christ the King Parish. I saw the Spirit move all these people. They seemed to love everyone with a deep love. They allowed their emotions to be free and hugged and kissed others freely. There was a true spirit of love for one another as Christ must have wanted us to have it. They prayed over a couple of people in unison, and some spoke in strange languages. The two people exclaimed that they were cured, and I could tell by their eyes that they believed they were.

I was moved to openly confess all my sins, but I resisted. Tears came to my eyes as I saw all this love. There were many people there, and when they prayed over my baby, I couldn't stand it any longer. I jumped up and ran outside. As I walked in the moonlight, I noticed lights in the church and entered. I begged the Lord loudly to cure my baby. I would do anything. I would even commit myself to the Lord again. "Lord, make me love you as I used to," I pleaded. "Make me trust in you. I have not asked you for much before this, but I beg this of you, please heal my little daughter Susanna."

My soul seemed to cry to me that I must do God's will; that I must commit my life to God as I had done once. Otherwise I felt my baby would not recover, and I would lose my soul. Somehow I knew I did not have much time.

"Lord, what can I do?" I prayed. "I have worked hard to raise a family, a beautiful family, and I have never asked you for any of the things that I saw other people asking for." I remembered the novenas where people used to ask for jobs, car payments, rent, and house payments. Then I again insisted, "Lord, I am only asking you for this. Please don't take away Susanna! What must I do?"

"How can I stop being a hypocrite?" I asked myself. "I am worse than a Pharisee. I know better. I have the knowledge of Jesus' Gospel of nonviolence and all I know and do is about war."

My whole life was unfolding before me, with all the sins I had committed, and I cried again in sorrow. When I finished, I thought for a long time about what this soul searching had shown me. I realized that because of me Susanna would never be cured, no matter how much my family prayed.

"How do you want me to serve you, Lord?" I prayed again. I studied my past all the way back to my childhood for an answer. How had I become a godless man with no peace? Where did I go wrong? Was I supposed to have been a priest? Was that the basis of my guilt feeling? No, I knew I was supposed to be a family man. What was it then? Where did I first lose Christ? Fears tormented me in the seminary, and yet I had a purpose for life. And no matter how tough things were, I had an inner peace with Christ. Yet I knew I was not supposed to be a priest.

Then I remembered. I had dedicated my life to working for peace on earth for all people and brotherhood and sisterhood for all races. When I left the seminary, I had felt that my calling to preach out against war was lost. I had even worked in a war plant since.

Then from my innermost depth I started speaking: "I was called to spread God's message of love to the Church. My duty was to teach Christ's church to instruct the youth that war is futile and against God's will. I had to teach God's church to love their enemies and set an example of how all people should live in peace. If Christians do not attempt to do it, then no one will, and the world will be destroyed. Even worse, it will the fault of the Church because they did not set an example."

"But, Lord," I cried, "What more can I do? No one would listen to me, not even the priests of your Church, so I gave up. If your Church does not want to instruct the Christian youth in your ways, then what chance have I? When your Pope, bishops, and priests justify wars even between Christians, what chance have I? Their own doctrine justifies war, "just war." But I never could understand why our catechism doesn't describe the conditions for a "just war," and never instructs the high school or college youth about when they cannot fight, even by the Church's own doctrine. They instructed us in everything else–stealing, divorce, abortion, birth control–but never a thing about war. Is that what you want me to do, Lord?" I queried.

A peace came over me then that I had not known for years. It lasted until I realized that I was incapable of doing God's work, and that I worked in a war plant, where I had been for years. "Lord, I can't do this. I'm a hypocrite. Where can I begin? Who would listen to me?"

First I have to stop being a hyprocrite; then maybe God will show me the way. I would have to commit myself to God and hopefully He would guide me.

So I prayed, "Lord, I will commit myself to you, but you must lead me, because I am a sinner and I am not capable of doing this except through your grace. Your Holy Spirit must guide me, because I cannot do it myself. Make me feel like those people at the prayer meeting."

I felt exuberant as I left the church and returned to the basement with peace in my heart. I felt filled with the Holy Spirit.

The next day I went to confession, Mass, and communion at the cathedral. I told the priest confessor of my great sin of omission, which had lasted 25 years. Even though he did not quite understand, I felt at peace when he gave me absolution.

The first thing I realized that I must do was to quit my position with Rockwell International.

Even though I could not stand the thought of working there, I did not want to quit my job because of my family, and now all of my own company's contracts were military too.

I began to devote all my time to getting civilian contracts for my own company so that I could feel secure in quitting Rockwell. My health seemed to deteriorate, and my wife made an appointment for me to have a physical examination.

The doctor discovered blood in my urine and stool and suggested that I enter a hospital for tests. When I called Rockwell to inform them of my situation, I felt happy, since this would give me an opportunity to get away, at least for a while.

I checked into the hospital at noon and had lunch. They informed me at lunch that there would be no more food until after the tests the following morning. Immediately after lunch I received an enema, and then another. This procedure was continued the following morning and then for four days. I wondered why they couldn't give me all the tests on one day. But each day, they fed me at noon, starved me, and then cleaned me out, all for a 20-minute test.

On the night of the fourth day I couldn't sleep. I wondered if they had found anything. Was something seriously wrong with me, like cancer? I had undergone three previous operations for my bad plumbing–my bowels. Whenever I drank too much wine, my kidneys hurt. A great many things ran through my mind. I would go to hell if I died.

It was at this point that I realized how many years I had wasted. If I died, I probably would not have a chance to go to heaven. I could have worked those past 25 years for Christ. I needed a drink desperately. Maybe a drink would help me sleep.

Late the following afternoon, the doctor entered my room with my wife and with the results of the tests. He began with the preliminaries, the x-rays, and the electronic tests.

When I saw tears in Dorothy's eyes, I cut the doctor short. "Okay Doc, just give me a straight answer. What's wrong with me, in language that I can understand?"

"You have acute cirrhosis of the liver," he replied.

I still did not quite understand what that meant, except that the man in the next room had died horribly from it two days before. I thought of my large family and was concerned.

The doctor explained, "Mr. Siemer, you told me you were a moderate drinker. Today, your wife informed me that you are a heavy drinker. This proves the results of our tests. If you stop drinking you may have a year. If you continue to drink, you will not last a year. It is your decision to make as to how long you will live." The irony of it was that while he was talking all I could think of was that I needed a drink.

I looked out the window and wondered how I could quit drinking. Even after he told me the results, I could not drive the need for a drink out of my mind. Then I asked, "Doctor, could I have just one glass of wine with each meal?"

His firm answer was, "No alcohol whatsoever—not even a glass of wine. If you can ask that question, you do not realize how serious this situation is. If you drink you are going to die, Mr. Siemer. I cannot put it any more bluntly."

The doctor threw up his hands and walked out the door. My wife stood by the window crying. Finally she pleaded, "Promise me you will never drink again."

"I can't do it", I thought. I can't live the life I live without alcohol. It would be impossible. I cannot face Rockwell and my conscience without all those necessary escapes when I drink. At that moment, I needed a drink. As I hedged and made a disbelieving joke out of it, my wife walked slowly out the door.

I lay there in silence looking out the window. For a long time I did not think of anything but the sunshine. I'm going to die! I'm going to die! For a stupid little thing like a drink!

I'll never see my grandchildren or my children grow up, and I'll go to hell because I have not done God's will. For the same reason, my little Susanna will never get well.

That night, I slipped out of bed and knelt on the floor crying.

All I could say was, "Please, Lord, help me! Please, Lord help me. I am too weak to do anything for myself. Please, Lord, help me." A nurse came along and helped me back into bed. I refused a sedative. I had to think about my whole life. I had to pray. I poured out my heart to God. In reviewing my life, I found that I had always considered myself a failure. And yet, I had raised a beautiful family and had succeeded in doing many, many things that other men would envy. Why? Why did I consider myself a failure? Why? Please give me peace. I need to continue drinking to live the life that I am living.

Then I remembered the promise I made to God long ago to serve Him. How many times I failed Him! I realized that I could never consider myself a success unless I lived up to the promise I made so many years ago. I knew I could not stop drinking. Then my soul cried out to me, "Commit yourself to Christ! Commit yourself to Christ first, and He will show you the way to peace. Let your salvation be in His hands." My daughter Maria used to tell me: "Commit your life to Christ, and He will show you the answer you seek."

I got down on my knees again and prayed, "Lord, into your hands I commend my Spirit! Lord, have mercy on me, a sinner. Lord, give me the strength. Lord, I can do nothing without your help. Lord, I will commit the rest of my life to your service."

I must have fallen asleep because I was awakened by the sun, and the world was beautiful. As I looked out the window, a nurse jokingly said, "Mr. Siemer, if you are going to insist on sleeping on the floor, we will have to put sides on your bed." After she left, I said the morning offering, "Oh

Jesus, through the Immaculate Heart of the Virgin Mary I offer all my prayers and actions of the day and . . ." I could not remember the rest of it. It had been so long that I had forgotten it. And so I said in my own words, "Jesus, do not let me sin this day and give me the strength to do Your will."

The old Catholic chaplain at Mercy Hospital came to give me communion. I stopped him and told him I was unworthy to receive unless I went to confession. I made a general confession and again confessed my sin of omission in not doing God's will. "Bless me father for I have sinned. It has been six months since my last confession." I told him of all the sins that I had committed by neglecting to do my duty, and that I had become intoxicated 100 times during that time. I asked him to pray for me because I was an alcoholic.

When tears came to his eyes I could not understand why. Then he said, "You have finally admitted that you are an alcoholic. I have been talking with your wife."

He gave me Holy Communion, and for the first time in years, I was really at peace. I felt so good that I wanted to jog down the halls. I was doing just that when I ran into the old priest making his final visit.

"Oh, Mr. Siemer," he said, "I would like to tell you something . . ." He stammered for a while and then admitted softly that he had been an alcoholic for 25 years. "You have much hope, son." he assured me. "I've seen your beautiful family on three occasions. But I must warn you. Only with Christ's help can you overcome this terrible affliction. Believe me, I know. When I awaken each morning, my first thought is of a drink. It never completely leaves my mind. Then I pray that I will have the strength to last one hour without a drink. Just without a drink until noon." For the first time, he looked me directly in the eye. I had wondered why he never did that before. Now I knew why. There was great sorrow there.

He continued, "I have been given permission to say Mass with grape juice instead of wine. I have not had a drink of alcohol in 10 years, but that does not change anything. In those 10 years, I never knew a time when I did not want a drink. So please pray for me." Tears came to my eyes too as I saw those many years of great suffering in his eyes.

"Father, you shall find that you have earned a great place in heaven when you join Christ there. It's how hard we try, not what we do, that counts. I have committed the most grievous sin of not trying. But I believe that the Lord has sent you to show me the way," I said softly.

"God bless you, son, and may the Lord be with you always. But do a favor for me? Please join Alcoholics Anonymous as soon as possible. Here is the booklet. And call me if I can help you. It won't be easy, except with the Lord. In fact, you can't do it without the Lord," he explained.

I returned to my room and read the little booklet. I was amazed that the 12 steps that alcoholics must conquer are the 12 steps one would have to take to reach Christian perfection. Conquering each step depended totally on Christ's help. The booklet stated that no step was possible without God. That is the answer to the impossible, I thought. The more I read of the 12 steps of Alcoholics Anonymous, the more I realized that they were steps for achieving "sainthood," and I only wanted to quit drinking. For your benefit I must include them here. The twelve steps of AA, which I read, are as follows:

1. We admitted we were powerless over alcohol—that our lives had become unmanageable.
2. Came to believe that a power greater than ourselves could restore us to sanity.
3. Made a decision to turn our will and our lives over to the care of God as we understood him.

4. Made a searching and fearless moral inventory of ourselves.
5. Admitted to God, to ourselves, and to another human being the exact nature of our wrongs.
6. Were entirely ready to have God remove all these defects of character.
7. Humbly asked him to remove our shortcomings.
8. Made a list of all persons we had harmed, and became willing to make amends to them all.
9. Made direct amends to such people wherever possible, except when to do so would injure them or others.
10. Continued to take personal inventory and when we were wrong, promptly admitted it.
11. Sought through prayer and meditation to improve our conscious contact with God as we understood him, praying only for knowledge of his will for us and the power to carry that out.
12. Having had a spiritual awakening as the result of these steps, we tried to carry this message to alcoholics, and to practice these principles in all our affairs.

These steps were the answer to my prayer, I thought. First I must seek God's help and then all things are possible. Maybe I can help to teach His people to love their enemies, but the idea seems impossible, for I have discovered how difficult it is for me to love my enemies. I failed personally because my need for a job made me a hypocrite for years. How could I speak out against unjust wars by Christians, or convince the American Catholic Church to preach its doctrine? They would look at my record and example and know that I did not believe in what I preached.

That night, I again read the New Testament from the Bible my children had given me. If I do not read the New Testament completely and regularly, I cannot put together the complete puzzle. After I first knew Christ and His message of love, I realized that message is perfection. Then I had a choice; to accept Christ's message or to reject Him. If I know His message and reject it, I will be even more unhappy than before. If I accept Christ and His message, I will be more at peace spiritually, but I will have become dissatisfied with the things of the world. I live to join Him in heaven. If I still continue to love Christ, I am forced to pick up my cross and follow Him. I must pick up my cross each morning for the rest of my life, because every day I must choose between Christ and the world. As an alcoholic, each morning I must painfully choose between sobriety, which is a fight against the terrible temptations, and escape, which leads to destruction.

I realize that as the Holy Spirit enlightens me more and more about Christ, I will have to do more and more for Him. Does this make me happier? No, because the more I am enlightened, the more responsibility I will feel toward God. Then I must choose between Christ and my wife and children, my mother, father, and friends, my job, and other things of this world. I must remember the statement, "For whosoever shall love his life shall lose it; and whosoever will lose his life for My sake, shall find it" (Matthew16:25).

Then, through the Holy Spirit, prayer, and the sacraments, I was shown God's most difficult task that I must do in order to be saved. This task will be the ultimate task for me, done in accordance with the talents and inspirations I have received from the Holy Spirit. When I reach my maximum endurance level, I must realize that I am on the brink and cannot maintain this level of endurance unless I pray constantly and sacrifice. Christ's maximum human endurance level was to choose to die on the cross.

The time had come for me to make that terrible decision. Now I knew how terrible it must have been for the Catholic parish priests in Germany to decide to speak out against Hitler, when he took the Jews away and killed them. I know some of them must have spoken out and made this great decision for Christ, and that it resulted in their deaths. The early Christians had to decide to love their enemies and die in the arenas rather than raise armies and defend themselves. They chose to die like Christ as an example to their pagan persecutors. And now I have reached that point in life when I must make this decision. I have decided to follow Christ. Am I happier? No, but I will be in the next life.

Then a strange peace came over me, a peace of knowing what I was supposed to do for the Lord. My mind was now dedicated to serving the Lord, and the Holy Spirit was inspiring me. First I must give up all the things that have separated me from Christ. Then I must strive for Christian perfection, and by my example, people will begin to listen to me. I must then appeal to the Catholic Church leaders to instruct the youth about war with the Church's own doctrine on just war. The spirit told me that I must appeal to the youth by writing a book that will be interesting to them and open their eyes to the fact that they have a moral right to decide when to fight for their country, only if it's right.

My mind was subjected to many thoughts as I lay there in my hospital bed, suspended between the dawn of awakening and the sins of my past. I knew that neither the Catholic Church nor my country would adhere to the words of my calling, and I would be a victim of scorn and mockery. These thoughts tore and shattered me, not knowing which way to turn, caught between doubt and belief. Who would believe me? Who would believe that on this day the Holy Spirit had called me again? I felt that people would not believe my story because they had not yet perceived that love is the only thing that will save the world–and save me from alcoholism. I also knew that I must change my life to conform to Christ's will, so I could live in harmonious tranquility, even if they tried to kill me.

Belief is a fine thing, but putting these beliefs into actions is a test of strength. Many are those who talk like the roar of the sea, but their lives are shallow and stagnant, like the rotting marshes. And many are those who lift their heads above the mountain tops, but their spirits remain dormant in the obscurity of the caves.

As I lay there, I shut my eyes and drew a deep sigh, as if my soul was sailing in the spacious firmament looking for a word to say. However, I found no words necessary, for the silence seemed to speak to me while I interrogated my soul.

I could not escape from the words "just war." By Catholic definition, there are no "just wars" anymore because of nuclear weapons and other weapons of mass destruction. So then why has the Church always taken such a hard stance on divorce, birth control, and abortion–but for centuries has not taken a stand against unjust wars? The Church could very well have condemned many unjust wars and excommunicated Christian participants; but it failed to do this.

Imagine if the Popes had never been allowed to fight or advocate wars. Then all those wars waged in the name of Christ would have been avoided, and the Popes would have been militarily powerless, like Christ chose to be. The Church has not once encouraged us or demanded that we must work out peaceful solutions with the communists; and yet the pure doctrine of communist socialism is more Christian in theory than materialistic and selfish capitalism.

The communists claim to labor in the name of all humanity, so that we may all live in a world community. Much as Catholics do in religious orders. With one-world rule, they could eliminate war. Because the Church neglected the physical welfare of the people, communists rejected the Church and Christ. They allowed themselves the right to use any violent means to justify the end, world peace and brotherhood. If we truly stood for peace we could not only put Christ in our daily lives, but we could also put Christ in communism by our example. Just as the early martyrs showed us Christianity by their dying.

It seems that all Christians, especially in America, believe that nuclear war is inevitable. They believe that nothing can be done to stop this war because it is outside the teachings of Christ and the Church. They still maintain that fighting in a war depends on the individual's conscience, but they do not define a "just" war, and they do not explain when we can fight as individuals. Catholic youth would have had a legitimate reason not to fight in the Vietnam War if they had been instructed in the Church's doctrine.

The Church does not preach that birth control, divorce, and abortion are up to the individual's own conscience. The advocates of these acts say they are in the realm of an individual's conscience to decide. Is the Church covering up for the hypocritical wars of the Holy Roman Empire, wars waged even by the Popes, or for the slaughter of "infidels" during the crusades for the purpose of gaining the Holy Land? The Vatican had an army until 1870.

The early Christians conquered the mighty Roman Empire with the love and blood of martyrs. Pope Leo turned back the conquering Attila the Hun at the gates of Christian Rome with love and God's help. Why then did we panic and fortify ourselves with the sword thereafter, and repudiate Christ's protection of love and example? For many years, the so-called Christians have been fighting unchristian wars! Yet through all this havoc and all this misunderstanding, I cannot believe that Christ has directed me to speak out on His divine doctrine of loving our enemies. I have persecuted my enemies in Christ's name, without knowing the meaning of my own persecution. I served in the military at 18, and since then, I have worked in a war materials plant for over 20 years and have sold arms to both the Arabs and the Jews, as well as to any other country that had the financial means to purchase them. I am presently Chairman of the Board and majority stockholder of a corporation that contracts to the government for construction at military installations. I consider myself to be the worst of hypocrites fighting wars, because I have helped prepare for war during peaceful times through the sale of weapons.

I left the comfort of my bed and stood in a darkened corner of the room. My spirit reached out and talked with Christ as if I were speaking with a brother or a close friend. On one occasion, I encountered myself praying, "Oh Christ, what have I, a sinner, to offer Thee? Why have You hounded me, oh Lord, to preach Your impossible doctrine of loving our enemies and those who will someday destroy us? Lord, I am far from being a peaceful man. I'm not even at peace with myself. Why have I been driving myself to alcoholism and sinful escapades in order to forget Your calling? I am totally unworthy! I am an unchristian capitalist in the worst sense. Then how can I preach Your doctrine of love for the communists or other enemies to the Church? Why do You beckon me unto this, when You have hundreds of Your priests, bishops, and even the Pope whom You could choose to enlighten with the power of the Holy Spirit to condemn unjust wars and forbid participation by Christians? Yet I have not heard one voice from the powerful pulpits forbidding our participation in unjust wars, or forbidding Catholic youth to fight, even for Hitler. The Church has chaplains in the services to minister to those who wish to fight, and who bless us before we kill our enemies in Christ's name. Why me, Lord, a sinner? Why not Your bishops and your Pope?"

At this very minute, I suffer from two broken fingers as a result of a drunken fistfight. I refused to have them set so they would remind me never to fight again.

What is peace? Is it manifest when two countries buy the strong arms of human beings and stockpile immoral weapons and live in "peace" by threats of mega-death? Or is it shown in submission of the body and spirit, away from those who dazzle our eyes with glittering medals? Oh Christ, full of love and mercy, stretch forth Your strong arms and show me the power necessary for peace. Will Your peace ever come to save humanity from the annihilation of the next immoral nuclear war? By Your Church's own just war theory nuclear war would be immoral. Help me, oh Lord, to be strong in this struggle against nuclear war. Assist me to be truthful and dutiful until death, and let Your will be done."

These are some of the thoughts that circled in my mind as I searched for a way to answer Christ's calling. Now I knew what I was supposed to do, but I didn't know how to work for peace. That night in the hospital I continued to pray for guidance until about midnight–and still there was no answer.

Then, as I was about to fall asleep, an inner voice seemed to say to me, "Write a book about your failures to love your enemies, and by your hypocrisy other Christians might see their own failures also."

A great peace came over me as I went to sleep.

CHAPTER 17

SECOND DECISION FOR CHRIST

When my wife came to visit me that afternoon, I told her that I had decided to leave Rockwell. That was the first thing I must do to change my life. I could no longer live the life of a hypocrite. I had committed the rest of my life to Christ.

"Well, what will we live on?" she asked, as a matter of fact. "You haven't sworn off drinking, so you will need money for booze," she complained. "As long as you have known me, I have had to drink. Why?" "I guess it's because you love the stuff. I don't know," she replied. "Your whole family drinks all the time. But now you are going to kill yourself, and you still won't give it up," she continued. I had forgotten about this immediate problem. because drinking did not bother me at that moment.

"Dorothy, I want to give up drinking, but I cannot give it up and continue working at Rockwell. Remember, when I first met you, I had a calling to preach against war?" I asked.

"Then why didn't you become a priest?" she queried. " You had a chance."

"Look, dear, I'm happy as a married man. It isn't that. It's my occupation. I'm a hypocrite. I can't live with myself unless I drink. I was supposed to have done something for Christ in regard to war that even I don't understand. But now I know. A voice keeps reminding me to do it. All these years I have lived with this, but I did not know how. Now my life and all the things I have done have a purpose. I'm really happy now!" I explained.

She studied me for a moment before she replied. "Tom, I always felt you would take off someday and leave me. It seemed as if you were searching for something else or somebody else. You always seemed so unsatisfied. You were never content or happy like other husbands or fathers."

"I'd never leave you, dear, except to serve Christ. Even if I serve Christ, I won't have to leave you. But something I have to do is to leave Rockwell International," I replied.

"Well, what about your insurance? Who's going to pay for the baby's operation? The doctor told me the other day that she would have to have the heart operation right away. Her heart is worse now," she told me. I had forgotten about Susanna's operation. For the past two years, I had kept putting it out of my mind. I got out of bed, and we cried in each other's arms.

"Honey, I'm sorry. Here you were worrying about the baby–and now you are worrying about me. I'm sorry. I promise you I will never drink again." I knew as I spoke that this was a promise I could not keep if I continued working at Rockwell. I made up my mind that I would not stay at Rockwell, even though I did not tell her. She had enough problems. I had made the commitment to Christ and I was going to live up to that commitment. At that moment, I knew that the baby would live.

During the two weeks that followed my stay in the hospital, before the baby's operation, we prayed constantly. I was at peace, even if temporarily. I felt that I was living with Christ again. My life had a purpose.

Some friends of my wife told her to take the baby to a priest in Dayton, Ohio, and ask him to pray for Susanna. They had seen many miracles there through that prayer group. I did not know it until later, but the priest, Fr. Maloney, gave Susanna the last sacraments in preparation for death. My wife was shocked at first, thinking Susanna would die. But Father told her that it had cured desperately ill people before. The whole Charismatic prayer movement in Columbus was praying for the child to be healed.

I had delayed returning to work because of my promise, but now the doctor urged me to go back. I begged him for a one-week extension until after Susanna's operation. I found myself constantly having to make decisions for Christ.

The morning finally arrived for the trip to the hospital. Dorothy dressed Susanna as she would dress a doll. She was so small and pretty. No one said a word, and the baby must have wondered what was happening. "Why are you crying, Mommy?" she asked. We hugged her as often as possible. As we left, the girls and Tommy cried.

The trip to the hospital was slow and sad. As Susanna saw the hospital building where she had spent time on five previous occasions, she began to cry. Once before, we had almost lost her to heart failure. Shortly after being checked into the hospital, we discovered she was not breathing. I ran into the hall to find the doctor and found a nurse, whom I dragged into the room against her will. She had just checked the baby, but she soon realized that Susanna was experiencing heart failure. An alarm was sounded and all hell broke loose. Extreme measures were being used as she was rushed into intensive care. If we had lost her, I know it would have been my fault, for lack of committing myself to Christ. Now that she lived, I was determined to adapt my life to the will of Christ.

As we entered the hospital this time, I was at peace. There was no longer that terrible feeling of guilt. For some strange reason, I knew she would be all right.

After two days of testing, the doctors were astonished to find that the huge hole in the interior of the heart had grown shut in a two-week period. Instead of major surgery, there would be a comparatively minor operation outside the heart to repair a duct that should have closed completely at birth. Praise the Lord!

A drastic change came over Susanna almost immediately after the operation. I trusted the Lord and knew she would recover.

Now I was definitely committed to my promise to the Lord to work for peace the rest of my life.

I immediately applied myself to the task of getting contracts for my own company so that I could leave the war plant. Every morning I would commit that day to the Lord. That was my only means of refraining from drinking. We won six construction contracts in two weeks. I tried to make enough non-military contracts to guarantee our income.

I should not have returned to Rockwell, but I kept telling myself that I wanted to leave gracefully. I also needed the money and the insurance until the contracts could be started. Again I was compromising my Christian principles.

As soon as I returned to Rockwell, I was given the foreign sales contracts for the HOBOS GBU-15 2000-pound guided bomb program. I noticed that the contracts for Israel did not specify the government of Israel. The contract specified that all deliveries were to be made to the Summids Warehouse

Company in Brooklyn, New York. I hesitated to ask. For two days, I did not know that this contract on paper was for the government of Israel. The oil embargo by the Arab states was still in place, and they would refuse to do business if they knew the truth, since we were attempting to sell other weapons to them. It was difficult to hide the facts after the Egypt-Israel War presented a need for Air Force planes to pick these weapons up every day and deliver them directly to Israel.

I was sick at heart, because now I realized I was directly involved in war again. One day, while I was pondering my hypocrisy, my co-worker on the program, a devout Catholic father of seven children, was holding a Charismatic Bible prayer meeting. He invited me to participate, since he knew I was a Catholic.

My response was, "Hell no, I'm too much of a hypocrite as it is. When you Christians stop depending on wars for a living, then I'll join." Everyone thought I had cracked up. That night I got drunk, but I didn't tell my wife. I explained that I was going to the cabin, it was Friday night. On Saturday, I went to confession, but found no peace.

An Israeli colonel was responsible for exposing the Israel contracts. He had been assigned to coordinate the deliveries in New York. This forced him to leave a beautiful, expensive apartment in Israel vacant. When he learned that our field representatives would be in Israel to instruct Israelis in the use of the 2000-pound E.O. guidance system, he decided to put his rent money to work. He made six calls to our plant and spoke with one of the representatives, a friend of mine. He even called me. The Arabs were not supposed to know that Israel had the weapon, let alone that there were American advisors. By the time the Colonel contacted Pete Paterson, the whole country knew that he was going to Israel and why. Pete never rented the apartment, because the rent was too high. Our weapons were going to be sold to Greece and Turkey. They may have used this weapon against each other on Cyprus. My position with the company had now become unbearable. I drank more and more, but I would never tell my wife.

As I sat there one day, I realized that under these conditions, I was in real trouble. I decided to go to the Medical Department for help. The nurse I had known for 20 years was surprised, because she had thought I was so easy-going.

I told her that I had cirrhosis of the liver. Doctors usually try to keep an employer from finding out. When I admitted to it, she verified it with my doctor, who refused to treat me anymore. He had tried to do me a favor, but I had unwittingly stabbed him by telling Rockwell.

Helen, the nurse, was very sympathetic, and asked confidentially why I drank so much as to become an alcoholic.

"What is bothering you, Tom?" she asked.

"I just can't stand working in a war plant," I replied. "I'm selling deadly weapons to any country that can raise the money. It's against my conscience, and I drink to forget."

Her reaction was "Are you kidding me? You can't be serious." I explained all the reasons why, and she responded, "You really do need help. Where did you get all those weird ideas?"

"From the New Testament," I answered.

"How can a guy who has worked in the same plant for 20 years suddenly decide it's wrong?" she asked. "You've got to be kidding me!" she repeated.

I knew then that I was losing my fight, and so I began to act neurotic. A Christian who explains why he is a complete pacifist is deemed a neurotic, it seems.

She recommended that I see a doctor who was an expert in these cases. He was in residence at Riverside Hospital. After our first conversation, I realized how he became the expert. He was also an alcoholic. He explained how he had lost everything: wife, children, home, car, and most of all, his license to practice medicine. One drink would wipe out three months of his life. He recommended that I join Alcoholics Anonymous, which I agreed to do. But I told him I could not return to the war plant. Every day I enter the door, I want to drink. When I do not work there, I do not drink. If he could not obtain a leave for me, I would resign tomorrow.

"Oh, don't do that! That's the worst thing you can do! You're unbalanced now, but when your senses return, you will understand what I mean," he promised.

I repeated, "If I do not get a personal leave approved by you, I'll resign tomorrow." He called the plant and spoke with Helen, who agreed that I should apply for a personal leave and she would have it approved. She stipulated the condition that I attend AA meetings at least once a week.

When I told my co-workers what I planned to do, they laughed.

"You don't know what an alcoholic is, Tom."

My boss continued, "If you're one, then so am I!" "Probably," I agreed.

I obtained the personal leave and was free. "What does it profit a man to win the whole world and suffer the loss of his soul?" I said to myself.

I was really impressed by the first AA meeting. It was pointed out at the beginning that it is impossible to conquer alcoholism alone. God's help and the help of the members are essential. They were all Christians and did not know it. AA was more Christian than any organization I ever belonged to, including Church organizations. These people lived each hour of each day fighting the devil. They knew that if they did not have God, they could not do it.

I was surprised to see so many of my friends at my first AA meeting. At every meeting volunteers would explain what alcohol had done to their lives. I felt sympathy for them, and yet, I was the one who had cirrhosis of the liver. I found it hard to believe that a person could go on a six-month drunk over one little drink. I never even enjoyed drinking at lunch with the other employees. A hangover from the previous night's drinking would kill my desire to drink. There were times when I felt I did not belong. But every week, I had to go to the doctor and act as though I couldn't stand it without booze. He encouraged me and gave me a bill for $25. My commitment to leave Rockwell practically cured me.

I continued to pray, asking God to help me see the path to His will. I did not know how to effectively preach against the Vietnam War. I knew it was not a "just war" according to the Catholic Church's doctrine. How could a war be considered self-defense when it killed innocent people in a remote part of the world 7,000 miles from our homeland? I envisioned what it would be like for Canada to fight Mexico in our country, destroying our cities and killing our children. We might gain the attitude that peace is more important than which country wins. Lord, forgive us for doing this to the Vietnamese. We will suffer for it someday. As Jesus said, "For all they that take the sword shall perish by the sword." (Matthew 26:52)

I still did not know how to accomplish God's will by writing a book. Every time I opened my mouth in Lions Clubs or in the Knights of Columbus meetings I was booed down and practically thrown out. "America, right or wrong" was their slogan. But the Vietnam War opened the eyes of many people who realized for the first time that our leaders could force us to fight in an immoral war, and that it was possible for us to lose a war because of it.

CHAPTER 18

SECOND ST. PETER'S WIFE

"There you go again; you always want to leave me. Why do you always give me that insecure feeling? Why do you have to leave me to serve Christ? Can't you write at home? Can't you serve at home?" my wife Dorothy asked.

"I'm a divided man at home," I replied. "The cars need fixing, the washer and dryer, the roof, and the children's problems. I can't do it. I've tried." I continued, "Look at St. Peter, he was a poor simple man trying to make a living as a fisherman. The Lord called him and he left everything to follow him across the countryside." But then I wondered what happened to St. Peter's wife. The New Testament refers to his mother-in-law, so St. Peter must have had a wife, although she is never mentioned. I had always thought of the Apostles as single men. I had assumed they were single when they left their nets to follow Him. Today, if Christ were to call me to follow Him, how would I explain it to my wife? I would probably tell Christ that I could not go because I have a wife and seven children to support. I also could not leave my business, because too many people depended on me. I might ask how much he would pay me, or ask for information on the fringe benefits.

St. Peter and his friends must have been very stupid to drop their nets and follow Him. What kind of excuse could Peter have thought of to tell his wife? "Dear, we had not caught any fish all day and this strange man came walking by and insisted that we put our nets in the water again. When I protested, He spoke with such authority that we felt compelled to obey Him. Dear, we caught so many fish that some of our nets broke. We did not know what to think, except that He was quite a fisherman, and He must have come from God, because of the miracle. When He told us to follow Him and He would make us fishers of men, we did what He said. He had everything going for Him, and He was a born leader."

St. Peter's wife may have responded with, "So you just dropped your valuable nets and followed Him? Do you expect me to believe a story like that? You've been gone three days! You were probably drunk again, or else you ran off with that whore Magdalene, who runs with Jesus' bunch. Do you know that I have to meet the mortgage payment this week? Who's going to run your business? Someone stole half your nets that you left on the ground, and your boat leaks and needs to be fixed. Joseph, the carpenter, came over to fix the boat and I didn't know what to tell him to do. Peter, you can't run off and follow this man. What will I do?"

My wife began to smile a little and I stopped. I really loved her. We hugged each other and I went on.

"Today," I said, "if a man was personally called by Christ, he would certainly have a difficult time dropping everything to follow Him. But St. Peter would have had as difficult a time then as now. I admire someone who can put his ideals before his family for Christ's sake. Modern Christian husbands and fathers have to do this everyday, and it is more complicated. I can refuse to cheat in business. I can refuse my wife's excessive credit-card purchases, which cause me to worry about the material things of the world. I can refuse my child a car for graduation. I can even send my children to a public school and save the high tuition of Catholic schools but the most difficult part of it all is to put Christ first in this modern materialistic society. I am so wrapped up in it that I feel I cannot miss one day's work." My wife continued to listen attentively.

So I continued, "Many young people have found the solution might be to have an abortion rather than marry and raise a family when it could cause a sacrifice of their education. It seems logical. St. Peter had all these problems facing him too, but he dropped everything and followed Christ. Lord, give me the strength to do this. I love my family, but I must serve Him first. Give me the strength, oh Lord. I love my dear wife and children so very much." I went on telling my wife, "I also wonder what happened to St. Peter's wife as he toured the countryside with Christ. What did she think when Christ accepted the prostitute, Mary Magdalene, into His close circle? What did she think when she heard from the priests and pharisees that the group included a band of sinners, tax collectors, and wine drinkers? I know what my friends would think, and what they would tell my wife." My wife was still smiling, and she hugged me again.

I prayed before my wife, "I have a most understanding wife, Lord, but I don't think she has the strength to understand Christ's call to me. At times I do not understand His calling either, and therefore, I need special grace. My wife needs special grace first. My wife is such a beautiful person, and she loves me and she loves God, so Christ will have to give her the understanding. As I think of my brother Ray, I also pray for him to understand. He will have to run the business by himself. We are in business together, and now the burden will be on his shoulders. Because I do not have much time, I must get on with the task ahead."

I said, "Dorothy, I must complete this story and I must convince the Catholic Church that as Christians, according to our own doctrine, we are not allowed to fight the next nuclear war. The Church must urge the people to come to terms with the communists, and must forbid Christians from participating in immoral wars or preparing for nuclear war. They have rejected this most important teaching of Christ, just as the Jews did. The Jews had wanted a great earthly ruler to protect them from their enemies and give them a great nation. The Jews also loved their neighbors, but they thought it right to kill their enemies. Christ warned the Jews for that reason, and Christ had also warned the Catholic Church because of its historical acceptance of and participation in numerous wars.

Christ allowed the Church to split apart in the Middle Ages because of it. Because Christians wanted to fight, He allowed Christians to fight Christians for centuries. He allowed Christians to hate Christians because they would not accept His basic teaching and the purpose of His life and example. The Syrians and the Babylonians loved their countrymen. The Jews loved their countrymen. Americans love their own. As Christ said, "For if you love them who love you, what reward have you? Do not even the publicans do the same?" (Matthew 5:46). The Catholic Church's first justification for war was based on self-defense. After tonight, I can understand why. It is in human nature, and now, I accept the Catholic Church's conditions that allow a man to fight a "just war" in self-defense. The next nuclear war, however, cannot be considered a "just war," according to the Catholic Church's own definition. In fact, at no time did Christ mention that we may kill in self-defense or for land or country.

He said, "Do not offer resistance to injury. When someone strikes you on one cheek, turn the other cheek. This will show the pagans we all have one Father in heaven." He presented this nonviolent message often, in many other forms.

Nuclear warfare is like two men holding a gun to each other's heads. Who can win? My grandchildren have a right to live too, and I must try to stop this great immoral war we are preparing for. Christians even believe that they should destroy their enemies, and themselves, if necessary, in the name of Christ. How wrong they are, and what great evil it is for the Catholic Church not to speak out against it! I must do whatever is possible to bring Christ's message to the leaders of the Church. I must make them give up their false security in weapons.

If possible, I will run ads in the paper. I must write constantly on the subject. I must speak to the hierarchy and the priests. I must spend the money I have set aside for my children's education.

I must make my family give up their economic security if necessary, as the Church needs to do. If this results in only two priests who really preach the true message of Christ, then it would be worth it. We Christians must begin to love our enemies and stand up and be counted as the early martyrs did. I just wish I were more worthy and had more time. But I am sorry, dear Dorothy, for all the trouble I am going to bring you."

Then I promised my wife that I would never leave her, no matter what happened. I may have to leave at times for a while, but I will always come back to her. "I love you, Dorothy, and without your help, I can do none of this. You are more of a Christian than I, and tonight proves it." My wife stopped crying and we were at peace. That was the first time I had ever fully explained to her what I was supposed to do for Christ.

I continued dragging out my personal leave with Rockwell. Finally, the old alcoholic doctor told me I must return to the plant. I had made my decision to resign. I would miss the security of the salary, insurance, and fringe benefits, but I had committed myself to Christ. Then one day, I read an article in the newspaper saying that Congress had canceled funds for the Rockwell Condor cruise missiles. It was a Navy contract for only 12 cruise missiles initially. The program had run for nine years and delivered a limited number of missiles for shipboard use. Then they discovered that they would not work. But the Condor guidance system did work, and was used in most cruise missiles.

The Navy Admiral was shocked to learn that he should not expect them to work without some modifications. "Then, why do I have them aboard my ship?" he shouted. "You mean we spent approximately $300 million for a few weapons that don't work?"

It was explained to him that the funds for the necessary modifications had not been approved. It was explained that the contract for the aircraft to carry the missile had also been canceled the year before. He could not believe it.

When Congress finally terminated the program, I called my boss and said, "This is your chance to lay me off, now that Congress has canceled the Condor program."

"Some people will have to be laid off, in some areas, but we will need more people to terminate the contract," he responded. "We're loading people up on it now, and it takes still more people to terminate it."

"You've got to be kidding," I replied.

"No, we're working on an estimate now for the Navy of what it will cost to terminate the contract. It will probably take a year," he answered. "It will probably cost more for the Navy to terminate the contract than to complete it."

I could not believe it, but it didn't matter. I just wanted to leave the company. It had served its purpose in providing work for highly paid engineers and generating stock profits for many years.

Then he said possibly he could lay me off, since the HOBOS antipersonnel cluster smart bombs program was delayed. "Would you, Mac? I would greatly appreciate it," I replied.

"Okay, I'll lay you off, but you will have to come in and terminate your medical leave. How about tomorrow, when we will be geared up for laying people off?" he asked.

"Sure," I said. "I'll be in at eight."

The re-entry medical examination to lay me off took less than five minutes. (When I was hired it took two days.) My layoff papers were waiting for me when I arrived at my desk. My co-workers were glad to see me go, since it gave them a better chance of keeping their own jobs. They also knew that I could stay if I had wished to do so.

I invited them to my cabin and the lake for fishing any time. I think they were relieved when I left, because I had become their conscience concerning war. I walked happily away from 24 years of hypocrisy. But it was not long before I realized that I could never completely serve God as long as I was a military contractor or a businessman.

In order to be a successful businessman, I had to psych myself to believe that a profit was all-important. I realized that everything I did had to be geared toward that profit goal. By being successful, I made enemies, and it was necessary for me to break the law at times. It was impossible to follow all the government laws and make money, or to build nuclear weapons and serve God at the same time.

The Condor cruise missile program, however, did create the first cruise missile guidance system that worked. (As a result, the Navy became the sole agency in charge of all the other services' cruise missile guidance systems.) But its propulsion system was very bad. At first it was made by Thiokol, Inc., which could not meet the specifications. Then the contract was given to Rockwell's Rocketdyne Division, which, after several years, could not meet the specifications either. Thiokol then sued Rockwell and the Navy for giving them an impossible specification. Rockwell backed Thiokol and both companies sued the Navy for giving them an impossible specification. Both companies made additional millions of dollars for nothing.

CHAPTER 19

THE FIRST BOOK

By the end of the year, the urge to do Christ's work was unbearable. I asked my wife to let me go away to write my book.

She reluctantly gave her approval around the first of February, 1977.

We had just started a new construction contract at the Defense Construction Supply Center (DCSC) in Columbus, Ohio. I had ordered the major material items used, subcontracted everything, and let my brother Ray run the job. My wife never believed I would really go until that day came.

Dorothy cried and cried. She would not believe that I was coming back. "My dear, I'll come back, I'll always come back to you. I love you now more than you know," I assured her. But I was really reluctant to go. I had never been away from my wife for a long time. "Why don't you give me three weeks to get settled, and then fly down and join me? You can then have a vacation while I write," I suggested. Her spirits were lifted and I left.

I headed toward Mexico with a mobile camper I had purchased. It was a strange world I entered, and I drove for miles in a daze. I really did not want to leave my wife and children. I should go back. But I knew I couldn't concentrate at home. I had tried many times before. I continued driving to warmer weather. The winter weather was so severe that it took a long time to reach warmer climes. As I drove, I thought about how I would write my book. Since nothing came to mind, I stopped at a church.

"Lord, I don't know how to write a book. I'm only kidding myself. If a book is to be written, then it must be written by You. Since I have no inspiration, I am leaving it up to You. If You do not guide me, then it shall not be written." I prayed with the ultimatum "either or else." I certainly never wanted this task.

As I drove into Texas, it all came to me in a flash. Why not just start writing about my own life, as an example to Christians, to help them see their failures through my failures? I had certainly failed a thousand times since I first understood Christ's message of peace. Besides, I would not be able to write a book in any other way than to tell of my own experiences. I was no theologian. I was no Doctor of Catholic Philosophy. I could only relate my own experiences.

I bought a notebook at the next town and began to write as I thought about my experiences. I began, in my own limited way, to tell the personal story of my failure to adhere to the sacred teaching of Christ to love my enemies so that by my example, other Christians will know of this failure.

I remember how at the age of' 18 I first began to realize that something was missing in my Catholic religion, an incompleteness. Something announced to my heart that we are all brothers and sisters with one Heavenly Father, and we should not fight wars.

In my early youth, I found the pleasures of life in the spirit, and the heart, and the body. I loved life and I loved the Lord. I drank life's riches and carefree happiness, until my soul encountered an awareness of the responsibilities of my life.

I yearned to be a flyer, sailing through the spacious skies, protecting my Christian country from despotism and tyrants of war ... by destroying other people.

Then I saw the terrible results of war and all my romantic notions went out the window. I had been enlightened by the Holy Spirit, which hounded me to speak out against the accepted "Christian" practice of war. This unique calling changed my whole life. I was never satisfied with my Christian Catholic religion after that enlightenment. I never knew total peace again until now, after I quit Rockwell.

Even though I have been a hypocrite, I was hounded by the Spirit for 25 years to speak out against the practice of war, and the Christian falsehoods concerning war, that lead far away from the truthfulness of Christ.

I almost hit a semi when I drifted off the road while writing. After the third close call, I got good at it; I became an expert in writing while driving. I reached the southernmost point of Texas before the weather got warm. I stayed at an old motel called Purdy's, which was built on the site of a Civil War fort in Port Isabel.

I chose this place because I was always inspired by the sea. It was on the island of Port Isabel and overlooked the Laguna Madre Bay.

The bay ran northward to Corpus Christi, Texas. Brownsville was about 20 miles inland on the Rio Grande Valley. Port Isabel was a quaint little Spanish shrimping village. Most of the people spoke Spanish.

The whole town got to know me as "the writer." Every morning, I would rise at seven and jog two miles to a little restaurant, have a cup of coffee, and jog back. I would awaken all the dogs on the way, and I could hear them howling as I ran. Then I would shower and dress and drive to the restaurant for breakfast. After breakfast, I would work on the book for 12 hours. At first, I taped it, but I could not find anyone to type from the tape. This led me to write the story in notebooks, painfully, in longhand.

I found a Spanish girl named Ottilia who could type. I rented a typewriter so that she could type the manuscript. But she typed it just as I wrote it.

Later I found another typist in Brownsville who did a very good job of proofreading before she typed. I attended Mass every other day, except for Tuesdays, which was the priest's day off. I called my wife every day at five. It was so pleasant to hear her voice!

The story really flowed. Every day I experienced the pain of writer's cramps. After the third day, I also experienced great loneliness. I missed my wife and children. Across the bay I could see the sign lights of the Hilton and the Holiday Inn on South Padre Island, about two miles away. A big beautiful bridge connected the islands, and Purdy's was at one end of it. It was like a beautiful path that could lead to my destruction. The fourth night the lights strongly beckoned me to join the "good life" again.

My room was as bare as a monastery, but it seemed to give me protection against the world, over there, of glitter and wealth. I was tempted, but I wouldn't go over the bridge. I had Christ's work to do first and foremost.

On the fifth night, a Saturday night, I could actually hear the bands playing across the silent black water. "Lord," I prayed, "When does a man stop being tempted? I have been tempted to do other things except Your will ever since I can remember. Didn't even Your disciples get relieved from temptation, after they had committed their lives to You and proved it? No, I guess You always want to prove our love like a lover. Look at Adam and Eve, Abraham and Isaac, King David and Bathsheba, St. Peter, the Apostles, the Martyrs. No, You have a history of tempting Your loved ones. Even the Lord's Prayer begs God 'and lead us not into temptation.' But it also says that if we fail He will 'Forgive us our trespasses as we forgive those who trespass against us.'" Those words alone are very powerful instructions for a Christian to become a pacifist.

But I was still tempted, and finally I decided to go over and just see what it was like. I was tired of writing and I needed a break.

Both hotels were beautiful and right on the Gulf of Mexico. I had a late dinner there in the dining room. About six couples from Canada were sitting at the next table, half-crocked. One thing led to another, and I joined their party. They were having the time of their lives. I ended up with a drink in front of me, and I protested. After a while I found myself drinking out of it just from habit. Then I had to buy a round, and before I knew it I was the life of the party.

One of the women asked me, "Are you a writer or something? Every time I go over to that souvenir shop by Purdy's, I see you sitting out by the bayside writing."

"Yes, I am a writer," I said proudly, even though I know the Lord was really writing this book.

"Well, tell me about it. I'm very interested. I thought of myself once as being a writer," she said.

All the others had decided to move to the dance room. "Aren't you going with your friends?" I asked.

"No, I just met them. My husband is up in our room," she replied.

"Does he have a hangover?" I asked jokingly.

She replied, "No, he's not feeling well. He has emphysema very bad. That's why we're down here. But he's been worse down here than in Chicago. He's a captain of detectives for Chicago."

"That's too bad, to come this far for a vacation and then you can't go out of your room."

"Yes, I'll have to go join him soon, but first tell me about your book," she asked.

We talked and talked until it was two o'clock in the morning. She knew far more about writing than I did, but she loved the plot. The next morning I got up to jog and my head just about fell off my shoulders. My mind was a complete blank that day, and I realized I could never drink if I wanted to write or live. My stomach was also bloated. My liver must have had another setback. I went to the 10 o'clock Mass, and since my mind wouldn't work anyway, I decided to take the day off.

I went over to the beach. The water was too cold for swimming, so I went to the heated pool at the Holiday Inn. Luckily I had my notebook and pencils, because as I walked the beach all sorts of ideas sprang into my head. I realized I had to write about my worldly side in order to show my failings. That monastery that I lived in wasn't the right surrounding for writing about the good life, or the bad side of my soul. But there at the Holiday, I was sinfully. I wrote for six hours by the side of the pool, until a voice yelled down from the balconies above. "Boy, don't you ever quit?" Then the voices of the other Canadians chimed in. I folded up my notebook, stuck it in my brief case, and dived into the pool.

I swam for awhile and then I got out, and when I went back to my lounge chair, Rosa was sitting next to it. Rosa was the woman I had talked to for so long the night before.

"Hi, Tom," she said. "You know, you look a lot thinner in clothes."

"Yes, I guess I do," I replied. "Where's your husband?"

"He couldn't seem to get his breath in this damp air. I feel so sorry for him, but he's happy just getting away from his job in Chicago. He's such a gentle old man for such a job, solving murders and all. Chicago's a tough city," she told me.

"Well, how old is he?" I asked.

"Oh, he'll be 60 this year. The poor thing. He's a bundle of nerves." Sixty, I thought to myself. This woman couldn't be over 35.

"I know, you're wondering how old I am. I was his secretary when he married me and I was only 28. We've been married for seven years, so figure it out for yourself," she said.

"He really did rob the cradle, didn't he?" I laughed, and we both laughed.

I showed her what I had written, and she liked it. It was the part when I was bumming around the country after I left the Navy.

"You were really a rascal, weren't you?" she asked.

"Yes, I have two distinct natures, good and evil. When I write about the good side of me, I write over at my monastery at Purdy's. But I can't seem to write about my bad side or the good times over there. I have to come over here, I guess."

"I can see why," she said. We talked about the book and swam some that afternoon. We really had a ball.

"Since this is your evil side," she asked, "why don't you meet me after dinner tonight and dance a little bit. Maybe have a couple of drinks. You're uptight and you need a break. I need a break, too."

"What about your husband?" I asked.

"Oh, he won't mind. He's been begging me to go out and enjoy myself. He feels sorry for me," she told me teasingly. "We can discuss the ending of your book. Come over about 9:30 and I'll meet you in the cocktail bar."

"Judas!" I said to myself, as I walked to the van. "How in the hell do I get into these situations?" I wrestled with my conscience all the way across the bridge, through the seafood dinner at Marchan's, and back to Purdy's. I tried to write. My mind and my page were both perfect blanks. My loneliness didn't help me in making a decision for Christ.

On the way back over the bridge of temptation, I crucified myself. I knew if I failed this time, it would be the end of me. I had to make this final decision. "Quo Vadis, Tom? Where are you going?" I remembered the title of that movie. I had to make a great decision to make things right *now*, and then probably 100 times again. I fell on my knees by the old bed and begged God's forgiveness. I prayed for an hour for strength. Then I got up and walked down the street to the telephone booth. I called my wife, and it was one o'clock in the morning where she was.

"Yes! Yes!" she replied to the operator, "I'll accept the charges." I know that because of my temptations, I shouldn't try to lead a good life without my wife again. Suddenly I heard her asking, "Tom! Tom! Are you there?"

"Dorothy, I need you badly; I can't stand living alone, without you, anymore. Please come down as soon as possible. Please catch the next airplane."

"Oh, that's the sweetest thing you ever said to me, Tom, that you needed me." There was a long pause before she said, "But honey, I can't get reservations until next Friday. That's the earliest time I can get a flight all the way through."

"Certainly there must be another airline?" I protested.

"No, there isn't," she replied, "I'll arrive there at three in the afternoon, on Braniff 's Flight #730."

"Dorothy, I love you!" and said, "People are saying that you went to Mexico and left me for good."

"Nothing could be farther from the truth! I realize I can't live without you. I'll love you more than ever, and I'll meet you at the plane. Please hurry, though! Give all my love to Susanna and the other children," I said.

"Susanna can come with me free. I've taught her to say she's only one year old, and she raises one finger.

"That's terrible, to teach a three year old to lie," I protested. Dorothy laughingly agreed. "But I'm going to hold her on my lap. What difference does it make?" she rationalized. "I love you, Tom, and I'll see you Friday. Goodbye, lover."

"Goodbye, lover!" I replied.

I was rather proud of myself for having beaten this great temptation. I knew I would have other temptations as I went through life, but I reasoned that none could be as great as I had overcome that night. Maybe I am strong enough to serve the Lord, I thought, or rather, the power of the Lord is strong enough to save me.

Early the next morning I left Purdy's and went to Brownsville. I checked into the Jardin Hotel, right on the Rio Grande River, and wrote for the next two days. From my hotel room at night I could see the happy lights of Matamoros, Mexico, and the people streaming across the international bridge.

I went back to Purdy's on Tuesday, the day after Rosa should have gone back to Chicago. I know it was only the circumstances of a good time that had brought us together.

I was inspired to write like I had never been inspired before. I had filled 200 hand-written pages. My writing fingers were so tired that I couldn't write anymore. I practically couldn't see anymore either. I had forgotten my glasses. I had both typists working for me now.

I waited impatiently for Dorothy and Susanna at the airport. Finally, the plane came in, and I anxiously studied the passengers as they got off. Finally, there were no more passengers debarking. Dorothy and Susanna had not been among them. I went to the airline office and asked about her. They could not tell me anything. Other people were asking about other passengers, too, who were also supposed to have arrived. Finally we were told that the plane had been oversold, but that another flight from Houston was due in at 8:30 p.m. I waited at the airport until then. I was so impatient that I drank five gin and tonics after I ate.

Dorothy and Susanna were the first to get off this flight, and I ran to them. We had a tearful, but happy reunion. And that night we became man and wife again. Susanna slept on the floor on pillows. Since it was Dorothy's vacation and since my rent was up at Purdy's, I insisted that we check out and go over to stay at one of the big hotels on South Padre Island. Naturally, she chose to stay at the Holiday Inn. We accidentally got a room with a balcony toward the sea. It was like a second honeymoon, except that we had the baby with us. But she was a joy.

That first night, after Susanna went to sleep, we dined by candlelight in the main dining room, and when the band started to play we went into the cocktail lounge. I forgot that the bartender and the waitress knew me. Dorothy protested doubtfully as they referred to me as "Senor Tom." "You must really have had a good time. When were you here?" she asked.

"No, I just ate here and listened to the music once." I ordered another 7-Up.

The next morning the sea and the sea gulls awakened me. I usually get up easily because I love the freshness of the mornings, which creates new hopes. I drew open the drapes just as the beautiful orange sun was peeping over the sea.

"Dorothy! Look at this!" I exclaimed, "Look at the dawn!" "What? What? Something wrong?" she asked. "Look at the sun!" I cried.

She fluttered her eyes open for a minute, said, " That's beautiful," and went back to sleep.

Now the whole sun was showing over the horizon, like the birth of a new world, a world that might possibly be at peace. I always believed that if there were a physical location for heaven, it would have to be the sun. Without God, there could be no life; and without the sun there could be no life on earth. The earth this morning was in beautiful conformity with heaven, and so was my soul. As I started to write again, I realized that I was condemning the Catholic Church, my own church. Then it struck me that in the last 25 years the Church might have changed its secret doctrine about fighting wars and the conditions for a "just war." And yet, I reasoned, if that is true, why did the Church still remain totally silent on the subject?

I knew that there were two things I had to do. First, to force the Catholic Church to instruct the youth about the Church's own doctrine concerning the morality or immorality of total war. Then, should there be another Vietnam, the youth can decide for themselves, with a clear conscience, whether they can refuse to fight and still be respected in the eyes of their parents, Church, and government. They wouldn't have to shamefully desert to Canada.

The second, and most important is to force the Church to condemn the total planning and preparation by the military for the next horrible atomic war. In such a war there will be no victor and millions will perish horribly in a human holocaust fought for the unchristian principles of both capitalism and communism. It appears this war is going to be fought without a single objection by the Pope. Nor will the Church make any attempt to condemn a war of annihilation as immoral and forbidden by the Church's doctrine concerning the conditions for a "just war," set down by St. Augustine and expounded by St. Thomas Aquinas. If nothing else, this might force the Catholic Church to seriously enter into the role of a mediator with Russia and begin to work out a Christian peace that would save the world from total spiritual, material, and moral destruction.

The situation now is like two men holding pistols to each other's heads. One is a righteous homeowner and the other an armed burglar. Would it be wise and sane for the homeowner to pull the trigger knowing he would die also? Wouldn't it be more sensible to immediately come to terms with the burglar and work out a solution?

We are beginning to be irrational as a nation. Now we are funding the development of a Rockwell neutron bomb, which, the military proudly announced, "will only kill all the people but will not destroy the buildings." We are constructing "doomsday planes" for the President and the military chiefs so they can fly around and direct retaliatory missiles at Russia in the event of war. This would lead a sane person to believe that there would be no safe place anywhere on earth. Our whole concept of self-defense is based on the premise that "If you destroy us, we will destroy you." This is madness, like the men with the pistols.

Isn't it rather ridiculous not to try to come to terms with your enemy, even to wholeheartedly attempt to? A sane person could reason this even without the help of the Holy Spirit. The Russian leaders might realize how insane it is too, if we, as Christians, didn't give them a bad example. The early Church conquered the mighty pagan Roman Empire by example. Couldn't today's Church compromise to save the world from nuclear war?

I am neither a psychologist nor a writer capable of convincing the great powers to come to terms. But the Holy Spirit is, and has done it many times in the past.

Even though the Spirit has moved me to write this simple story, self-interest has made me complete it. I have a selfish desire to see my children and my grandchildren enjoy the right to life. As long as they have just the right to live, then, I don't care whether they are capitalists or communists—just so they are Christians. Christ will not die again, no matter who rules the world.

I was eager to get back to Columbus and confirm the Church's doctrine on the practice of Christian warfare. I felt that my story was completed, except that I must spend the rest of my life serving Christ by educating the youth in regard to war... educating them with their own Catholic Church's doctrine. I had wasted too many years. Always, while I was writing, a voice seemed to keep telling me to hurry. Probably this sense of urgency was because I didn't have long to live.

"I don't know what the future holds for me, but I know who holds my future. Without God's help, I can do nothing. If this is not His will, then I shall fail," I told Dorothy.

After Sunday Mass that day, I decided to stop at the Catholic newsstand in the back of the church to see whether the Pope or the church had condemned the neutron death ray bomb as an immoral weapon and said that it couldn't be built by Catholics. I guess he was too busy, because all the headlines read, "Pope still condemns masturbation as a serious sin." I said to myself, "The end of the world is being planned and here we sit, thinking about masturbation." I flipped open the final magazine in disgust, and on the back I read the following:

> "The Church, through her bishops, must speak, no matter what the fears, what the opposition, what the criticism. Unless she does, the notion of Almighty God's having anything to do in the affairs of nations, and of individuals, may be lost. And the idea of a social order based on the Christian principles of justice and charity may be abandoned as an unrealistic, impractical, visionary illusion."
>
> Bishop Donal Lamont, South Africa
> (*Purchase People*, 1959).

I looked at the date again and said, "Hurry, Dorothy! I don't have much time!" And as an afterthought, I added, "And neither does the world!" I decided to appeal to the U.S. Catholic Bishops and to the Holy Father.

CHAPTER 20

THE VOICE OF GOD

From the day I left the Rockwell Missile Division I had been wondering why neither the popes nor the bishops had ever forbidden me to build nuclear weapons. Because of the guilt I felt and because I had been told I did not have long to live, all through 1978 I hurried to write to every single American bishop. I spent hundreds of dollars sending them technical information about the great danger of cruise missiles and other new offensive weapons such as the Pershing II and the Trident II missiles.

In late 1978 I wrote my first letter to the Pope, appealing to him to ban nuclear weapons. Pope Paul VI died after he would have received it, on August 6, 1978, the anniversary of Hiroshima. I was very sad, because Pope Paul VI had seemed close to banning nuclear weapons. Pope John Paul I was elected shortly after Paul VI's death.

Maybe he would have made some important changes, but we will never know, because he did not last. He wanted to change the Vatican Curia. I remember passing out the letter I had written to Pope Paul VI, which I also sent to

Pope John Paul I, at the cathedral in Columbus, Ohio. It was there that Sharon Abercrombie of the *Citizens Journal* became interested in my story. She took a picture and wrote an article about me warning the Church.

I cried when I learned that Polish anti-socialist Karol Wojtyla was elected Pope John Paul II. The last thing the world needed, it seemed to me, was a Polish super-patriot as Pope. All the Polish knew was persecution of the Church and constant fighting. The Polish had a tradition of hating the Russians 800 years before communism.

I would have thought the Pope would hate the Germans even more. They had ravaged Poland much more than the Russians had. However, that was not the case. The cardinals must have elected him because they knew that he would never give an inch to the communists… or ban nuclear weapons, I thought sadly.

One day in early January, 1979, I was praying before the Host in St. Joseph's Cathedral when for some strange reason I felt an urge to go to Mexico. At first I thought it was just a desire to go to the place I had bought across from Mexico on the southern tip of Texas, or maybe it was because I had a desire to get away from the cold winter. Later on, while reading the newspaper, I read that Pope John Paul II was going to be visiting Mexico on January 23rd. I immediately felt that I should go there and try to appeal to the Pope personally. I proceeded to make arrangements for the trip that day. My wife, my daughter Monica, and sweet little Susanna, then age six, went with me. We drove to our place in Port Isabel, Texas, and from there to Mexico City.

I had heard at Rockwell that the United States was proposing to put first-strike Cruise and Pershing II missiles in Europe. I knew exactly what that meant, since I had worked on the cruise missiles. The "Euromissiles" could strike a Russian missile silo with pinpoint accuracy.

Obviously these were offensive weapons; the silos would be empty if Russia launched first. The plan was to put them on the borders of Russia. The U.S. was also going to build 27 Trident II submarines with 24 missiles each: 408 warheads, each accurate enough to strike a Russian missile silo.

Russia would be forced to take equivalent measures, putting both superpowers only eight minutes away from destroying the world.

It crossed my mind that an "infallible" Pope could ban these offensive first-strike nuclear weapons and save us.

What if the Pope would ban the making, training for, and use of nuclear weapons from the Chair of St. Peter? If he said it "ex Cathedra" all Catholics would have to believe it, especially the 52 million in America. It would become a matter of faith for 800 million Catholics of the world. Hey! That could possibly save the world from nuclear destruction!

Our first night in Mexico City we stayed in the Holiday Inn. It had a big crack from top to bottom caused by an earthquake the week before. The next night we moved to the quaint, old, and safe Geneva Hotel.

I was sleeping when I must have heard Monica give a scream. I woke to see the bottom of the drapes and curtains leaning out two feet from the wall and swaying back and forth. The whole world was moving back and forth. I was glad we had moved from the seventh floor of the Holiday Inn. The earthquake registered 6.9 on the Richter scale. The following days I went to two newspapers, *Excelsior* and *El Heraldo*, and placed hundreds of dollars worth of ads appealing to the Pope and the Latin American Bishops Conference in Puebla to ban nuclear weapons and nuclear war.

I had prepared a big sign to carry before the Pope around the huge square, or Zocalo, which was in front of the City Hall and the Mexico City Basilica. I cut corners to get into position and held the sign in front of him It simply said,

"Dear Holy Father–Ban the nuclear weapons–Ex Cathedra." I was so full of faith and hope then. We all went ahead of the Pope to Puebla, about 80 miles east of Mexico City over a beautiful mountain range. We arranged for ads in all the papers there. We also went to the Shrine of Our Lady of Guadalupe. I had always wanted to see the sacred image of the Blessed Mother, supposedly imprinted on an Indian's cloak in 1531. It was fascinating to think that this was just the way the Blessed Mother of Jesus Christ looked in her own eyes.

Always before the Blessed Mother had been described by someone she had appeared to–as for a police composite drawing.

In this case, it was said, she herself had imprinted her own image on the cloak or mantilla of the poorest of Indians, one called Juan Diego. The cloak was made of rough cactus fiber. Juan Diego was one of only a handful of baptized Christian Indians in Mexico in 1531, only 10 years after Cortez had conquered the Aztecs, humiliated Montezuma, and murdered him.

It was explained to me that the Indians had become totally dissatisfied with the cruel regime of the Spanish Catholic Conquistadors. Even those Indians of other tribes who had helped the Spanish conquer the dreaded Aztec nation objected to the cruelty. The Spanish had destroyed their temples and their culture and made slaves of the Indians. The Spanish only wanted gold, and ruled by torture and death. So the Indian nation was about to revolt. The situation required a peacemaker.

Juan Diego was going to Mass one morning when he heard beautiful music coming from Tepeyac Hill, where the Virgin Mother of all the Aztec gods was believed to live. Juan Diego climbed the hill, and there the Blessed Mother appeared to him. She instructed him to go to the bishop in Mexico City to tell him that she wanted a home built, so she could be among her humble people and watch over them. Juan Diego had to wait a long time, but his persistence paid off and he succeeded in seeing the bishop. The bishop listened patiently, but told Juan he would have to bring proof from the Virgin.

There is much more to the story, but eventually the Virgin Mother had Juan pick roses from the hill, in cold December, and arranged them in Juan's cloak. The bishop's servants saw the roses and took Juan Diego to the bishop, who was with guests. When Juan Diego opened the cloak, the roses cascaded onto the floor and the image of the Virgin Mother appeared on the cloak, before the eyes of many witnesses.

This image was the picture I was looking at that morning–the picture that caused the conversion of nine million Mexican Indians in just a few years.

"Another story," I thought. The image didn't impress me at first because the Virgin wasn't beautiful. But as I gazed at it, I saw great humility in the face and figure. If I wanted to paint a portrait of humility, it would be exactly this picture!

The picture combined all the symbols of the Aztec Indian culture with the conventional Christian images of the Virgin. She stood before their mighty god the sun, but didn't block it out. She was supported by the moon, their second-ranking god. The number of stars on her cape was the exact number of their tribes. The cape was also blue, which only their royalty could wear. To an Aztec, she was obviously "a woman with child" because of the brown maternity belt she wore. From a distance she was dark like an Indian, but because of the rough fiber of the cloak, her complexion changed to light when you came up close (like those little plastic pictures that change as you look at them), which made her both Indian and Spanish. There was a discreet little metal cross on a band around her neck.

I remembered thinking about the Immaculate Conception. I never had given it a thought before, and therefore I had assumed that Jesus Christ was the Immaculate Conception. But then I realized that the Blessed Mother, had said, “I am the Immaculate Conception.” And she was! That meant that God the Father must have planned her conception long before she was conceived, because you can’t have retroactive “immaculate conception.”

Therefore, she was the mother of Jesus Christ, the bride of the Holy Spirit, and now the special daughter of the Father. No human woman could be loved as the Mother, the Bride, and the Daughter of God at the same time. So she was loved by God the Trinity more than any other creature, and was an example of total love in one human being.

I had never had a devotion to the Blessed Mother before. I had actually disliked saying the rosary because I was made to as a child. But as I stood there crying I accepted Her as my Mother and the rosary as a great source of serenity—and self-discipline—just as Gandhi’s weaving must have been.

We went back to Puebla to meet the Pope. I had printed up leaflets to distribute to the South American bishops. My wife Dorothy and Monica were afraid to help me at first, but then they came over and handed out leaflets too.

My wife overheard them saying that I was a communist and I would be taken care of. She came over and begged me to stop, but I continued. Some of the bishops were very indignant, and so were the police.

The next day I got really close to the Pope, but again the crowd blocked me as we entered. It was impossible to speak to him because he said Mass on a balcony on the second floor. I was threatened twice. That afternoon I wept as I sat with my wife and daughter at an outside restaurant.

I had not given any appeal to the Pope and I knew he was the only one who might quickly change the hearts of the Christians who were in favor of nuclear weapons.

Despondently, I had started to write a final desperate letter to the Pope. I wanted to complete it and try to get it to him before he left Mexico. I told my wife that I wanted to go to the lovely Chapel of the Rosary in Puebla and pray to be inspired. Then I would go someplace on my own for a few days and not come back until my appeal was written. I was surprised when she agreed. Maybe it was the tears in my eyes.

When I came out of the Chapel I didn't know where to go. As I looked down the street towards the poor section of town, I saw a huge lighted H in the night sky. I walked towards it and saw that the "H" stood for hotel (not for heaven). It was the June Hotel. I got a room on the third floor. As I walked in, the first thing that struck my eyes was a large cross drawn with an ink marker on the wall over the writing table. I sat down and took out my pen and papers and began to work on my final letter to the Pope. I was very desperate and despondent as I wrote:

> *29 de enero 1979*
>
> "Puebla, Mexico
> Su Santidad Juan Pablo II
>
> By the grace of God and the Son Jesus Christ and His Holy Mother the Virgin of Guadalupe, Bride of the Holy Spirit, I implore you. The Lord Jesus Christ is greatly offended because you, and the leaders of His Church, continue to be silent about God's clear commandment to teach all nations that we must love one another, even our enemies.
>
> Christ, represented as the dove and always as the lamb, the most defenseless of

> creatures, commands you, by the example of His defenseless death on the cross in the hands of His enemies, to immediately enforce the Church's teaching concerning a just war. This teaching already forbids Christian Catholics from planning to use the atomic bomb against the entire populations of whole cities. You cannot profess to be as a little child unless we become dependent on God, our Father who made us all brothers and sisters, and stop depending on the atomic bomb for protection.
>
> The Pharisees could not accept this teaching of Christ. They would not teach the Jews to love their enemies, the Roman conquerors. The Jews hated the Romans, and were going to rebel as soon as they could. But you are worse than the Pharisees because you have the Gospels and the example of the early Christian martyrs. +*You have destroyed the effectiveness of My teaching. You must teach them everything I have commanded you. This missing piece, or peace, makes the whole puzzle of my teaching incomplete.*+
>
> The nations of the world are thirsting for a way to peace. Peace is in their hearts. Many non-Christians trust Christ's teachings, but they don't trust Christians, who have fought in the name of Christ for nearly 1700 years. They are not hypocrites, but you are, because you knew better and yet you are afraid to teach them."

I started to write, "I order you to immediately forbid all Catholics and other Christians from intending to use the atom bomb against entire cities in the name of self-defense."

Then I suddenly stopped. "Hey," I remember saying to myself, "I am writing in the first person. I can't do that!" I realized that I was writing as if I were God commanding His Church. Then an inner voice seemed to tell me to continue to write as I had been doing and not to change anything. The thought flashed through my mind that I would suffer, and I accepted the suffering.

I began to write what I had written before. Then I was shocked to hear a REAL voice dictate to me what to write. When I subconsciously hesitated, the voice grew louder and louder until I began to write again. I understood that I had to write what it said.

THE WORD OF GOD
SU SANTIDAD JUAN PABLO II

"You have destroyed the effectiveness of My teaching. You must teach them everything I have commanded you. This missing piece, or peace, makes the whole puzzle of my teaching incomplete." (Then the voice came in.)

THE VOICE OF GOD

+I order you to immediately forbid all Catholics and brother Christians from intending to use the atom bomb against entire cities in the name of self-defense. I want you to instruct them that it is evil to justify atomic warfare and the probable destruction of most of the world. I want you to teach them that they must come to terms with their enemies and begin to promote all possible peaceful negotiations.

You disregard God's commandments and cling to war, which is human tradition. Teach them to carr y out ever ything I have commanded you. You must be made perfect as your heavenly Father is perfect. Whatever you declare bound on earth shall be bound in Heaven. Speak "ex Cathedra." You must do it. My little child, I know this will be most difficult for you, and my heart grieves for you and My church. You think now that you have peace because of the bomb. But you are mistaken. You have not put peace in the hearts of men and women by your lack of instruction. My servant of servants, you must be brave.

I will help you. Pick up your cross and follow me. My burden is light. My sorrow is great. My time will come, but you must help me save millions of souls. This is the only way you will convert them until I come. Do not lose any more souls to hell because of this. I know your trials are already great, but this must be. My Church cannot go on like this. I have been ignored too long. I grieve greatly for My people. The world will not know Me unless you do this. My Mother grieves for all Her people. I should end it all and stop her suffering. But I have promised, and My Father grieves. The world does not know My message yet, but I have promised the time. You must instruct all nations.

In my name, peace will come about, if you do this. There is no other way. I grieve for you, and for my people. It will not be easy. Father will be against son, and son against father. Brothers will hate each other. But in the end, more souls will finally be at peace. Pray for Russia!

I have used my enemies many times to chastise my people. I am using a sinner now to instruct you.

You must be made perfect as an example because you would not listen. The world must come to the feet of My mother or Her Bridegroom may destroy it. She is your only hope, the Lady of Guadalupe, My mother and My bride, who begs me every day for her children. She is sorrowful, and she fears that I may turn on them. They are pathetic, going to and fro, not knowing from where they come nor where they go. I am sorry sometimes that I made them, but they are My children, and I am their Father, so what can I do?

The universe is mine but the free love of man is not. You must help me. I created them out of love and gave them a free will to love Me: My worst mistake. For love has to be given freely or it isn't worth anything. Teach My children to love Me and I will make your burden light.

The angels envy your free will. Since I first contemplated love through loneliness, and created man to love and want to be loved, it has been a trial. I did not need this, nor does my Mother need all her sorrow. You have sinned grievously, but I love you because I am your Father. Say no more and be done with it. Do it and great peace to the hearts of people who heed your words and come to me. Your Mother saves you now, but if you persist, even she will not be able to.

Teach as I have commanded you. Women may yet bring peace to the world if they will have the heart of My Mother.

Do not tempt My servant Thomas, for he is the weakest of the weak, and the strongest of the strong. His mind and heart are simple, though, and he understands My simple words and example. He is a complicated man but he will finally find peace, if not in this world. He knows My simple message of peace now after all these years. You must be as clever as snakes and as peaceful as doves, and he is both.

It you would have listened to Me, I would not have had to speak through such a worldly one. I will take him to heaven, but he has been a pain. Still, his heart has always been clear, and he believes in Me. Why do I always have to speak through the weak and the foolish to confuse the wise? Do not write any more encyclicals. Enough is enough! Speak simply and command my people.

Why? Why do I always have to speak through such simple people and sinners? Do not be complicated, be simple like him. He doesn't know any better than to take Me word for word. Must you always complicate and then ignore my simple commands? I was born in a filthy stable, wet my pants, loved my Mother, honored my father Joseph, and was truly a man. I was simple, My life was simple, My disciples were simple. Peter was the dumbest of them all but he was simple enough to take my words literally, and he loved from the heart as Thomas does.

Do not complicate this command, or the world will be destroyed. Do not fear when you read this. If you act upon it. I will protect you. Be My little child. Do not waste time or your time will be at hand. God knows all, and I will guide you. Be on your way immediately; be about Your Father's work. Do not refuse Him or He will not be as tolerant as I. Know Your God. Know Him with your whole mind and body and heart. Do not offend Him. He is your Savior, He is your God. Do not complicate or condition this command. It is the only way to bring more souls to heaven. Do not turn away or the world will be lost soon and many more will be damned. I love all my children, but justice commands that I do this.

Please, keep My Father, through justice, from doing it. End My mother's sorrow. You don't know how it grieves me to see her suffer.

She is a loving mother and will bear anything for her children. But I cannot bear to see her suffer so much. Such a beautiful woman is she. I have loved her from the moment I first contemplated her. She is my joy or you would have been destroyed a long time ago.

The world is at peace but only in her heart will people see what I have commanded you. Speak quickly! Do not be afraid. My beautiful mother will protect you. She has promised and anything she has promised I will fulfill. Peace is only in the hearts of those who know Me. Pagans will war till the end, but my people shall not. Feed my sheep! Feed my lambs! Know your Shepherd. Know that my Father is love. You were created by love and you will be saved by love. The Father knows me, and I know true love. You have it in your heart but you are weak like Thomas. Lord have mercy on him. Each day he breathes and is good is a miracle—but he persists and so must you. Do not turn your back on Me or you will be most sorry. Do not turn your back on him or on My words. Act immediately or else it will be too late. Your time and his is now. He has been trying for so long, but he is so weak. Do not let the communists worry you. They must be saved, and this is the only way. They are not My enemies; they are also My children. Do not run when I talk to you. Listen to me, you are My voice. I promised to speak through you until the end of time. Do not let me down, oh simple striving child. I know how hard you are trying. But this is the most important thing you have to do. Drop all else and come to Me. Heed My command: Love one another as I have loved you. Do you think it was easy for me to die on the cross? No. It was the most difficult thing I ever did, even loving you and My people. I felt the nails like any man. I felt My flesh being torn away like any man who was hanging from nails through his hands. I did it to show you an example of the sacrifice My people must make to bring peace to the world.

Woe is Me! My heart can hardly bear your insults. Man has become so wicked that I should destroy him. But for the sake of the elect and because I have promised, I will continue to accept your sins. But I don't know how much longer I can bear to see my Mother in such pain. I have said enough. Thomas, do not write anymore. He will listen to you. Give it to My Church immediately. Peace be with you, Thomas. Give it to the Archbishop. Sleep now. Your work is finished. +

I was exhausted when I finished. I put down the pencil and that is all I remember.

I woke up the next morning in a very strange environment. I looked down on the bed sheet and there were many pages of roughly written script. Then I remembered!

How could this be happening to me? I never expected anything like this in my life. Luckily, all the pages were hurriedly numbered. There, too, was the neat letter I had started earlier, before the Voice came into my life.

I began to write what the Voice said in legible script, adding it to the letter. The Voice answered all the questions I ever had about my Catholic faith and about God. The Voice told me to appeal to my Catholic Church and to the Pope, the Servant of Servants, the leader of the Church, to ban any justification for nuclear war.

When I woke up I knew that I would never forget what the Voice sounded like, especially when I wanted to differ with what it said and it would rise in volume. But at that moment the sound of the Voice was stricken from my mind forever.

I only had the memory and the pages of what the Voice dictated before me as proof. When I had finished adding what the Voice had said I finished the letter by signing a statement in which I swore that this was truly the word of God as I had heard it, on this date of January 29, 1979. So help me God.

I went downstairs to call my wife Dorothy to come and join me. While I cleaned up the papers and the room I could only shake my head.

Dorothy arrived with a knock on the open door. We hugged and kissed. Then I started to tell her every detail of what had happened to me the night before. She looked very wide-eyed when I told her I suddenly heard this Voice that began dictating to me how to write my letter to the Pope. I was forced to write down what it said to me because it became louder and louder as it waited on me. When I would fall behind it grow louder and then waited for me to catch up. I prayed that I wrote down everything correctly. These are all the pages I wrote as the Voice spoke, the Trinity voice of God, because it talked like the Father, the Son, and the Holy Spirit at different times.

"Wait a minute, Tom. Are you trying to tell me that you actually heard the voice of God?" We were still sitting on the bed. Until now she had listened to my story.

. "Well," I answered, "this Voice sounded like it was contained within me. From what followed I reasoned it to be the combined voice of the Holy Trinity. Listen to some more."

Dorothy shook her head. "God said he made a mistake? Good Lord!"

"Well, He made humans, did He not? In the Bible He said He was sorry He ever made us! Saying He's sorry is the same as admitting He made a mistake, is it not? Even if He did it out of love. Do you mind if I go on?"

"He wet His pants! Come on, Tom!"

"Dear, the Voice was only saying that Christ was human."

"How would Jesus ever call St. Peter dumb?"

"Well, Peter was pretty dumb. That is to say, he was simple and uneducated. Fishermen are some of the most uneducated men. The Voice called me simple!

The Voice said, "He will listen to you (meaning the Servant of Servants, the Pope). Give it to My Church immediately." Did God mean to give it to everyone, to the Pope only, or to the Archbishops? He must have known I was terribly tired, because he said, "Sleep now. Your work is finished." And I immediately fell asleep.

With a little ornery smile, Dorothy asked, "Tom, I hate to ask this dumb question, but what did the Voice sound like?"

"Dear Dorothy, when I woke up and looked at the writing paper in amazement, I said to myself, 'I shall never forget what the Voice sounded like.' At that moment it was completely stricken from my mind."

"Now that is too much!" she screamed.

"No, dear, I remembered what I was told, but I could no longer remember whether it was a high pitch or a low pitch."

"Did it sound like Charlton Heston?" she asked sarcastically. "I only know it sounded like begging and it sounded frustrated at times. I remember it would get exasperated when I mentally questioned what it was saying–when I did not understand. Maybe that is why it called me simple. The rest of the prophecy warned again that if the Pope and the Church did not morally forbid nuclear weapons and war the world could be destroyed."

"Well, Tom, what happens now? What archbishop will you give it to?"

"I will give to the Archbishops of Puebla and Mexico City, and when I get back home I will immediately give it to my Archbishop, Joseph Bernardin of Cincinnati, Ohio."

"Well, go on with your story. I'm really fascinated now–or have I gone off the deep end?" she exclaimed, as she rolled her eyes back in her head.

"I don't know what to think about this prophecy. Being new to this sort of experience, I really believed that God had instructed me. What an incredible thing! I have been directed to write a letter to the Pope!"

We left Room 309 of the hotel and went walking to join Monica and our friend Pablo, who were waiting for us at the park of the Zocalo. As I passed a poor little market I saw a Xerox machine, which had been put in the middle of the sidewalk to attract customers, between a table where they were selling fruit and another selling vegetables. I made four Xerox copies of the message. "Dorothy, what do you think of it?" I asked.

Dorothy hesitated, looking into my eyes for the longest time. Finally she said: "If you absolutely want me to . . . I can say it was a prophetic message for the Pope and the Church.

However, I really also believe that you have taken on an impossible task, one which is much more than your strength. Why don't you give it up?"

"I cannot, Dorothy. I believe more than ever that now only the Pope or the Church can save us from nuclear war. How can I abandon the fight? Christians just do not know how evil it is to fight nuclear war. The Church has always kept silent."

Dorothy looked away. "I don't know Tom, I don't know . . ."

I asked Monica to go to the newspaper *El Heraldo* and tell them to stop publishing the ads, and also to ask for the names of the Archbishops of Puebla and Mexico City. Monica came back without her copy of the letter. She said that the journalist with whom she had spoken knew English and had kept it in order to write an article. I did not like the idea, because I wanted to give the letter to the Pope before anybody else could read it in the newspaper. So I went to see the journalist and the editor. Both personally knew the Archbishop of Puebla, Dr. Pacheco. They promised to give the original letter to the Archbishop. He gave it to the Pope on that same day without knowing what was in it. When the article and the inspired letter to the Pope were published in the Mexican newspaper, I made photocopies of it in order to pass it on to all the bishops attending the Third Latin American Bishop's Conference.

Then I waited to see if the Pope would react in any way. At 3:30 in the afternoon, all the bells started to ring in the city of Puebla. The result was deafening. I saw thousands of people lining up along the road. I did not know what could justify such a concert of bells. It crossed my mind that maybe the Pope had spoken, declaring the use of nuclear weapons a mortal sin for Catholics. The more the bells rang the more

I convinced myself that a miracle had taken place. The Pope had read my letter and the Pope had acted!

I was thanking God with tears in my eyes for saving us from nuclear danger when Dorothy and Monica came up to me and asked what had happened. I was so moved I could hardly talk or explain it to them.

"Oh, no!" Monica said. "It is only the International Bicycle Race from Mexico City. The leading group is crossing into Puebla just at this moment."

"Are you kidding me, Monica?" I said despairingly. I knew it was true as I watched the first bicycles whiz by. I still had a lot to learn about the Church. The Pope went to Oaxaca and we went back home.

The prophecy had also mentioned the heads of the Church and the bishops, but it did not say which bishops. So I had to make sure the letter was also given to Archbishop Ernesto Corripio Ahumada of Mexico City. Later, in the United States, it had to be given to my Archbishop, Joseph Bernardin of Cincinnati, who was the President of the U.S. Catholic Bishops Conference and later was the chairman of the committee of bishops in charge of the pastoral letters about nuclear weapons and war. I gave it also to George Fulcher, the auxiliary bishop of my city of Columbus, Ohio, who was later president of the bishops committee for spreading the Pastoral Letter. Then I gave it to my Bishop Edward Hermann, who later agreed to go on a peace walk and protest with me in front of Rockwell. Sometimes you *do* experience the surprise of seeing seeds you planted grow.

I was smiling to myself as Dorothy said, "Did you tell the story to many people? I hope not, because, you know, most do not believe in this type of prophecy."

"Dorothy, I have only given it to the reporter and Archbishop Pacheco of Puebla, who promised to give it to Pope John Paul II."

CHAPTER 21

GIVING GOD'S WORD TO THE CHURCH

We made copies of the prophecy and we handed them out to the Latin American bishops going into the Seminario Palafaxio in Puebla at CELAM III. I then went into the pressroom with my bought press pass.

A little dark bishop came up to me and asked most humbly,

"Will you help me tell the world about the murders and disappearance of thousands in El Salvador? I have proof. I am Oscar Romero."

I could not tell him my "newspaper" was two pages, so I took him to Roy Larson of the *Chicago Sun*, who listened as he documented the murder of the Salvadorans. Afterward Roy told me it could get the Archbishop killed. "They would never dare," I told him.

The next day the humble Archbishop Romero was back and again asked me to help him. You could not refuse to help him once you looked into his eyes. So this time I took him to Ken Briggs of the *New York Times*. The Archbishop convinced him that the squads had killed 30,000 people in E1 Salvador. Ken's editor told him it was not newsworthy.

Instead of eating, every day the Archbishop would come at lunchtime for me. Another time I took him to Jaime Fonseca of the Catholic News Service, who really did listen to Archbishop Romero.

Every time I listened to Romero I was struck by the sweet and humble tone of his begging, by his despair, and at the same time, by his obstinacy in wanting to help his people. Every day at lunchtime, when the other bishops were sitting at the lunch table, he would be back to speak to any international journalist who would listen to him.

CELAM III tried to stop Christian Base Communities from evolving into political camps where the doctrine of Liberation Theology would be preached to impoverished majorities. Oscar Romero, if asked, could list the tenets of this movement that now had over 100,000 "comunidades eclesiales de base" throughout Latin America. They work in the spirit of the Gospels and draw many ideas from Marxism. Some of its theologians identify the poor in the Gospel with the poor and landless today.

After CELAM III, the CIA began to pour billions of dollars in military aid into El Salvador, Guatemala, Nicaragua, Chile, and most of Latin America to fight these Christian communists. The Vatican poured so many millions into Argentina to stop the leftist- socialist takeovers that it collapsed the Banco Ambrosiano of Rome. The irony of it all is that it was Catholic priests who were the leaders of these rebels.

At home I could not find anything in the Prophecy that did not apply to the pure logic of Christ's teachings. As soon as I had given the letter to Archbishop Joseph Bernardin, I realized that everyone was going to consider me crazy. One day I would try to forget about it altogether, but the next day I would read it over and feel more convinced than ever. The first real trial I was facing was my own family. I wanted to take time and think about it, but my daughter Monica accidentally gave a copy of it to my nephew, Jimmy Siemer.

His family soon began to poke fun at me, and I was very upset. I felt that the Pope and the bishops should have been the first to know. One night my nephew Jimmy came to dinner. Jimmy was taking a course in the New Testament, and he was convinced too that a Christian who builds, uses, or justifies nuclear weapons not only fails to love his enemy but also fails to love his family and himself. That night at dinner Jimmy unexpectedly said, "I'll go with you, Uncle Tom, and help you spread the prophecy in the Church."

I finally had somebody on my side! Thank you, Lord, for this sign. I told Jimmy that I was going to trade in my new car and get a van to go across the USA appealing to each Catholic diocese and bishop, leafleting the churches and talking to bishops with the following:

THE MISSING PEACE

THIS WARNING WAS GIVEN TO POPE JOHN PAUL II AND THE CHRISTIAN CHURCH DURING THE POPE'S VISIT TO MEXICO IN 1979.

(Picture of)
LADY OF GUADALUPE
Queen of Peace

"Let these shameful weapons be banned. Let this terrible art, which consists of manufacturing, multiplying, and storing bombs to terrorize people, be outlawed."

Paul VI's Message on the 20th Anniversary of Hiroshima

(Text of the Prophecy follows)

Jimmy left Ohio State University, and on May 1, 1979, we embarked on our voyage across the United States with 500,000 pamphlets of the complete prophecy, which was called " The Missing Peace." We also had thousands of copies of an article by Fr. Richard McSorley, S.J., of the Georgetown University Peace Center, entitled "It's a Sin to Build a Nuclear Weapon." It described how most would die horribly if we had a nuclear war. The religious seemed to prefer the scientific facts and the scientists to relish religious moral doctrine.

I knew my wife would not be happy about our campaign, so I decided not to ask. I just did it. I was filled with zeal, and Jimmy was enthusiastic too! I had a reputation in the family for living an exciting life and he wanted to experience something different. He also was filled with the pure Gospel of nonviolence, just as it had been before the theologians and intellectuals got hold of it. My daughter Monica went with us to the first few dioceses.

We had tested our leafleting strategy at eight churches in Springfield, Ohio. We couldn't find the ninth and last one, and were driving out of town at eight p.m. when we saw a little church with open doors. Mass was being said inside. We put our literature on all the cars outside, and as I walked in the front door the Priest shouted the day's gospel from the pulpit, "Why did you doubt me, Thomas?" I wept.

We developed a pattern of action as we went from city to city. We would arrive at a new city on Monday morning and go directly to the Catholic diocesan newspaper, where Jimmy would tell them about his Uncle Tom and give them previous press clippings. I would then ask the editor or city desk man if he thought we'd all be destroyed if we fought a nuclear war. Then I would tell him that he had a duty as a journalist to tell the public of the great danger. We also went to the lay newspapers, but later in the week. Catholic papers all had a Monday or Tuesday deadline, because they were printed on Wednesday, mailed on Thursday, and in the churches by Friday or Saturday. This schedule couldn't be altered. If we were stopped from leafleting we would show them the newspaper article, or we would ask with indignation, "Didn't the bishop's office call you?" They would usually give us permission to continue.

We would park the van in the parking area of the biggest, best, and busiest motel in the city. Jimmy and I would rest on Monday afternoons. On Tuesday morning at poolside in the sun (we always went north in the summer and south in the winter), we would mark all the Catholic churches on a big city map in a spiral, working out from the center.

We had to start from the center because the poor people usually live in the inner city and go to Mass early before going to work. In the suburbs they always went to Mass later. We would go to five or six churches every weekday morning, and we would sleep in the van at the motels or the large all night drive-in restaurants. We had curtains that could slide around the glass in the van. Sometimes the police would try to see us with lights and rap on the van, but we would stay quiet and they'd leave us alone. There were also times when people would try to break in, and I would say in a deep slow voice, "I'm going to give you just two seconds to get your hand off that door or you're dead." They would disappear! They didn't know we were nonviolent pacifists.

We had time after masses at night to visit peace centers and peace people. But we usually went to Charismatic prayer meetings. We had bought an international guide to all the prayer groups with the contacts and locations. Jimmy would tell the leaders or core groups how his uncle had been called by the Holy Spirit to do peace work after he was freed from alcoholism and death and gave up his hypocrisy for Christ.

Then, of course, they would ask what my hypocrisy was. I would start telling them about the horrible weapons, anti-personnel "smart bombs," I helped to develop at Rockwell, which were used in Vietnam. And also about developing nuclear cruise missiles, which I proved were first-strike weapons.

"I had a year to live and the Lord saved me if I promised to work for peace. Alleluia! Praise the Lord!"

During the morning we would stuff all the pamphlets into the missals and song books and church periodicals inside the dark churches. Every once in a while we would be caught by a little old lady saying the rosary, who looked terrified, and we would have to explain to her satisfaction that we were legitimate servants of God.

On Fridays, or sometimes Thursdays, at noon, we would go into the bishop's office building (the chancery) on the pretext of seeing the Peace and Justice Director (who we could never find). We would hide in the men's room until all the secretaries went to lunch. Then we would sneak down the halls to the Bishop's or Cardinal's office and enter unannounced. He would look up as I asked him, "Do you believe we would all be destroyed if we fought a nuclear war?"

The answer was usually "Yes."

I would then say, "I am here to help you instruct your people that it is evil to plan for a nuclear war." The Bishop would usually listen at first and then answer in one of the following patterns: either "My son, we must have a balance of power," or "Nobody will ever use them—they're only for protection," or "Go tell it to the Russians—go to Moscow and tell them."

But most were just too busy and would send me to their Catholic newspaper or their Justice and Peace Commission. Some would say that they supported Pax Christi. Jimmy and I had never heard of it, nor could we find it, so we thought. it was some sort of a disease until we ran into some very strong groups in St. Louis, Chicago, and Washington, DC.

Jesus always said that a nonviolent Christian would have to be as clever as a serpent and as peaceful as a dove. If you are committed to nonviolence you really must be awfully clever—and awfully, awfully nice, nowadays. The early Christians used to dig catacombs underground in order to say Mass and worship. They had secret signs and codes.

Therefore, I never felt bad about using con game tactics to spread Christ's nonviolent gospel. Jesus said you would be persecuted if you taught the real Gospel, and you will be. So you better be clever, because Jesus was also against suicide.

Saturdays and Sundays were like a three-ring circus. It was really hard on our nerves sometimes to go to 60 and 70 Catholic churches without permission. We would dress like bankers—we got all our clothes from welfare stores. I was very stocky, and these stores had a better fit than my old well-known clothiers.

We would pass ourselves off as ushers if we arrived right before Mass. We leafleted until everyone went in, then we would take off as the congregation all turned to look at us at the same time. It took them about five minutes to get seated and to read the leaflets.

The article in the Catholic newspaper would help us, because we would show it to the ushers and priests. People would point at me as they recognized my picture in their paper. This way everyone thought we had the backing of the diocese and the bishop.

Once my dear wife agreed to help me pass out literature. She ended up being chased by a bishop across his lawn in

Northwest Washington, DC. He caught her, but we were armed with the truth.

The same Bishop caught me in the parking lot and said, "You have to take the leaflets off each car."

I looked at him, and as always, I said, "Do you believe we'll all be destroyed if we fight a nuclear war?"

He studied the leaflet and said, "Well, yes."

"That's all the literature says, Your Excellency. You have not given us permission to do this, but someone needs to do it. So when they come to you, just say you didn't give anyone permission and you won't be responsible. Look, I built nuclear weapons for 23 years at Rockwell and I was given a year to live, so I must do this."

He looked up as Jimmy continued leafleting the cars and said, "Forget it! God bless you!"

In Washington, DC we also appealed to Cardinal William Baum. I was talking to the Chancellor on the bottom floor, keeping him busy as Jimmy slipped up the stairs and down the hall. He opened a door and there was a man sitting at a desk working. He looked up at 19-year-old Jimmy and said, "What do you want?"

For the first time Jimmy was at a loss for words. He stammered out, "I am here to see the Cardinal."

"I am the Cardinal," the man said. Jim handed him the leaflet and ran!

After Cardinal Baum went to Rome, Archbishop James Hickey replaced him. We went to his Mass and reception for the southern half of the diocese, in St. Mary's, at the very tip of Maryland. We had talked to the Archbishop many times, and he really took a liking to my nephew Jimmy.

The Mass was being said in a space between two long driveways lined with trees. It was in front of a monastery. I drove down the left side and parked the van, which had a huge sign on it, at an angle next to the altar. Everyone turned to read "Catholic doctrine forbids me to register for a nuclear armed service. James E. Siemer." Jimmy was a military draft resister.

The sword-carrying Knights of Columbus immediately charged us in full uniform. I had told Jimmy to jump out and run as soon as we stopped, but they caught him. If it hadn't been for Marjorie Hyer of the *Washington Post* asking the photographers to take pictures, we would have been arrested in the communion line. We said we knew Archbishop Hickey, and I even showed them my Knights of Columbus membership card. When we got in line to meet Archbishop Hickey, we were under guard until he saw me and waved. The guards suddenly melted into the crowd when Hickey said, "It is good to see you, Jim and Tom."

I remember the time we went to Washington in 1979 for the U.S. Bishops Conference at the Capital Hilton Hotel. I was astonished to see huge expensive displays advertising the Army, Navy, Air Force, and Marines, each manned by two chaplains at all times. They were ranked all along the great golden mezzanine leading to the ornate conference hall. At the door by the entrance I saw a beautiful bronze table, so I took out my pamphlets and literature and placed them on the table. I sent Jimmy down to our van to get the posters we had used to appeal to the Pope in Des Moines, Iowa. We then dragged the table over to the door. Immediately the Hilton police seized us. Just at that moment Archbishop Tom Kelley came by, and I shouted, "Bishop, they say we cannot display for peace!" And I pointed to all the military displays.

The Archbishop, who was then executive secretary of the U.S. Bishops Conference said, "And why not?"

The Hilton police said again, "No displays allowed! Only the military!"

"Wait a minute, and I'll ask a higher authority."

He came back after a little while with an issued order to allow us to stay at the entrance. We took shifts and never left the table alone in five days for fear they would remove it. Other peace people came and gave us their literature too. I gave the prophecy to the Apostolic Nuncio, Archbishop Jean Jadot, who promised to give it to the Pope personally, and he did so in Rome. I have proof.

That night Jimmy and I leafleted over 2,000 Hilton hotel rooms in order to reach all the bishops. In every town or building, he would always take the even numbered floors and I the odd, which was perfectly natural. (As Flannery O'Connor once said, "You shall know the truth and the truth shall make you odd.") The next morning there were a lot of guests with pamphlets and disturbed faces appealing to the hotel management. At that Bishops Conference in November 1979, we had heard that the European NATO countries were going to vote within a month for the United States to deploy its first-strike Cruise and Pershing II missiles in Europe. I was shocked. How could they deny those missiles were first strike—especially the Cruise, a sneak attack weapon to strike the Russian missile silo? If Russia launched first, the silos would be empty. I could not believe that in 1979, Western Europe was going to allow this deployment. Didn't they realize the danger!

I told Jimmy that we must go to Rome and make sure that the Pope had received the prophecy from Mexico. Then I went to Ohio State University's language departments and got translations into Polish, French, Italian, Spanish, and German.

Professor Jerzy Krzyzanowski helped me rehearse the appeal in Polish so I could speak to the Pope, but all I could manage to remember was "Swiety Jan Pawel: Zabronic Bronie Nuklearne." I asked for and received letters from American bishops requesting a private audience for me with the Pope.

I was filled with confidence as I prepared for the trip. If the Pope got the prophecy, and if the technical reasons for the great danger were explained to him, he would surely ban nuclear weapons. I also had to get proof from my parish priest that I was a practicing Catholic. That was certainly a crazy rule. I wondered if the Pope only saw practicing Catholics!

Then we got to Rome by way of Iceland and Luxembourg. We immediately went to the North American Catholic College's tourist branch hotel, called Casa de Maria. We saw a Polish nun named Sister Irene Soberjer and really impressed her with the letters from the American bishops.

"We are going to give you and your nephew special passes so you can see the Pope," she said. After having also talked to Father Vincent O'Keefe, second in command of Casa Generalitia Jesuitas, at 5 Borgo San Spirito, we went to dinner.

We felt very honored walking across St. Peter's Square as we were directed and into the Nervi Auditorium for our private audience with the Pope. But where were all these other people going? We were directed to the front section of a huge hall. "Is this the private audience?" I asked. "There must be 6,000 people in here!"

I went down to the second row and sent Jimmy back farther along the center aisle. The Pope came in the back entrance, and as he got close I was cut out by three little nuns who elbowed through and sneaked right between me and the rail. So I whipped out the big sign I had folded and hidden in my coat and flashed it in front of him. "Dear John Paul II, please ban nuclear weapons ex Cathedra. Change the course of history!" I had never seen such a pained look on the Pope's face, or such an expression of hatred as was on his assistant's face.

I stuck the sign back in my coat quickly as the guards looked for it.

The Pope went up the marble steps and sat on his throne. Some private audience I am having with the "Servant of Servants," I thought. I gradually became exasperated as the Pope spent one whole hour talking about sex. I had a priest next to me who laughingly interpreted what he was saying in Italian. The world is about to be destroyed by nuclear weapons and he worries about sex and contraceptives and the details of the rhythm system!

I looked at the prophecy I had in my hands. It was in Polish, but I knew every word by heart. I looked back at the Pope and I remembered the promise I had made to personally give it to him. I realized that this was the closest I was ever going to get to him. It was now or never.

The people stood up for a benediction and I noticed the seats were set in concrete. I was just five seats from the end. Should I? I'll probably get shot. I'm going to do it anyway!

I prayed and a great peace came over me as I made up my mind to run up to the Pope. When the people stood up again, I was going to run on top of the seats, jump the barricade, sprint up to him, and give him the Missing Peace Prophecy.

I saw that the front guards were looking in opposite directions. I was over the barricade as if in a Walter Mitty dream. I ran between the guards and up the steps, expecting a shot to ring out any minute. The Pope tried to shelter himself from my knife as 6,000 people screamed. The knife turned out to be a Polish letter of peace. I knelt at his feet, putting the prophecy in his hands. He was quite relieved, and soon called the Swiss guards off of me one by one with a protest, "No, No, No!" As I stood in front of him, he said, "I bless you in your work," in deep guttural English, then motioned me off to the right.

Now I had to deal with the Vatican police. They questioned me and were surprised when they searched me to find the letters of introduction from the U.S. Catholic Bishops. I could see them discuss it and make gestures. They seemed unable to decide what they were going to do with me. After half an hour or so, the phone rang. The Chief said, "Si, Signore!" He showed me the door and ordered one of his men to take me to a gate on the other side of the Vatican—the museum side. The gate opened and I was free. I took off fast and kept on running for a while. I knew the Vatican police often let people go through that gate only to hand them over to the Italian police, but this time, nothing of the kind happened. I went back to the pensione where my friends were waiting. It was January 16, 1980. We celebrated our victory.

The next day the Italian newspapers said I had been taken to jail for my own good. Both English and American papers gave the same version. They did not state my cause, only that I was an American. They didn't give my name. They said I was in jail for safekeeping. I knew it was only a matter of time before it would be true.

I did not like the situation. I had given my message to the Pope and had no desire now to end up in jail instead of going back to my family.

After much discussion and consternation, Jimmy and I agreed that I should leave, or in other words, run, in case the police came after me. It seemed the most reasonable solution. I decided to go first to Father O'Keefe at the Jesuit House and ask for his advice and help.

As I reached his street, Borgo Santo Spirito, I saw a police car waiting in front of the Jesuit Headquarters. I immediately took the first train I saw at the station. It went to Naples. There was a sign in the Naples station directing me downstairs to a train to Sorrento. I stayed for a day in Sorrento until I saw a newspaper with my picture on the front page. I bought it and caught a bus over the mountains to Positano. A day later I went by bus to Amalfi.

If I stayed only one night in a hotel I did not have to give them my passport. I remembered Arafat of the PLO saying, "Never sleep in the same bed twice and they will never catch you."

In beautiful Amalfi I got a room in a pensione. It was on a back street, but my front window overlooked the town square and the cathedral. I did not have to show my passport, so I stayed three weeks with a family who owned the pensione and hid me.

In the meantime, dear Jimmy had gotten the U.S. Embassy to help find me by first going to the jail I was supposed to be in. I was not there, and the press, with Jimmy's help, immediately picked up on the story of my mysterious disappearance.

With the help of Jerry Filteau of the Catholic News Service, Jimmy was able to keep my story on the front page for three weeks. The articles clearly stated the great danger of the nuclear Cruise missile deployment in Italy and told my whole story.

I then decided to leave Italy without going back to Rome. I chose to cross the border to the French side close to Genoa. I bought a cheap skiing trip to the Alps. I had noticed on the pamphlet that there is no direct route from the Italian coastline to Limone, and the train to Limone Piemonte had to go into France, then back into Italy. We had to change trains right on the border, so I got off and passed the checkpoint walking, side by side with a German tourist loaded with suitcases. I kindly volunteered to help him to carry his skis and boots, and the station police did not even ask for my passport. I was now on French soil.

That was the beginning of my tour around Europe. I had decided to warn the whole of Europe of the danger of first-strike nuclear weapons. What a task! The first time I ordered 10,000 pamphlets in Marseilles, I couldn't speak a word of French.I looked up and down the street until I saw a sign that said "IMPRIMERIE OFFSET." I went inside and came out a half hour later having ordered the pamphlets printed in French from a guy who could not speak a word of English, and having ordered them folded. My arms were tired from miming the words.

I remember Paris, and the first time I leafleted on Sunday in front of Notre Dame Cathedral. I would leaflet for 10 minutes to the people going in the entrance at the right-hand door. Then I would hide my pamphlets inside my coat, go to the exit on the left-hand side, and leaflet until the people coming out had the pamphlets in their hands. Then I would go back to the other entrance and leaflet again, alternating. I saw three priests looking about for me, so I went and got a cup of coffee. Then I continued the same procedure over again until the police made it impossible.

At the second cycle of door changes I heard a police siren coming toward the Cathedral. As I reached the coffee shop across the street, five gendarmes unloaded rapidly from a van and ran towards the doors. After 15 minutes they left and I continued the procedure, only this time inside the Cathedral, about halfway down the church, from behind a pillar. I had learned to keep changing positions every five minutes and to pull the pamphlets out of my inside coat pocket. I was just stepping through the doors again as eight gendarmes ran in. Finally it got too hot, or I was too "hot," to continue, so I went to the Sacre Coeur church on Montmartre. There, I continued the same procedure as at Notre Dame until the police showed up.

I went to Saint Denis, and this time the police didn't bother me, but the prostitutes did. The Pastor at Saint Denis had a calling to evangelize the prostitutes who worked the five streets around his church. He had large posters and pamphlets calling for the girls to join his conversion program: off their backs and into legal professions! I went out the side door of Saint Denis and had to walk five blocks past all these beautiful ladies ready and waiting, but it was Sunday and I was a good Christian.

In Madrid, all the big, well-to-do Catholic churches were in the Falange or Fascist areas. The Communists, having lost the Civil War, were consigned to the slums of the southern part of the city. Their churches were rooms in apartment buildings and slum wrecks. I was well received there, even during my accidental visit to the Communist Party headquarters. The leader got a great laugh out of it, but still ordered the members to help me leaflet the churches. They reluctantly complied. The Falange areas were in northeast and west Madrid, and they were tough. Here, of course, the pamphlet was in Spanish.

I devised a plan to leaflet the Catholic churches in Madrid which consisted of taking a cab to all the churches in the neighborhood while the cabby waited. Then he would rush me to the subway, I would race across town and get five more churches by cab, then I would rush on to another section by subway. The last church I went to in Madrid, which was across from the American Embassy, must have been warned, because there were police all over the place. I got inside without being seen and leafleted in the usual way. Mass was over, and I saw a sunlit golden door at one side. As I made my way toward it to leave, I passed four priests standing by their confessionals, so I gave them each a leaflet. My bravery was a mistake, because the exit went into a sealed patio. I turned immediately to go back through the church, but two strong custodians trapped me in the back of the church, and as I pulled free to go out, one guard struck me with his fist in the back and knocked me down. The people coming out of Mass looked astounded as I fell to the steps. I got up and the other one shoved me while both were calling at me, "Communist propaganda!"

As I said, "No, Jesus Christ's propaganda," they knocked me down again. I struggled to the corner, turned it, then ran as fast as I could to the next alley, and kept turning at alleys until I saw a coffee shop. I ran to it and walked into the far back and half hid. I was shaking until I suddenly recalled the words of Christ, "Rejoice when they persecute you and beat you for my sake, because they also did that to the prophets; they did it to me." Rejoice in this situation! I wondered whether it was right to cause so much hatred. Then I looked up and saw a crucifix, and I wept for joy. I guess it was because I realized it was the first time I had ever suffered bodily for my belief in Christ. Remembering that He said we must suffer persecution as the first Christians did, I was truly filled with joy.

In Koln, Frankfurt, and Bonn I used the same procedures, but the German Catholics were even less tolerant than the Spanish.

I followed with Belgium. The Netherlands had many peace organizations, so I was well received and spoke everywhere at conferences.

I treasured anybody who was loving. I had nobody, so everyone I met I loved with my whole heart, and they seemed to sense it, even though I didn't speak their language.

I left Belgium by ferry for London. When I got off the train at Victoria Station I saw a sign that pointed to Westminster Cathedral. I knew it was one of the few Catholic cathedrals of England. It was Saturday night so I leafleted the evening mass. On Sunday I went back to leaflet the Cathedral (and Cardinal Basil Hume's house also). I kept moving from door to door in the Cathedral until a priest suddenly caught me and asked, "What are you passing out?" He grabbed my pamphlet, which had a picture of the Blessed Virgin on the front. I could tell he couldn't see. He wore glasses an inch thick, poor man, and held the pamphlet one centimeter from his eyes. "Father, it's a devotional prayer to our dear Blessed Mother,"

I said.

He looked at it, gave a smile, and said, "Well, if you see any communists passing out stuff come in and get me. I'll be by this door." "God bless you, Father!" I shouted after him.

I loved the Irish because they were either in church or in the bar next door. The churches were open every day all through the week. There were many well-attended masses—ideal places for leafleting.

Eventually I decided the time had come to go back to the States and continue the appeal to American bishops. Jimmy was waiting for me. I have so much to thank him for! He sacrificed a lot. He even had the church organize a Mass at the Cathedral for me.

We immediately went to Chicago, where the yearly bishops conference was about to start. I don't have much to report about that conference apart from our amazement at hearing the beginning of Cardinal Cody's opening speech, He was apologizing to the bishops for having not yet had the usual bottles of wine and fine liqueurs placed in their hotel rooms.

Again we traveled from diocese to diocese, but I had to stop for a while in Texas to sell my winter house. The money was never enough for the peace movement. It was the only property my wife gladly allowed me to sell. She had always felt lonely when we spent our winters in Port Isabel, because she was a talkative, warm person and most of the regular inhabitants only spoke Spanish. She also greatly missed her family. I made a lot of money from the sale, but my wife had an active part in spending it fast. She thought if I ran out of money I would come home and find a job again. She wanted me next to her, but she also wanted me to live according to her view of a good Christian rather than mine, that of a crazy prophet.

When I went home to my family they were always very happy to see me. I continued to mail the Voice's message to the Pope, and to all of the bishops of the Church.

We were now into 1980 and almost four years had gone by since I was supposed to die of cirrhosis of the liver. I had almost forgotten about my impending death, since I was now free of the fear of dying in a state of sin. Getting rid of the hypocrisy had almost completely eliminated my yearning for alcohol, and my liver had gradually recuperated, I guess. Anyway, I was filled with energy and enthusiasm.

Speaking the truth always gives one great joy. It was such a change for me to work with people committed to peace and love after so many years in the dog-eat-dog atmosphere at Rockwell— and all the killing in Vietnam.

I had grown a beard, which was surely due to an unconscious desire for physical evidence of the change that had occurred within me. I really was a different man now, and my wife had a very difficult time getting accustomed to this man.

It was painful for me to see shadows of disapproval gradually growing on my daughters' and Dorothy's faces. During all those years at Rockwell I had enjoyed—and needed—their total love and admiration. They had even overlooked my drinking because they knew I was totally reliable. I had never once failed to respond to their physical needs or requests.

Now, not only had I stopped making money for the family, but I was spending it fast for peace and they were beginning to suffer from it—mostly Monica. She was extremely intelligent and really wanted to go to college. I had talked her out of it. "Who needs another intellectual at a time when nuclear war is threatening to destroy us all?" She was really too young to accept my priorities and go around the country in a van crusading for peace, so I think she resented me for a long time. She finally settled down to work for the Georgetown University Peace Center with Father McSorley. The other children accepted my poverty. I used to tell Monica that no dummies without degrees ever designed or built a nuclear missile. The "intelligentsia," I told her, is responsible for all these weapons of mass destruction.

By the end of 1980 all my children had organized their lives except little Susanna.

Maria had married Ron Horn, the wonderful boy whom she had helped start a Charismatic religious community for the youth at St. Rita's Camp. They had an outside wedding in August and it poured down on hundreds of guests just as the priest gave the final blessing. I cried and cried at the wedding, because Maria was my first daughter and the first to get married. I hated to "give her away."

Maria had always been levelheaded but also capable of having a good time. She was famous for throwing the biggest party in the history of her school. She had invited the whole school (500 students) to our property across the street from home on the occasion of the school winning the state basketball championship. They won the next year too. She managed to get married despite all my efforts to discourage my daughters' boyfriends. I always talked very coldly to them and pretended I couldn't remember their names. You have to do that when four of your daughters are homecoming beauty queens!

Tina had wanted to be a movie star since she was born. She always wanted to wear lipstick and make-up to school when she was a little girl. Every morning her mother would wipe off her make- up, and every morning the two of them had a fight over it, until I found the answer. One day, as I drove her to school, I pointed out that there was a nice little mirror in the car and it would be wiser for her to make up after she left the house. Tina lost her self-centeredness and limelight dreams when religion entered her life, and it changed her whole character. She married and all of a sudden she was ready to accept the heavy responsibilities of being a mother. From then on family came first for her, as it always did for her own mother.

Lisa, the lovable heart, was studying to become a nurse. I know each of her patients will be looked after with the greatest warmth and dedication. I know that every time a patient of hers dies some of her will die with them.

Marcia was looking around for a good job at the time. I always have to laugh when I remember her as a child. She could never be threatened to do something. Spanking her would do no good. You had to reason with her heart, and then she would gladly obey.

My son Tommy was a Christian, one who never said a word against my calling. He was dedicating his whole life to social work with simplicity and a great heart.

My nephew Jimmy returned to America. He thought and operated in every way as I did, except I was a religious fanatic on a guilt trip and he wanted to do things normally. He went to the Ohio University at Athens.

He wanted to enjoy life a little bit. He wanted to live, and I really didn't. I guess I wanted to be a martyr. I don't blame him for his choice. He is now giving conferences about his experience as a conscientious objector. He managed to get hold of slides showing a vast selection of nuclear weapons. He got them from the Pentagon files using a trick. He pretended to be the aide to some general who needed the slides to explain the lecture he was going to give that night. (Jimmy had overheard him discussing the lecture.) Can you imagine the face of the General when he found out eventually that his slides were being used for pacifist conferences!

I decided to create a Peace Center in the basement of the Church of the Holy Family, 584 West Broad Street, in Columbus, Ohio. It was supposed to be a fund-raising center to help finance my peace campaign.

The Parish priest, Father Francis Schweitzer, had offered me the use of this place. It was adequate as an office and had many rooms for conferences. So I set up my desk and files there happily, but for me this was only a parenthesis. My principal goal was still the appeal to the Church and the Pope with the prophecy.

I had no money at the time. I had already spent $100,000 of my own money going around the United States in my appeal to the bishops. My wife was fighting any new expense with all her strength.

A Buddhist peace group came to town on a pilgrimage. They wanted to demonstrate in front of Rockwell, and John Myer tried to convince me to give a speech, since I had worked there. I didn't feel like doing it. I didn't feel I had the right to point the finger at the people who had been my colleagues for 23 years. I didn't feel I was less guilty than they were. My responsibility was proportionate to the management job I had performed in the missile division. Yet on the day of the demonstration, there I was, in front of the gates at Rockwell, asking myself how I could convince my former colleagues to change professions. I knew they would have to be forced to stop building nuclear weapons.

Rockwell was now building the B-1B supersonic nuclear bomber. I knew its design was already 12 years old when they began to build it. The Pentagon had awarded the B-1B bomber contract to Rockwell because it was the only company with experience. North American Rockwell had built the previous B-70 supersonic bomber. The B-70 could hardly stay together on the ground and was barely able to fly to the Air Force Museum at the Wright-Patterson AFB, Dayton, Ohio. Someday I expect that a great scandal will be made public involving the B-1B nuclear bomber that was supposed to take the place of the current, 35- year-old B-52 bomber.

All the states were now organizing nuclear freeze organizations out of the National Freeze Campaign office. The Freeze Movement in Ohio was centered at Holy Family.

My former colleagues were the least appropriate people to talk to. We had to convince the farmer, the baker, the students, and the retired people that they had nothing to gain from the production of nuclear weapons—that the 50,000 nuclear weapons in the world were already more than enough to destroy it 10 times over. If we could make ordinary people really be aware of this, popular opinion would put pressure on the government to accept the Freeze. Then, later, an industrial conversion would automatically come about. If Rockwell, for instance, couldn't build any more missiles, would they fold up and go out of business? No! You better believe they would immediately propose to design and build huge rockets to load 40 nuclear warheads and launch them to the sun, where they would explode harmlessly. In other words, if forced to, they would begin to invent all sorts of new things for peace— synthetic foods, rapid transit, whatever. You can't keep a good capitalist down.

I too had to surrender to the evidence that totally giving up nuclear weapons was premature. It required too deep a culture change. For the time being I had to concentrate my efforts on the very simple and primary platform of the Freeze Campaign. Of course the American war industry immediately started to fight us with all its resources.

Richard Celeste, the new Governor of Ohio, supported the Freeze Campaign. His wife Dagmar joined us on a peace march to Rockwell. They were in trouble.

In October of 1981 I took another trip to Europe to appeal to the Pope, to participate in the great peace marches against the Cruise and the Pershing II, and to attend a conference in Nassogne, Belgium, as coordinator of Pax Christi Ohio, our state chapter of the international Catholic peace movement.

Pope John Paul did react, but politically rather than spiritually. He sent teams of well-known scientists associated with the Pontifical Academy of Sciences to meet with world leaders, including President Reagan and the late Soviet President Leonid Brezhnev. The text of their message: "The conditions of life following a nuclear attack would be so severe that the only hope for humanity is prevention of any form of nuclear war."

But the real miracle that originated the Catholic Bishops' Peace Pastoral occurred at the bishops' conference in Washington, DC, on November 1980. Certain peace bishops had proposed to the assembly that the conference should issue a statement on the immorality of nuclear weapons. Two notable military-chaplain- type archbishops, Hannah of New Orleans and Cardinal Cook of New York (who was the Military Vicariate over all chaplains), spoke against the move on the grounds that it was interfering with the defense and political policies of the government. They said the bishops had no right to do this. I was so happy that I wept when I saw most of the bishops respond immediately by rising from their seats voicing protests. Then the president of the conference agreed to name a committee to draft a pastoral letter concerning Christian morality in regard to nuclear weapons. I knew that once these honest spiritual leaders committed themselves to face the issue they would be compelled by their honesty to seek the truth and spread it—no matter how painful the answer might be.

On that day I knew the U.S. Catholic Bishops were going to condemn nuclear weapons as being immoral. Before the next bishops conference I was able to talk to the chairman of the pastoral committee, Archbishop Joseph Bernardin, at Notre Dame and outside the Vatican in Rome at Villa Stritch. The Rome meeting occurred just two weeks before the November 1981 meeting of the bishops in DC. The Archbishop was concerned about the committee being neutralized by Bishop Gumbleton (a pacifist) on one side, and Bishop O'Connor (in favor of nuclear weapons) on the other side. (Bishops Fulcher and Reilly were neutral at the time.) Bernardin stated that he didn't want to chair this committee because he already headed the Canon Law Committee. I told him point blank that the pastoral was the most important thing he had to do in his life.

We talked of this serious task as two friends for over an hour.

Two weeks later the Archbishop issued a very strong statement. It was the beginning of the November 1981 U.S. Catholic Bishops Conference. It was also at that conference that I talked my friend, Chief Milo Yellow Hair, and his partner, Glen David, into marching their Indians for Peace through the lobby of the Washington DC Capital Hilton Hotel and into the U.S. Catholic Bishops Conference. As the Indian drums died down, the conference secretary agreed to have a press conference and hear the Indians' peace appeal—after all, they were American citizens, too. I had marched with the Indians across Ohio, and Milo, who was the nicest, biggest, ugliest Indian I ever loved like a brother, owed me a favor.

It worked so well that the next day I got my friend Utsumi, whom I had helped to lead a Buddhist pilgrimage across Ohio, to come to the hotel. He arrived with his Buddhist friends and they beat their prayer drums in the Hilton lobby until the Bishops agreed to hold another press conference, this time to hear the Buddhists' appeal! During the following year I continued to appeal to all Catholic religious orders, particularly the good religious Sisters, to write to their bishops in support of a strong Pastoral against nuclear weapons. The women's orders were the most active religious group in the peace movement.

While a million people were preparing to march in New York on June 12, 1982, I arrived at St. John's Abbey in Collegeville, Minnesota, instead. I was very disappointed to miss the march, but as usual my duty was with the bishops. I parked my crazy van, with large signs appealing to them, in the middle of their private conclave. I felt like a fool for three days as I hid in the bushes and popped out to talk to the bishops as they walked between buildings. Archbishop Bernardin came out to my van looking for me. He called my name and I came out of the bushes to see him.

He proudly showed me a copy of the first draft, and for some strange reason, instead of rejoicing, I asked him if it could still be changed. He acted surprised but said the first draft could still be changed by the bishops. Ten minutes later the college alumni association was trying to have my van towed away.

We peace people were not happy with the first draft that Archbishop Bernardin had showed me, which was later issued at the closed meeting of the bishops in Collegeville. I immediately helped form a coalition of Catholic Workers and peace groups, and tried to enlist the aid of the National Freeze and the Bethlehem Peace Pilgrimage. The pilgrimage was led by Father Jack Morris and Father George Zabelka, who had been the Hiroshima bombing crew's Catholic chaplain. I had initially made up a large flyer imploring Catholics to write or contact their bishops for a stronger pastoral letter calling for an immediate halt to the production, deployment, and use of nuclear weapons. The coalition was later named the "Catholic Bishops' Freeze Appeal," and the flyer was sent out to all Catholic organizations and religious orders.

The Bethlehem Peace Pilgrimage walked in all of the towns and cities from Kansas to Washington, DC, handing out this flyer. We planned for the pilgrimage to arrive in DC the day before the bishops conference opened. We would walk around the White House first and then to the Capitol Hilton for an all night prayer vigil for the bishops. The Bethlehem Peace Pilgrimage did not get much publicity as such, but pictures of the march ended up in *Time* and *Newsweek* and in all the papers across the country.

The Church was slow as ever, but a few bishops were starting to support the Freeze. Archbishop Raymond Hunthausen was the first to promote tax resistance, and Bishop Matthiesen promoted work resistance.

I traveled around Ohio starting new sections of the Freeze. In every city, I arrived with the addresses of two or more people who had worked for the Reverse Arms Race. I called them on the phone and asked them to add more names to my list until we organized a meeting of interested people in a restaurant, a good old American tradition. Following this method I instigated peace groups in 42 cities.

The U.S. House of Representatives passed the nuclear Freeze, but it failed in the Republican majority-controlled Senate.

At the United Nations in 1982, 118 countries voted for the Freeze in production of nuclear weapons. Only twelve countries voted against it and with the United States.

Maryknoll missionary priest and great peace activist Roy Bourgeois telephoned me one day and asked me if his film crew could come to Columbus and begin making a film about my conversion from war to peace work. He asked me to find him a church with lots of light and said that he would arrive in Columbus by plane on Saturday.

I said "Sure" thinking he was joking as always. But he called me back that night and wanted me to talk to his director, Robert Richter, who said, "Tom, I need a church with lot of stained glass. And I also need a demonstration at Rockwell."

It just so happened that Hermann and Fulcher, the Bishops of Columbus, were walking with us to Rockwell that week by way of a protest at the abortion clinic. I said. "Great! Meet us at the airport with a van."

They arrived and the whole crew stayed at my house for 10 days. Roy loved my family, especially my 9-year-old "Susanna Banana," as he called her. Much to my surprise the film, entitled *Gods of Metal*, was nominated for an Academy Award in the documentary category. Fr. Bourgeois went on to organize and then lead the protests against the School of the Americas (since renamed), which teaches and trains Latin America militaries in the art of population control by torture and other immoral, oppressive measures, including assassinations like that of Archbishop Oscar Romero and many other religious. Fr. Bourgeois has been engaged in numerous peaceful, creative non-violent actions, which resulted in many months of prison time. Today he is still continuing to lead that organization from just outside Ft. Benning Army Post in Columbus, Georgia, and continues educating people on this issue around the country. He is the greatest!

GODS OF METAL

PRODUCED BY ROY BOURGEOIS

MARYKNOLL FILMS,
MARYKNOLL, NY
DIRECTED BY ROBERT RICHTER MA

And the Lord told Moses to
say to the community:

"Do not abandon me and worship Idols. Do not make gods of metal and worship them. I am your Lord and God." Leviticus 19

A 27-minute documentary about the nuclear arms race and people of faith who are trying to stop it

NOMINATED FOR MOTION PICTURE ACADEMY AWARD, 1982

The arms race is analyzed from a Christian perspective, showing the economic and social effects on people in the United States and the Third World, especially the poor.

The film shows what individuals and groups are doing to halt the arms build-up and gives practical suggestions on what each of us can do to help create a world of peace.

GODS OF METAL SPEAKER

TOM SIEMER, witnessing before the Rockwell International Columbus Division, is one individual in the film who has converted from war to peace work. Tom was a "Charter Member" of Missile Administration and worked there for 23 years before leaving in 1976 to work full-time for peace. "The B1-B nuclear bomber—able to

> fly under radar—and our missile guidance systems—now with such incredible accuracy requirements—could only mean that *THE PENTAGON IS DEVELOPING A FIRST STRIKE NUCLEAR ARSENAL. WHY WOULD YOU WANT TO HIT AN EMPTY RUSSIAN MISSILE SILO?*
>
> For reservations write or call the ENVIRONMENTAL PEACE ACADEMY.

Then, the pastoral committee released the U.S. bishops' powerful second draft of the Peace Pastoral. Without naming the Nuclear Weapons Freeze Campaign, the draft enthusiastically endorsed its platform. This was a direct stand against the nuclear weapons policies of President Reagan and Company. Catholic peace groups were happy with the second draft of the pastoral letter.

The Reagan Administration immediately launched a campaign against the draft. Three counter-freeze Catholic "peace organizations" were suddenly formed. The bishops still voted in favor of the draft 199 to 12, with 68 voting to accept it with minor changes. But then I was shocked by the complacency of the peace movement. They all thought that since the bishops had already issued an acceptable, strong pastoral letter draft, there was no danger of their slipping backward. But having worked at Rockwell, I knew that billions of dollars were at stake for the military-industrial complex. I knew they would not hesitate to spend a few million to stop a nuclear weapons freeze. I also knew that the millions of militarists in the Catholic Church (along with millions in other Christian churches) were still in shock and had yet to voice their reaction. In fact, President Reagan immediately tried to force the hands of the Bishops with maneuvers such as new statements on prayer in schools and tax reduction for families who send their children to private Catholic schools.

You can see why I insisted and insisted we should keep up public pressure on the bishops and on the Pope.

Being on the Ohio State Nuclear Weapons Freeze staff since its beginning, I immediately contacted the National Freeze Clearinghouse in St. Louis end begged them to send out an urgent appeal to the Catholic bishops to endorse at least the Freeze, if not all of Christ's teachings. I was finally invited to conduct a full workshop on how to lobby the Catholic bishops at the National Nuclear Freeze Conference to be held in St. Louis on February 4-6, 1983. I again sent out flyers to all the Freeze groups across the country and to all the Catholic religious orders and peace groups.

We were able to form a network of Catholic activists across the country by following up on contacts after the workshop. But the bishops, at least according to Bishop Hoffman of Toledo, Ohio, were still getting letters three to one against the strong peace language of the second draft. A coalition called Catholics for Peace had been formed in Chicago by 117 Catholic organizations, yet I still begged everyone to do more. It was now or never.

Most of the National Nuclear Weapons Freeze Campaign remained sleepily unconcerned until the pastoral committee issued the third pastoral draft on April 1, 1983. They were shocked to find that the Bishops' Pastoral Committee had changed the Freeze's call to HALT the production, deployment, and design of new nuclear weapons systems to the much milder CURB. They were also extremely puzzled to see that the bishops' committee again "tolerated" NATO's first use of nuclear weapons in case of an attack with conventional weapons by the Soviets.

The Reagan Administration and Catholic militarists appeared to have won. But truth has a funny way of imposing itself on people who are committed to honesty.

The peace people began to stir and slowly regenerated the zeal they had deployed before the victory of the Pastoral's second draft. Thousands of Catholics—and Protestants—began to write and contact the bishops. The Pastoral Committee quickly issued a statement that the word *halt* would be used again in place of *curb*. It was a sign of things to come. The Spirit was moving.

On the morning of April 25, my friend Gary Houser and I loaded my van for the trip to Chicago. On our arrival we had a meeting with the leadership of the 8th Day Center for Justice Freeze people and the AFSC (Friends) of Chicago. The next day we had more meetings with Pax Christi's Fr. Jim Gower, and other leaders at the national headquarters, and then with the newly formed coalition of Catholics for Peace. We obtained thousands of flyers announcing the prayer ser vice at Seneca Park and the pilgrimage to the bishops' conference at the Palmer House Hotel. I couldn't understand why many wanted to direct it to the Federal Building Plaza instead. They were timid. I guess I used to be timid with the bishops too, in the beginning.

Gary and I went around to all of the Catholic colleges, particularly De Paul and Loyola, leafleting and urging people to attend the pilgrimage and the vigils. I had the largest signs ever on my van, and during rush hours we toured the downtown Loop areas. Thousands of people saw our huge appeal to the bishops.

I sweated blood writing a final appeal letter to the bishops. I was in extreme distress every time I tried to write the bishops a letter to hand out at their conferences. They, however, always expected one from me. I think they had grown accustomed to me. But how far can your appeal go without being disrespectful? I just had to let the bishops know that they must speak the truth in regard to Christ's teachings and nuclear weapons or lose all credibility as leaders of the Christian Church. Imagine trying to say this in a nice way!

> Dear Bishops, Apostolic Successors,
>
> By taking on this topic of nuclear weapons, you have boldly moved yourselves and our church into the world as a focus of moral leadership, and have been seen as such in many countries. [We were careful to praise them first!] You have not only created focus, you have provided hope. You have told all that the Catholic Church is capable of taking on moral issues that few really want to touch and honestly debate, and you have shown that the issue can and should be pursued until there is but a single answer: a yes or no. In this age of weaponry capable of the mass murder of millions of innocent civilians, the issue is stark, and the answer is equally stark: NO! Christianity must now apply the absolute—not the absolution—to the making, deployment, and threatened use of nuclear weapons. If you, through qualification and argument, permit the making, deployment, and use of nuclear weapons by Christians, you will have become "blind guides." Your arguments will be no different however theological than the arguments around nuclear weapons "counting" when sufficient already exist to kill everyone a hundred times over.

Peacemakers for Christ—Thomas Siemer & Gary Houser

As we drove my van around downtown Chicago, people who saw it in the movie *Gods of Metal* would wave to me and say, "I saw you in the movie! God bless you," or, "Keep it up!" It brought me to tears a couple of times. Since the healing of Susanna and since I was in the peace movement I had learned to cry. Now tears often came to my eyes as I accepted alternately the experience of intense happiness or intense distress, instead of removing all emotion or blocking things out of my mind as I used to do at Rockwell. These shameless tears were a great joy and liberation.

On Saturday, April 30th, I tried to call up anyone I knew who could be influential in lobbying the bishops for peace. On Sunday we went to the Palmer House at 8:00 a.m. to see if we could find some peace bishops coming in early. I still had to get some bishops to agree to present thousands of signed petitions. Sixteen peace bishops had been contacted and asked to receive them and to speak, but no one was coming in early on Saturday except a few "hawks." I asked Bishops O'Connor and Ahern and Cardinal Cook, but all three refused.

God must test the endurance of peace people, because rain started to pour down as soon as the prayer service at Seneca Park began. Then followed a pantomime. Did you ever try to watch a peace pantomime group in a rainstorm? I was thinking we needed some hot oratory instead. Still, 2000 souls stayed on. It was a witness to perseverance for peace.

I went to the staff of the U.S. Catholic Bishops' Conference to get my customary press pass. I had acted like a "real gentleman" at the past November meeting because of the strong second draft. I felt like doing something crazy again this time, but I promised that if they gave me a pass I would behave. They are a great bunch of most capable people. They were hesitant at first, but the word came down from above to allow me in the conferences.

The Benedictine Sisters for Peace had a prayer vigil that night, and had invited me. I was so tired that after my head nodded a few times I went over and lay down in a corner. I slept from midnight until 6:00 a.m.—the fastest all-night prayer vigil I ever attended.

On Monday morning at 9:00 a.m. the bishops celebrated the liturgy of the Mass in the light of 27 television cameras. We had decided to pass out our strong letter to the bishops as they went into their first conference, because there was only one door there.

The letter was folded so the picture of a crucified Christ by Rembrandt was on the cover, on quality paper. A message was also printed in huge letters which must have struck them right in the eye. Dear Bishops: DO NOT BECOME AS BLIND GUIDES WHO STRAIN OUT THE GNATS AND SWALLOW THE CAMEL, WHO BAN CONTRACEPTIVES AND ALLOW NUCLEAR WEAPONS!

We had chosen the role of prophets since everyone else was trying to be nice. We did smile a big peace smile when we gave it to them. Only a very few Bishops appeared startled and none of them attempted to tear it up. How could a bishop ever tear up the picture of a crucifix in public?

On Monday we were joined in our lobbying efforts by the great peace theologian and author, Richard T. McSorley, SJ of Georgetown University. I was glad to see my friend Dick because he had so much influence with many of the Bishops. Father Fran Meehan, a likewise distinguished and friendly theologian from St. Charles Borromeo in Philadelphia, showed up with Mary Lou Kownacki and Anne McCarthy, both Benedictine nuns.

The formal bishops conference started at 11:00 a.m. with an address by the President, Archbishop Roach, followed by motions to limit debate for the numerous planned amendments. Other rules to speed up the process were accepted by the body. Archbishop Joseph Cardinal Bernardin then gave an address in support of a stronger pastoral letter.

As soon as they assembled after lunch they proposed to debate and vote on the amendment to change the wording from *curb* back to *halt* the construction of new nuclear weapons systems.

A vote was called to accept the whole pastoral letter. Archbishop Roach called for a secret ballot vote, and by a margin of 238 to 9 the U.S. Catholic Bishops changed the course of history. The greatest decision by Christians not to fight war in over 1,600 years was made in Chicago on May 3, 1983. The Catholic Bishops in so many words had decided that Catholics may not morally make, deploy, or use first-strike nuclear weapons in accordance with the teachings of Jesus Christ. The Pastoral, however, is not based on faith; it is based on the "just war" theory, because it still allows weapons for defense. Yet it is at least a base from which to start developing a theology of peace. So praise to the U.S. Catholic Bishops, but also praise to those Quakers, Friends, and Mennonites who always kept the belief in the thin thread of nonviolence running through the many years of Christian violence.

I am not at all satisfied with it. Still, I am happy because no one will be able to find in it any condoning of nuclear war, the preparation for nuclear war, or the threat of it. The Bishops have adopted a new position of nuclear pacifism. I am happy because, after six long years I am suspending my appeal to the Bishops. They will not move again until the Pope does. Now I must appeal to the Pope. Our Catholic faith teaches us that only the Pope, the successor of St. Peter, can morally bind us from the human tradition of war. I am not satisfied with the Pastoral because it still allows some kind of nuclear possession and a "just war" theory with conventional weapons. It is a monument to theological ambiguity. I believe that only the Pope can possibly stop deployment of the destabilizing first strike Cruise and Pershing II missiles in Catholic Europe, and stop "Star Wars" in space.

The Bishops insulted not only my intelligence but God's also by stating: "Nations can possess nuclear weapons as long as they show evidence of getting rid of them." I thought,what a copout! If they have them, they will use them on earth and in space, or threaten to.Otherwise, why would they keep them? I knew the Bishops would never say anything stronger now until the Pope himself took the initiative.

All through these actions I kept studying the Voice's message that I received in Mexico in 1979, and I kept learning more and more about my faith. My first question answered was, "Why did God make us?" The prophecy's answer is: "Since I first contemplated love through loneliness, and created man to love and want to be loved, it has been a trial."

I asked, "Why does God tolerate us?" The prophecy answered it for me. "You have sinned grievously, but I love you because I am your Father, so what can I do? The universe is mine but the free love of humans is not."

I always wondered about Mary, Christ's mother, and her role in our redemption. I always wondered why the Immaculate Conception was so important. The Prophecy also answered all that for me when it said: "Such a beautiful woman is she. I have loved her from the moment I first contemplated her." That was the answer for me.

Why is she always the one who appears at Lourdes, at Fatima, at Guadalupe in Mexico, and in numerous other times to guide and save her children? Why not God Himself? Again, the prophecy answered it for me. "She is your only hope, the Lady of Guadalupe, my mother and my bride who begs me every day for her children. She is sorrowful and she fears that I may turn on them!... I did not need this, nor does my mother need all her sorrow. Your mother saves you now but if you persist even she will not be able to."

My big question always is, why does the Catholic Church not teach the pacifism Christ ordered in the Gospels? The prophecy states: "The world does not know my message yet but I promised the time. You must instruct all nations in my name. Peace will come about if you do this!"

After 2000 years we have not yet received the message of Christ.

It is true. This is the missing peace I was first inspired to write before I heard the holy Voice. "You have destroyed the effectiveness of my teaching. You must teach them everything I have commanded you. *This missing piece,* or peace, makes the whole puzzle of my teaching incomplete." Pacifism is missing in the Church. "I order you to immediately forbid Catholics and brother Christians from intending to use the atom bomb against entire cities in the name of self-defense." This is the real command of the prophecy. It is a command to the Pope and the bishops of Vatican II, the highest Church authority.

Then the prophecy said, "My Church cannot go on like this," and "I want you to instruct them that it is evil to justify atomic warfare, and the probable destruction of most of the world.... You disregard God 's commandment and cling to what is human tradition—war."

Then the Voice asked the Pope, or "Servant of Servants," to make this proclamation: "Whatever you declare bound on earth shall be bound in heaven." These are the words of Jesus to St. Peter and his successors. But then the Voice went on to say: "Speak ex Cathedra," and also, God said, "You think that now you have peace because of the bomb. But you are mistaken ... You have not put peace in the hearts of men and women by your lack of instruction." Then the Voice goes on to name the Pope as responsible: "My Servant of Servants, you must be brave."

But, why did the Voice ask me to give this message to the Pope instead of giving it directly to the Pope or a bishop? The Voice said: "If you only would have listened to me I would not have had to speak through such a worldly one. Why do I always have to speak through the weak and the foolish to confuse the wise? Do not write any more encyclicals. Enough is enough.

Speak simply and command my people." The Voice went on: "Why do I have to speak through *him?* Must you always complicate and then ignore my simple commands?"

Then the Voice gave a serious warning. "Do not complicate this command, or the world will be destroyed." And later it said. "Do not complicate or condition this command. It is the only way to bring more souls to heaven. Do not turn away or the world will be lost soon and many more will be damned." The Voice admonished us with: "Peace is only in the hearts of people who know me and all my commandments. Pagans will war till the end, but my people shall not." Then the Voice spoke directly to the Pope and said: "Feed my sheep. Feed my lambs," as Jesus said to St. Peter. I will never stop believing in God because of this prophecy.

The American hierarchy was becoming increasingly opposed to the Administration's hard-line nuclear policies. In the final draft of the Pastoral Letter—*The Challenge of Peace: God's Promise and Our Response*—the U.S. bishops bluntly took issue with their government's position on when a nuclear first strike is admissible. The letter condemns certain Reagan Administration views as "immoral"; it calls for a total nuclear arms freeze and describes the United States position on nuclear deterrence as "unsatisfactory from a moral point of view." Reagan's supporters were outraged. A White House aide reportedly asked whether "the Bishops plan to oppose Russian nukes with their crosses." After the draft was released the President urged his personal envoy to the Holy See, William Wilson, to use, in Wilson's words, "every avenue open to get the Pope to make the American bishops realize what they are doing."

I kept studying the Voice's message and learning more about God and my Faith. I do not know of anything in my past that would make God speak to me to warn the Church and the Pope that the Church needed to ban the justification for nuclear war, except that I had become a pacifist.

There must have been something. I grew up around guns and hunting. There must have been something, I kept saying to myself, because I grew up in the United States when war was very popular, during the years of World War II.

I joined the Navy just after I turned 18, but my primary reason was to learn to fly. I realized I had made a big mistake after only two weeks in boot camp at Great Lakes, Wisconsin, while waiting to become a naval aviation cadet. I realized that the main purpose of my training was to condition me to follow orders blindly and without thinking.

It was not my nature to shoot first and ask questions later. Every stupid thing I was ordered to do I questioned.

But the real purpose of boot camp was to teach us to kill whoever we were ordered to shoot or blow up. That is the part I could not accept. I realized that I could never kill anyone. The Gospel my ex- protestant mother read to me said we were not supposed to kill our enemies, but love them. She had been a Methodist before marrying my dad and becoming a non-Bible-reading Catholic.

My anxiety and my feeling of ineffectiveness were increasing every day. I desperately wished I could do something that would change public opinion once and for all. I would have given my life if necessary.

I knew even that would not do much good. At times, though, it seemed the easiest solution, compared to the effort of speaking day after day in meetings without ever seeing a result or a clear sign that people were finally going to impose their common sense on their governments. I was wondering what was left of my faith. It certainly had received many blows since I had first rested my hopes and trust in the Pope and in the Church. I really had thought that at Christmas the Pope might celebrate the birth of Christ by banning nuclear weapons and war. But, as usual, nothing happened.

Many of the strong Catholics in the peace movement began to ask me, "Why, why must you depend so much on the Pope and the Church? Our Church is light years away from applying Christ's nonviolent teachings. Forget the Church! Forget the Pope! Do your peace work with serenity. Give conferences—educate the people to the great moral and physical danger. Stop torturing yourself for nothing. The Pope, Cardinal Casaroli, and the rest of the hierarchy will decide to move when the people decide to first. You know the Church has always been the last to pronounce itself, as it was against slavery and segregation." The prophecy kept me believing.

They didn't understand why this contradiction was so difficult for me to accept. Jesus said that He left His teachings in the hands of the Church, and I believe the words of Jesus. I believe all the words of Jesus, not only the ones that suit me—as most Christians do, for instance, when they dismiss non-violence by considering it utopian. My total faith demands to see all the teachings of Christ respected by the Church and the world. That and the prophecy have driven me for the last seven years. If Christians can't give up nuclear weapons first, why ask anyone else? Still, of all the people who were working for peace, only a very few agreed to help me appeal to the Pope. The thought that I wanted him to speak "ex

Cathedra" seemed to irritate my friends. They considered it too "dictatorial." At times I wondered whether they realized how critical the world situation was.

I was desperate and I did not have much money, so I printed my "Papal Peace Appeal" on a four-and-a-quarter-inch by eight-and-a- half-inch hard card, as follows.

PAPAL PEACE APPEAL

P.O. Box 15633, Washington, DC 20003

DEAR CATHOLIC AND CHRISTIAN

WE REMIND THE CHURCH THAT BY ITS SILENCE CHRISTIANS ARE PERMITTED TO JOIN ANY ARMY (EVEN HITLER'S, ETC.) AND START KILLING ANY ENEMY (EVEN CHRISTIANS) FOR ANY CAUSE (EVEN GULF OIL) WITH ANY KIND OF WEAPON (EVEN SUICIDAL NUCLEAR).

THE GREATEST VIOLENCE IS NUCLEAR WAR. IF THE POPE CAN BAN CONTRACEPTIVES TO SAVE LIFE BEFORE IT EXISTS, HE CAN ALSO BAN CATHOLIC JUSTIFICATION FOR NUCLEAR WAR, WHICH NOW ALLOWS CATHOLICS TO GO INTO THE NUCLEAR MILITARY SERVICE FOR WAR.

THE CHURCH HAS 1752 CANON LAWS BUT NOT ONE APPLIES TO WAR. THE GREATEST HERESY IS ALLOWING CHRISTIANS TO BELIEVE THEY HAVE A RIGHT TO FIGHT A NUCLEAR WAR. THE FALLOUT

WOULD KILL ALL, AND THE COST ALREADY STARVES AND KILLS THE POOR.

PLEASE JOIN US! Your signature—

Send this appeal to Pope John Paul II, 00120 Vatican City State, EUROPE

I have printed millions of these cards in five different languages and, when I had the money, I have mailed the cards to the Pope, cardinals, archbishops, and bishops of the world at least every six months. In the meantime, during the week I would put this card in the missalettes in every Catholic Church that I could. On Saturday evenings and Sundays I would pass them out. I would also pass the card and the prophecy out at every U.S. Catholic Bishops conference or meeting.

CHAPTER 22

THE "FAST FOR LIFE" OR DEATH

I was losing my sanity trying to think of something effective to do. It was shortly after the U.S. Bishops Catholic Conference summer meeting. In this summer of despair, my wife, my brother Jim, and his wife and I went out to dinner at the Schmidt House restaurant in German Village. We were talking about the various financial projects my brother Jim was working on.

My wife Dorothy interrupted us with a sudden sarcastic laugh, "Well, my husband Tom retired six years ago, and he doesn't plan on ever getting another job."

It hurt me, so in reaction I blurted out, "Dorothy, I'm going to Rome to appeal to the Pope by fasting. I am going to join the Fast for Life going on all over the world."

I went on, "My prophecy is to the Pope, and I must go there and try to see him." I didn't tell her the details of the Fast for Life, but they made me love her more because I would miss her and probably not see her again. The Fast for

Life was planned to be a fast until death, if necessary, to stop deployment of the Euro-missiles.

I left for Rome one week later to begin the Fast for Life—my last peace action. I had given my wife the property and complete power of attorney over everything else we owned, some apartments and other property.

What I had given her would provide a decent income for the rest of her life. She could get a simple job to supplement it. I wasn't worried about myself either. I thought if the Lord wanted me to work for Him, He would take care of me—and he always did after that. He never would give me an excuse to quit working for peace, or to loaf because I had no funds. He would also take care of my wife and children.

I had started the fast at the White House in Washington, DC, on August 6th. On that day Phil Berrigan (the famous activist who, with his brother Dan, a Jesuit, had raided military draft centers during the Vietnam war and burned draft records) had organized a peace protest at the White House with Liz McAllister and 15 other people. I was late, so I got into the White House tour just as they were picking up the protestors and hauling them out. I sat down and began to sing, as required by the good old nonviolent tradition.

At lunch I stated proudly "Since I'm on the Fast for Life, I'll just have tea or juice or something to drink. Kathy Shields, Art Laffin, Monica Siemer, Jimmy Siemer, and Fr. McSorley were there.

"But isn't that a Gandhian fast?" Phil asked.

"Yes, it is, I think. But what exactly is a Gandhian fast?"
"That's only water, Tom."

"Only water?"

"Yes, didn't you know?"

"Oh! What did I get myself into? OK, give me some water." I think I had really gotten into the fast because there wasn't anything else going on at the time and the nuclear danger was so great. I couldn't stand inactivity. Also, I had decided to fast in Rome primarily because it was a good opportunity to appeal to the Pope.

Imagine all that free food on the plane and not being able to touch it! Again, I flew Icelandic Airways to Luxembourg and took an overnight train to Rome. I weighed over 222 lbs (or 100 kilos) then and I thought I would be able to fast for a long time. I was already starving by the time I got to Rome. It was the worst time of the fast for me. Later I realized that our day-to-day hunger is mostly appetite caused by a habit of routine eating. The body really rebels against suddenly not receiving its customary food. So the first five days almost killed me. I remember getting off the train and suffering when I looked at all the food in the windows, remembering the times I had eaten my way across Italy as a tourist. I love Italian food, and especially the wine.

I had been in Rome in 1950, 1975, 1980, and 1981, and each time I threw coins in the Trevi Fountain—why not—wishing to come back. I thought, if they don't stop nuclear weapons this will be the last time. It would really be a shame to destroy beautiful Rome, even though Rome is the symbol of 1,680 years of Christians fighting wars against Christians.

It was a difficult time for me, but still I was filled with hope. I really thought my fast was going to move the Pope. I started discovering Italian politics. I learned that the communists and the leftists were already against U.S. first-strike cruise missiles, and they represented over 38% of the country. So all we had to do was change the other side—whoever they were—and there would be no missiles in Italy. The other side was primarily the Church and the Christian Democrats. It certainly was a great paradox for the Christians to be for nuclear missiles and the atheists against them!

I had a terrible time finding the church where the fast was supposed to be taking place. Everyone said it was just past the Coliseum. But they did not say it was up the hill and behind the bushes, and all I could think of was food. There were many Arabic and Black people lying around the bushes and the fountain. I looked at the ancient facade of the church and saw the Borghese name inscribed. I climbed the high steps, and inside the right- hand arch was a beat-up old banner saying "Digiuno Per La Vita." I went into the courtyard and could not find the entrance, until a door opened on the right and someone wearing a "Digiuno Per La Vita" badge and long hair greeted me with a big smile and said, "You Thomas Siemer?" I nodded affirmatively.

"Me Lorenzo Porta of the League for Draft Registers. Come in! Come in!"

Those pictures on the wall must have been 500 years old! The place was like a museum without formal upkeep or maintenance.

Lorenzo motioned, "This is Rita Sanvitore and her sister Roberta, from Milan. They are in M.C.P. (the Movement of Christians for Peace)."

Looking up from her typing, Rita said, "Ciao." She was necessarily all business at the time. Later we became close friends and I called her my little Mama, because she was always taking care of me.

"This is Donata and her husband Tony from Naples," Lorenzo gestured. You could see peace on their faces. Then he said, "And this is Franca—she is a Hebrew." Franca gave me a nervous smile. "And this is Turi Vaccaro from Comiso." Turi must have been just out of jail, because his hair was only half an inch long. He gave me a big Sicilian smile.

Pointing, Lorenzo said, "This is Ubaldo Geravisone, a Worker Priest and very active in the National Peace Committee. Thomas, you want to stay in this room with the support group, or do you want to sleep in the next room, reserved for fasters only?"

I realized Lorenzo was the only one who spoke reasonable English. It was going to be a lonely life even to the end. "I'll sleep with the fasters," I said. It was getting late. There was no one else in the room and no beds, and I could not sleep without a mattress. I told Lorenzo, who offered to get a mattress from the Little Sisters of Calcutta in the same building. He returned with an old mattress. "Thomas, this is for you.

Can I get you anything else?"

"Yes, could I have some sheets and a blanket, please?" I begged. "He looked at me in disappointment and said, slightly exasperated "No—there is none."

"Where are the other fasters?" I asked. "Most of them are eating." said Lorenzo. "They're what?" I asked, astonished.

"Well, they aren't fasting now. We have been here four days now. I am Mascimilliano and I fasted for three days. Roberta and Rita are fasting for seven."

"Good Lord," I said, "that apple you are holding looks so good!" He quickly hid it.

"Well, is there anyone else fasting?" I questioned.

"Well, not at the moment, but others are expected," Lorenzo replied. "There are support groups who take turns fasting in other cities. But it's been six days since August 6th when we started."

"You mean there is no one else fasting here?"

Lorenzo nodded affirmatively. "Only Rita and Roberta. Italians don't like to fast."

"What's that good smell like garlic and meat coming from the next room? What are all those people in the hall carrying food for?" As they came down the corridor they waved and closed the door on me as if I were some sort of a prophet. (I knew they were really trying to hide the sight of food from me—but they could never hide the Italian food smell!)

At dawn a gnawing stomach awakened me. I stepped over to the door and down the hall to the old church thinking I would find someone saying Mass there. The church was dark except for a sun ray shining through a little top window. It settled on the picture of a fat little pope. I stopped a custodian as he was walking through and he said, "No Mass—vacation!"

I walked back to my room and lay there praying. I prayed constantly during the fast, for the first time since I had left the seminary. People started to wake up and I moved to the large patio on the roof of the kitchen. There were people out there sitting in a yoga position on an old rug. I sat with them, but at 100 kilos I couldn't begin to sit in a yoga position.

They were seriously discussing something and nodding toward me. Finally Lorenzo said something directly to me. "Thomas, the other Fasters for Life have called to get you to guarantee that you will fast to the death."

"You people can only fast for less than seven days and you are worried about my sincerity? You fast to the death, and I'll be your support group and provide you with everything!"

They all got together in another huddle. Then Lorenzo asked me again if I would declare that I would fast to death for the cause, as had the others. I thought, well, what have I got to lose? I certainly don't want to live any longer than I have to—no wine and now no food! So I answered "Yes, with the same dedication as Charles Gray, Dorothy Granada, and the others, I am determined to fast to death."

Lorenzo translated for the support group in Italian while I waited for their verdict. Then I added, "OK, I will fast as long as the others, I promise."

Lorenzo said, "Thomas we have agreed to accept you as a Faster for Life and will telephone the other Fasters." "Bless you, my child, bless you!"

Padre Anselmo, the head of the Calmandolese Church of San Gregorio, was extremely friendly until my letter to the Pope was first printed in the communist newspaper *Il Manifesto*. But after he read it, Padre Anselmo almost threw us out of the San Gregorio church!

I remember him saying, "Thomas is a saint, but Lorenzo and Ubaldo, you should be kicked. You can't live in the Pope's house and point the finger at the Pope. You must leave this church immediately!" He was very angry that an open letter to the Pope first appeared in a communist newspaper.

Father Anselmo changed his mind when he started to receive congratulations from the rest of the Calmandoles Order. He relented and let us stay. He really supported us when we had articles in the Catholic newspaper *Avennire*. Those totally won his heart. I had already fasted for a week when Hedi Vacarro walked into my life. I remember that her first words were, "You're not a faster! You don't know how to fast!"

"Well, you fast then, and I'll support you," I replied.

"I cannot fast. The doctor said I am too thin already. But, if you are going to fast you must not pray alone."

"Hedi, I pray all the time and go to Mass every day."
"We must all pray together," Hedi insisted.

I could have told her that the support group wasn't too crazy about Charismatic praying, but she didn't listen. She pushed everybody into a circle and began to pray.

"Oh well, we'll humor her," Lorenzo said. (Lorenzo would do anything but eat meat.)

Then suddenly Hedi said, "You must all sing now," and started a Charismatic song which she sang completely by herself. I didn't know Italian and no one else knew the song.

At the conclusion she practically picked me up and demanded that I be in the fasting room by myself in quiet solitude. There she gave me some poems she had written and insisted that I read them. She was the most forceful peacemaker I had ever met. Later I found out that she was German Swiss, and that explained it. Still, she was very likeable.

Hedi had worked for peace in Rome for 20 years and had a broken down library as a memorial to that effort, with the records going back the whole way. It must have been discouraging for her, after all these years of dedication, to see how difficult it was to find people really committed to nonviolence. Still, she always had at least a dozen disciplined followers. To achieve this, of course, she needed some leadership qualities. These she did not lack. Hedi, being Charismatic, thought she received her instructions directly from God. Under these circumstances it was quite difficult to contradict her.

Since the Franciscans had already established a peace group, run by Fr. Marco Malagola and Fr. Ken Viego, a Pakistani, I went to their motherhouse on a beautiful hill overlooking Rome. Fr. Vaughn, the director of the order, did see us, but sent me to his assistant when I tried to explain the great danger of the cruise missiles. The assistant was an all-business-type religious executive. There are so many in Rome!

As days went by I continued writing letters to the Pope, many requesting an audience, but to no avail. I never understood why the Pope hadn't banned nuclear weapons for political reasons, if nothing else. It is true he had banned contraceptives and abortions and not too many people paid attention to him on those issues. But everyone knows if we fight a nuclear war we'll all be destroyed, and people want someone like the usual father image to try to stop them. The tremendous evil of nuclear weapons is the obvious truth, and people recognize the truth when they are presented with it.

The Pope would probably get the Nobel Peace Prize and be canonized! And, think of the third world countries where the government starves the people year after year to buy more and more weapons! Imagine how many new converts would flock to the Church if the Church condemned weapons and those who chose them! The world's population is expected to double in the next 20 years, and the masses of starving people will turn into the most terrible and powerful force the world has ever known. The Church had better be on their side! An absolute statement by the Pope would corner the righteous Catholics; they would lose the "God is on our side" argument they always use to convince simple, naive people. The fascists and power-seekers would probably walk right out and the Church might be "condemned" to poverty again, but it would be completely free.

On the 32nd day of the Fast, we decided to have a walk to the Russian Embassy to protest the shooting down of the Korean Jumbo Jet. But I collapsed in front of ' the Russian Embassy. I remember leaning on the car hood feeling dizzy before I fell. The next thing I remember is lying in the street looking up at a lot of people, and Lorenzo holding my feet up in the air. Then I found myself in the wardroom of a very bad hospital—surrounded by unbelievable dirt and filth. People were lying around bleeding with no bandage changes, and we were stacked in beds beside beds. I thought I had traveled back in time to the 18th century. Journalists took pictures of me lying in the hospital bed. It was in all the papers the next day.

Dr. Francesco Tullio, a homeopathic peace doctor, came to see me, and his eyes were filled with admiration. He said it was a glorious thing to be able to give your life for the cause. He hugged and kissed me. "I fasted once for a couple of days, but it affected my efficiency and I stopped. You are great!" Then he waved to me as he ran out.

I refused to take intravenous fluids the first day, and a strong-willed young doctor came in the second morning with an intravenous glucose bottle and two big orderlies. He said in broken English, "You die with your liver if you don't eat. You will have spasms and die. You cannot refuse." Then he set up the bottle and the needle. I struggled with the attendants but was too weak to fight. "This only keeps you alive and doesn't affect your fast. But you must have sugar for your liver."

There was a man who came in with me who was dying in the bed across from mine, and they were trying to scrub the floor around his wife and children. As he gasped for his last breath and his wife began to cry uncontrollably, a floor scrubber looked up and drew the curtain around her just a little bit. He still stretched his mops under the curtain to get under the dying man's bed.

Tullio tried to get me out of the hospital to a better place. Others (including Lorenzo) wanted me to fast in the apartment- office of Digiuno Per La Vita, in Trastevere. As I lay there starting to gradually lose control over my senses, I began to realize for the first time why people who really starve to death, not out of a free choice like mine, become so passive and eventually resigned to their destiny.

"Hunger is the worst form of violence," I said to Lorenzo, "because it deprives a person of the sacred right of thinking, developing a consciousness of their own identity, and recognizing the self as a human being. It is the ultimate violence to let entire populations starve to death without doing anything to prevent it. And yet the studies financed by President Carter in 1979 had shown that 12 million people starved to death around the world each year. Now, in only four years time, the number has climbed to 40 million.

How is it possible that instead of saving these human beings we keep choosing to invest money and the best scientific brains into building six nuclear weapons a day in the U.S. alone, and who knows how many in other countries? How is it possible for anyone to hear this data and still continue to live life the same way as always, minding their own business and only concentrating on solving little daily problems? Christ said, 'Ask and you shall receive'—but we ask only for ourselves. Unfortunately 'It will be poured to you according to the size of your container,' and we have chosen to be very small containers, incapable of opening up to let the world's suffering in. We make it impossible for God to pour down the torrents of vital strength, indispensable to start healing the suffering. Do we ever think it is only by pure chance that we were born on this side of the world? Do we ever think that our child could have been one of those starving children, had he or she been born by accident on the wrong side?

How is it possible that we don't all take to the streets shouting together, 'Enough, forever!'—shouting so high and loud as to bring down governments, as to change once and for all this world of indifference and death?"

"Thomas, you are a good man and a good socialist," Lorenzo said softly.

The next day I was moved to the Clinica Santa Lucia on the outskirts of Rome. That is where several American bishops came to me and advised me against fasting to death. Bishop Leroy Matthiesen and Mike Kenny both told me that Cardinal Caseroli, Secretary of State, had called the Casa di Maria, where they were staying, each day to inquire about my health. (I guess he didn't want to have a corpse on his hands.) The bishops insisted that to fast to death for any reason is a violent act, and said, "Christians, as we all know, cannot use violent acts to do good."

I replied, "Do you know, I can't tell an American Catholic Christian nuclear missile from a Soviet atheistic missile? The Christians have been as violent as the communists have been in the world arena in recent years. I think it would be difficult to tell the Christians from the Romans—and from the lions!"

Good Bishop Maurice Dingman of Des Moines, Iowa, said Mass for me at the clinic. I was really so weak I could hardly lift my head off the pillow.

After 38 days of fasting with only water, I finally received a letter from the Pope's secretary. The body of the letter said, "Your request for an audience with the Pope has been noted and will be given consideration. Yours in Christ."

I was beginning to wonder whether it was useful for me to die.

From a practical point of view, did it make sense to die when I could do so many other things for peace?

When I began to stop thinking rationally and was not seeing things clearly, I realized I was dying. I tried to tell Lorenzo and Ubaldo that I wanted to stop the fast.

Lorenzo said, "Wait, I will get another doctor's opinion." Francesco insisted that he would look after me, since the hospital would not take responsibility to keep me any longer.

The good little Sister Teresita and a friendly old patient who could not talk or hear helped me. So did Maria, a beautiful 35- year old nurse who did not understand a word of English. Then I received the most important phone call of my life from France. Solange Fernez phoned to tell me the other fasters in Europe might agree to end their fast on the next day. Would I agree to end the fast also?

Hedi said to me, "Dorothy Granada and Charles Gray are on another line. Solange is also on another line. All want to end the fast on the 40th day, tomorrow, if you do."

All my friends were crowding into the room. Ubaldo said: "The Russian Ambassador asks how you are, Thomas.

You passed out in front of his embassy protesting the downing of the Jumbo Jet in Korea."

Gianni Novelli added, "I am showing your movie, *Gods of Metal*, dubbed in Italian. You must quit, Thomas, you are dying." I said softly: "I want to end the fast too, at 1 a.m., September the 16, 1983." Everyone cheered happily.

Sister Teresita said, "We should not fear our enemies anyway, because the worst they can do is send us to Paradise."

Someone said: "I am Bishop Dingman, Tom, do you remember me?" I opened my eyes in surprise and said: "Hi, Bishop Dingman, and hi to you too, Bishop Matthieson."

"We just came from Cardinal Casaroli, who will be very glad you are stopping the fast. He asked us to come see you." He also said that the Pope sent his blessings, and to say he has received 'The Missing Piece,' and now says it is time for you to go back to your wife and your children."

"Star Wars" is not my real concern. It has always been the missing piece, the Church's failure to teach about Jesus' unconditional love. It was always about this prophecy I received from God in Mexico to get the Pope and the Church to ban the justification for violence and war, especially nuclear war. Sweet Sister Teresita was very happy with my decision. During the last days she had tried to tempt me with glasses of milk left on my bedside table at night, as if by mistake. "Come on, drink a little milk," she used to say, "I will not tell anyone." Anna Luisa L'Abate from Florence and her husband Alberto were very loving too. Anna Luisa stayed with me day after day. She slept in the bushes in the park of the clinic at night. At 40 years of age she was like a little bird—so flighty and unsteady—but so loving. She would beg me each day to end the fast, but I would tell her and the doctors, "Just one more day." Then the next day I would say "Just one more day. This is the last day," and so on. Now this bold action was really over.

At first they were surprised. Then they joyfully accepted the idea and hugged me, laughing and relieved after all. I understand their first reaction. During those 40 days they and I had shared the conviction that we were doing something really strong for peace—and now we would all have to face the everlasting and despairing question again. "What more can we do for peace now? What can we do next for peace?"

Much to our sorrow, at the end of November 1983, parts of the first cruise missiles assigned to Italy arrived at the U.S. Air Base at Sigonella, Sicily, not far from Comiso. On December 8, 1983, I asked my friend Hedi Vacarro, a leader of the MIR peace activists in Rome, to take me to see the American Base. I had to insist for a long time before she finally agreed. When we arrived at Sigonella Hedi's friends were holding back. It was forbidden to go near the base. Cement blocks closed the road. I left the car and walked in the direction of the standard Navy checkered water tower, which I recognized immediately. Hedi followed me.

We entered the gate of the base without stopping, and I immediately started shaking hands with a group of American soldiers. Then, taking advantage of their surprise, I said, "My name is Thomas Siemer and I have come here to pray that you never receive the order to launch these cruise missiles. I know that you never want to receive an order that would mean the death of millions of women and children in Russia and also of most Europeans and Americans. You know perfectly well that the enemy would counterattack and destroy your wives and children. So let us kneel down and pray for God to protect us all." They all knelt down with me. After the prayer I shook hands with them again and one soldier offered to take us back to our car.

The next day, Sunday, I was invited to debate with the bishop of Ragusa, Bishop Riso, in the Cinema of Comiso, Sicily. I spent the whole morning handing out leaflets at the church corner. After the meeting the Bishop hugged me and told me that I had convinced him that the cruise missiles were first-strike weapons.

After I returned to America in 1985, I continued to try to get a formal audience with the Pope and to publish the prophecy in five languages and sent it to the Pope, the Curia, and every Catholic archbishop in the world. In the meantime the years went by fast, very fast, living with my family and working for peace in Columbus, Ohio, and Washington, DC.

In 1992, I was fasting on the steps of the National Capitol to commemorate the 500th anniversary of Columbus' arrival and the subsequent annihilation of most of the indigenous people, down to the horrific U.S. Latin American policies of that time. I was called home because Dorothy was very ill. This time it was serious. When the doctors began what they thought would be fairly routine gall bladder surgery, they found cancer of the small intestines, colon, liver, lungs, and lymph nodes. I spent the next two years caring for Dorothy, and she died surrounded by love.

My wife had spent the last 10 years working in soup kitchens and food pantries and helping to staff the peace center at Holy Family Church. She was the best woman I ever met in my life, and the most unselfish. Hundreds came to her funeral, and the paper printed stories on the loss to the community. Her children loved her immensely and gave her great joy by following her example of love and generosity. She has 34 grandchildren.

Much to my surprise, at Christmas time in 1998, the Pope gave me hope. I could not believe it. On the occasion of his 1998 Christmas message, Pope John Paul II expressed his conviction on the matter of the death penalty. He prayed that "Christians can help to strengthen and renew throughout the world the consensus concerning the need for urgent measures to defend human life and end the death penalty."

A month later, during his apostolic trip to the Americas, the Holy Father re-emphasized that teaching. "There must be an end to the unnecessary recourse to the death penalty," the Pope said. "This model of society bears the stamp of a culture of death and is therefore in opposition to the Gospel message. Faced with this distressing reality the Church community intends to commit itself all the more to the defense of the culture of life." ("Ecclesia in America," January 1999)

Four days later the Pope included a similar appeal in a St. Louis, Missouri, homily: "The new evangelization calls for the followers of Christ who are unconditionally pro-life to proclaim, celebrate, and serve the Gospel of Life in every situation. A sign of hope is the increasing recognition that human life must never be taken away even in the case of someone who has done great evil." "Praise the Lord" I shouted. "If you cannot kill the killer by capital punishment then you cannot kill anyone, even for your country."

This is the Fifth Commandment that God gave to Moses for the Hebrew people. But the Hebrew leaders applied it only to Hebrews, and therefore permitted Jews to kill Gentiles, Christians, and Muslims. The Israelis do not have capital punishment to this date. Because of this rule, Hebrew leaders had to have the Romans kill Christ, who said, "We must even love our enemies."

On June 11, 2000, the U.S. Catholic bishops stated: "The death penalty offers the tragic illusion that we can defend life by taking life." They said this in a letter to George W. Bush on the day that Timothy McVeigh was executed. Again I reasoned that if the Pope and the Catholic Church will not permit us to kill a killer who had killed 168 innocent people, how can it allow us to kill for our country two million people in Viet Nam, and so many thousands more in Iraq?

Or, how can we build, prepare, and train for nuclear war that will kill billions of innocent people? Christian morality dictates that if we intend to do something evil, like fight a nuclear war, we have already done it morally.

The Vatican II Council stated that, "Any war aimed indiscriminately at whole cities and population centers is a sin and a crime against God and mankind, and merits unequivocal condemnation." Making our nuclear weapons and training our nuclear military to launch on orders, we have already committed ourselves to fighting a nuclear war that is condemned by the Church.

On September 11, 2001, the world was physically and morally shocked when terrorists intentionally crashed two hijacked civilian airliners into the World Trade Center Towers in New York City, killing approximately 3,000 innocent people. Another hijacked airliner was crashed into the Pentagon, killing more. On October 7, 2001, before the United States had proof of who were the terrorists responsible for the attacks, President Bush and the U.S. military launched a war of revenge, with hundreds of military aircraft bombarding the country of Afghanistan, killing untold thousands of civilians and destroying their country while saying that they were only trying to kill one terrorist, Osama Bin Laden, and a few members of his Al-Qaeda network.

Because of this attack on Afghanistan, President Bush was made a national hero by the American people—specially Christian and Jews, who the Administration claimed supported the attacks. Naturally the American people were very hurt and angry, but at the time the U.S. government had not yet presented to the American people or the world the evidence of just who was responsible for the terrorist attacks. Going after the recognized Taliban government of Afghanistan, regardless of its reputation, seemed more like vengeance than justice to me. The attacks on the USA were terrorist acts, to be sure, but nevertheless, as Christians we cannot respond in kind.

The Taliban government, however, was one of the most extremist in Muslim fundamentalism. The Jewish and Muslim extremists cause most of the violence in the Middle East. How strange it is that all the combatants, including the U.S. Christians, strongly believe in the One God Creator, which makes all us religious brothers and sisters and children of the one same God.

There will be no peace in the Middle East unless the Palestinians and Jews reach a fair agreement, hopefully guarded by Christian peacemakers. Ther e should be an immediate meeting of the Jewish, Christian and Muslim religious leaders, preferably in Jerusalem, the city of Abraham, the father of all three religions.

Instead of condemning the bombing of Afghanistan, and this form of collateral revenge on the Taliban government and civilians, at its November 15, 2001, meeting, the US Catholic Bishops Conference supported the U.S. government's actions. I stood up in their midst and shouted, "The Pope said we cannot kill the killer by capital punishment, so how can we kill for our country?" I was physically removed by the police, but for some reason the sergeant was sympathetic with my cause and let me go.

In the meantime, the Pope continued to speak adamantly against capital punishment and all killing, and encouraged a peaceful solution to the Afghan War. At the same time the Pope was saying this in Kazakhstan, the Vatican spokesman, Joachim Navarre Vals, was saying, "We at the Vatican are not pacifists, and we support the Afghan War."

I still believe that the Pope and the bishops are our best hope in getting the Church to commit itself to the missing piece of the Gospels of Jesus Christ. The only reason I believe this is because God told me so in the prophecy I received in Mexico in 1979. I believe because of what Jesus said, "Thomas, you believe because you have seen. Blessed are they, Thomas, who have not seen and who believe," meaning those who have read the Gospel of unconditional love and lived by it.

I do not know how much longer God can tolerate the silence of the Church in regard to war, especially nuclear war. I am sad to say, popes and bishops make great moral pronouncements like they are now doing against capital punishment after all the civilized countries do it first—like they did against slavery and segregation. But I was happy with the Church's weak stand against capital punishment, because it was the first step to ending all killing.

Then, to my great sorrow, President Bush, on December 13, 2001, announced that he had formally notified Russia six months in advance, as required, that he was withdrawing the United States from the Antiballistic Missile (ABM) Defense Treaty of 1972. He had committed the USA to breaking the treaty with Russia that kept the nuclear peace for so long in order to build a new Star Wars National Missile Defense (NMD) and put nuclear weapons in space. We are back to the beginning, and I am back to the first chapter of my story, beginning with the Pope's Star Wars Report. *

It has been 17 years since the Pontifical Academy of Sciences studied and condemned the Antiballistic Missile Defense in space. The American Catholic Bishops, the clergy, and the faithful do not know of this papal report condemning the NMD "Star Wars," or they would protest. It is now the year 2002, and still the big battle rages in the U.S. Congress over continued funding and development of the NMD. We are still in Washington, DC protesting the funding, because Star Wars is really a cover-up for designing and building a whole new generation of exotic, offensive nuclear weapons, so we can threaten anyone, anywhere on earth from space.

But the immediate danger of the NMD is that it gives the American people the illusion that they have a defense system against nuclear weapons and therefore they can fight any war, anywhere they want, without fear of nuclear retaliation. This is totally absurd.

It has been 19 years since the U.S. Catholic Bishops' May 3, 1983 Peace Pastoral condemned first strike and first use of nuclear weapons. Furthermore, the bishops' conditional acceptance of the possession of nuclear weapons was based on the country's showing evidence of getting rid of them, and that condition has not been met. Nineteen years is an excessive amount of time to get rid of a few thousand nuclear weapons. Also, the Peace Pastoral did not approve the development of any new nuclear weapons on earth or in space. Yet, the U.S. Catholic bishops have continued to remain silent, even when Bush is for a first-strike nuclear war.

It has been 23 years since God spoke to me in Mexico and told me to go tell the Pope and the bishops to morally ban the justification for nuclear weapons and war. All the while the Pope has remained silent, while more and more countries have acquired nuclear weapons, even some terrorist countries. Why does the Church continue to remain silent when the United States is proposing to deploy new nuclear weapons in space, thereby causing a new nuclear arms race?

** NOTICE CONCERNING THE POPE'S STAR WARS REPORT OF 1985, in which the Pontifical Academy of Sciences condemned the Antiballistic Missile (ABM) defenses: The only documented reference to this January 1985 meeting is in Volume 14, Page 560, of the Vatican's ORIGINS, published by the Catholic News Service in Washington, DC. The Vatican's Star Wars Report has not been released as of Jan. 16, 2003.*

I believe that all God wants is for the Pope and bishops to make a simple, clear edict, such as the following, ex Cathedra:

EDICT

To all Cardinals, Bishops, religious, and faithful:

As the successor of St. Peter and the apostles, we again bind you to what has already been commanded by Our Lord Jesus Christ in the gospels, and the College of the Pope and bishops at the Vatican II Council, when they passed the following position of the Catholic Church.

ANY ACT OF WAR AIMED INDISCRIMINATELY AT THE DESTRUCTION OF ENTIRE CITIES OR EXTENSIVE AREAS ALONG WITH THEIR POPULATION IS A CRIME AGAINST GOD AND MAN HIMSELF AND SHOULD BE CONDEMNED UNEQUIVOCALLY.

Therefore, as Pope, I bind nothing new, which has not already been commanded of you. But, to clarify for you this existing law of the Church, I am proclaiming this new law from the Chair of St. Peter, ex Cathedra.

IT IS A SERIOUS SIN AND IT IS FORBIDDEN FOR CATHOLICS (AND ALL HUMANKIND) TO HELP BUILD, TRAIN FOR, USE, DEPLOY OR IN ANY WAY COMMIT THEMSELVES TO THE USE OF NUCLEAR WEAPONS OR OTHER WEAPONS OF MASS

DESTRUCTION, NOW OR IN THE FUTURE.

POPE DATE

I believe that if the Pope and Church would make this clear commitment, it would set an example and it would be the beginning of all religions coming together for a lasting peace on earth. The religious leaders of the Jews, Christians and Muslims could come together in their sacred city of Jerusalem to make the prophecy of their holy prophet Isaiah come true:

There shall go forth instruction, and
the word of the Lord from Jerusalem.

He shall judge between the nations,
and impose terms on many peoples.

They shall beat their swords
into plowshares and their
spears into pruning hooks;
One nation shall not raise a sword
against another, nor shall they
train for war again. ***Isaiah 2.3-5***

THE END

EPITAPH

by Rita A. Clark

The message from God may stand alone, but to say "God told me to tell you," as Tom Siemer does, people cannot accept.

They cannot accept that God would speak to anyone, even though there are many examples in the Bible, the Torah, and the Koran. God spoke to the first man, Adam. God also spoke to Eve and later to Cain, Eve's son. God asked him:" Where is your brother Abel?" after Cain had killed Abel. God spoke to Noah so that he would make preparations for the deluge which was to come because men had offended God. God even said He was sorry He had made man.

Messengers were sent to Sodom and Gomorrah to warn them that unless they changed their wicked ways they would be destroyed. Many times God told prophets to go warn the people that their sins were serious and they needed to change or be destroyed. Jeremiah was told by God to tell the Israelites that they would be conquered and exiled because they had failed to observe the mandate of the Jubilee years and of the Sabbatical years.

In the Book of Job God even spoke to Satan before he allowed Satan to tempt Job. Similarly, God told Jonah to go tell the Ninevites that they must change from their violent ways or be destroyed. They listened to Jonah and were saved.

Now that we face the danger of total nuclear destruction and still persist in building more nuclear weapons, and even put them in space, how could God abandon us? I believe God is warning us through Tom Siemer.

Tom and many others believe that the so-called "terrorists" have nuclear devices. Tom thinks that before they start blowing up Haifa or Tel Aviv to win the West Bank of Palestine, he must appeal one last time to the Jewish, Muslim, and Christian leaders, before millions are killed and contaminated by nuclear fallout.

We must appeal to all religious leaders, especially Christians, before New York or Washington, DC are blown up by the hatred for the USA that our economic policies, interferences, and invasions of many foreign countries inspires. We must make this appeal before the United States begins to build a very costly National Missile Defense, which will waste trillions of dollars, as well as our greatest minds and natural resources that should go to help the starving masses. This is an evil waste when we know that the population of the world will double in approximately 30 years. We must attend to the starving people first.

It becomes a diabolical waste when we know it will not work. Our scientists condemned it in 1972 and the USA and USSR signed a treaty to prohibit the building of an Antiballistic Missile Defense. It is without merit because low flying aircraft, Cruise missiles, even Volkswagens and vans can carry nuclear devices underneath space defenses. It has, however, broken the ABM Defense Treaty of 1972 and is causing a new nuclear arms race.

This is the reason Tom Siemer appeals to the Christian Churches to lead the way, because of their Gospel of nonviolence and Jesus's call to love our enemies.

Why did God pick Tom to warn the world of a nuclear holocaust? Why did not God talk directly to the Pope, or to a cardinal, or at least to a saintly man? Tom is an ordinary man. However, after reading of his past, one realizes that he learned from an early age about the nonviolence and peace message of the Gospel. Later on in his life, in the seminary, he learned the rules and ways of the Church, including the just war theory. Finally, while working for the Rockwell International Missile Division for 23 years, he became an expert in the high-tech field of nuclear weapons, creating a serious conscience problem. At that point his education was complete and a choice needed to be made.

Tom Siemer decided to work for peace, and I believe God did speak to him. Tom believes that after his book is finished and published his peace work will be finished and he will die. Therefore, this book is his epitaph.

Printed in the USA
CPSIA information can be obtained
at www.ICGtesting.com
LVHW022323140924
790997LV00001B/120

9 781643 673400